D1017343

Praise for *Heisman*

"I didn't get the chance to know Coach Heisman, but having an opportunity to win the award has allowed me to learn about him. Probably the first thing you learn about is his integrity and the way he conducted his life. I have been impressed with the men who have won this award and hope that I live up to the name Heisman as they do. It has been an honor to be a part of an award that stands for integrity and excellence!"

—TY DETMER,
BRIGHAM YOUNG UNIVERSITY HEISMAN WINNER, 1990

"My greatest honor has been to win the single greatest award in all of amateur sports—the Heisman Trophy. This trophy is named for one of the best college football coaches ever to pace the sidelines, John W. Heisman. As I am one of the few Heisman winners to become a coach, I consider it a huge privilege to represent the coaching profession and the Heisman Trophy."

—COACH STEVE SPURRIER,
UNIVERSITY OF FLORIDA HEISMAN WINNER, 1966

"I am honored to be the recipient of the 1969 Heisman Trophy, which is named after a true coaching legend. John Heisman was dedicated to the game of football and the athletes who played it with passion and integrity. He was a man of excellence, principles, and sportsmanship. This book is a tribute to his enduring legacy."

—STEVE OWENS,
UNIVERSITY OF OKLAHOMA HEISMAN WINNER, 1969

"In this book we finally find out the history of John Heisman and why the most prestigious trophy in America is named in his honor."

—ARCHIE GRIFFIN,
OHIO STATE UNIVERSITY HEISMAN WINNER, 1974 AND 1975

"Winning the Heisman Trophy was one of the most memorable events of my life. And to this day the December announcement of the winner captures the attention of the entire nation. Since 1935 the Heisman Trophy has been awarded to the most outstanding college football player in the country. Most people easily identify with the name Heisman because of the award but don't know much about the history of the man it was named after. This book tells the story of the incredible life and accomplishments of the man and the coach John W. Heisman."

—JOHN CAPPELLETTI,
PENNSYLVANIA STATE UNIVERSITY HEISMAN WINNER, 1973

"When I won the Heisman Trophy in 1959, I didn't know anything about John Heisman or the Heisman Trophy. I knew Heisman was involved with the Downtown Athletic Club of New York at one point in his career and had been an accomplished and successful college football coach. If it's not the most important trophy in sports, it has become the most recognized trophy over time. When you're playing football, you're playing for the moment. To be recognized as the most outstanding player of an era was a wonderful experience. Looking back fifty years later, it was a wonderful experience to be recognized for your efforts and your team's efforts. I can't wait to learn more about John Heisman."

—BILLY CANNON,
LOUISIANA STATE UNIVERSITY HEISMAN WINNER, 1959

"To be a member of the most prestigious fraternity in sports is a supreme honor. As a new name is added to the trophy each year, winning the Heisman becomes more important to each past winner. All of us are grateful to John W. Heisman; this book outlines the remarkable history of the man and the trophy that carries his name."

—JOE BELLINO,
UNITED STATES NAVAL ACADEMY HEISMAN WINNER, 1960

"I was born in the same year as the first award of the Heisman Memorial Trophy. Within that year, our first athletic director, John W. Heisman, passed away. In my position as athletic director at the Downtown Athletic Club, we annually met with and honored our nation's best college football players. In 1971, I was fortunate to meet Coach Heisman's family, William L. Heisman and his son, John, and became keenly aware of the great man's reputation and some of his influential history. I am glad that Coach Heisman's life story is now being told and I'm glad for the Heisman family that tells it."

—RUDY RISKA, EXECUTIVE DIRECTOR EMERITUS
OF THE HEISMAN MEMORIAL TROPHY TRUST AND
COAUTHOR OF *40 YEARS AT THE HOME OF THE HEISMAN*

"Leon never put a monetary value on the Heisman Trophy. He never felt comfortable trying to capitalize on receiving it. To him, that trophy represented the hard work of his teammates and his coaches. He felt there were a dozen guys on his 1949 team who were befitting of the honor. To him, the trophy stood for character, perseverance, and integrity, and it marked him for the rest of his life. He felt an obligation and a reverence to the tradition of the Heisman. To never disgrace what it stood for. To bring honor to those who came before him and to those who would come after him. He lived his life with that heavy responsibility and he instilled those values in his children and grandchildren."

—KEVIN HART, ON BEHALF OF LEON HART,
UNIVERSITY OF NOTRE DAME HEISMAN WINNER, 1949

"Like many young boys, I dreamed of winning a Heisman Trophy. But I never once considered the impact it could have on one's life. Now I can almost imagine one of us winning something like the Nobel Peace Prize and still getting introduced as a former Heisman Trophy winner. It's an honor and a title that sticks, and it opens many doors in life. I pray I am a good steward of the platform I've received from winning this prestigious award. I can't wait to learn more about John Heisman, the man behind the trophy."

—DANNY WUERFFEL,
UNIVERSITY OF FLORIDA HEISMAN WINNER, 1996

"The Heisman is arguably the most iconic trophy in all of sports, and certainly one of my life's proudest achievements. As recognizable as the statue is, many do not know the storied history of the man it was named after, Coach John Heisman. This book explores the life of a legend."

—DESMOND HOWARD,
UNIVERSITY OF MICHIGAN HEISMAN WINNER, 1991

"The Heisman Trophy and its winners are forever a part of the history and lure of college football. This book provides readers with an excellent examination of the life of John Heisman, the trophy's namesake. After reading *Heisman: The Man Behind the Trophy*, you will know a lot more about the history of college football and learn why the Heisman Memorial Trophy is simply the greatest honor in all of American sports."

—GINO TORRETTA,
UNIVERSITY OF MIAMI HEISMAN WINNER, 1992

"Winning the Heisman Trophy made me appreciate the importance of coaching and teamwork. You don't win Heismans by yourself and you don't win national championships by yourself; it's always in conjunction with others that you make your greatest accomplishments and teamwork makes your dreams work! John W. Heisman taught us that success in athletics is more about finding a world-class coach and studying him like a scientist. It's not about being brilliant or bright, it's about surrounding yourself with the right people. It worked for me."

—JOHNNY "THE JET" RODGERS,
UNIVERSITY OF NEBRASKA HEISMAN WINNER, 1972

HEISMAN

HEISMAN

THE MAN BEHIND THE TROPHY

JOHN M. HEISMAN
WITH MARK SCHLABACH

HOWARD BOOKS
A DIVISION OF SIMON & SCHUSTER, INC.
New York · Nashville · London · Toronto · Sydney · New Delhi

Howard Books
A Division of Simon & Schuster, Inc.
1230 Avenue of the Americas
New York, NY 10020

Copyright © 2012 by John M. Heisman and Mark Schlabach

First Howard Books hardcover edition October 2012

HOWARD and colophon are trademarks of Simon & Schuster, Inc.

For information about special discounts for bulk purchases,
please contact Simon & Schuster Special Sales at
1-866-506-1949 or business@simonandschuster.com.

The Simon & Schuster Speakers Bureau can bring authors to your live event. For more information or to book an event, contact the Simon & Schuster Speakers Bureau at 1-866-248-3049 or visit our website at www.simonspeakers.com.

Designed by Renato Stanisic

Manufactured in the United States of America

10 9 8 7 6 5 4 3 2 1

Library of Congress Cataloging-in-Publication Data

Heisman, John M.
Heisman : the man behind the trophy / John M. Heisman and Mark Schlabach.
   p.   cm.
      1.   Heisman, John W. (John William), 1869–1936.   2.   Football coaches—United States—Biography.   3.   Football—United States—History.
4.   Heisman Trophy.   I.   Schlabach, Mark, 1972–   II.   Title.
   GV939.H38H45 2012
   796.332092—dc23   2012017657
[B]

ISBN 978-1-4516-8291-5
ISBN 978-1-4516-8293-9 (ebook)

John M. Heisman

FOR WILLIAM AND HELEN HEISMAN,
PARENTS EXTRAORDINAIRE, THE MEMORY
OF THEIR LOVE SUSTAINS ME STILL.

Mark Schlabach

TO JACK SCHLABACH, MY SON AND A FUTURE HEISMAN
TROPHY WINNER IN WHATEVER HE DECIDES TO DO.

Contents

Foreword

I was ecstatic to win the Heisman Trophy during my senior season at the University of Florida in 1966. It is a tremendous award and certainly the most recognized trophy in all of American sports.

My greatest individual honor is winning the Heisman Trophy. There were a lot of tremendous players in college football in 1966, like Purdue quarterback Bob Griese, UCLA quarterback Gary Beban, Syracuse running back Floyd Little, and Notre Dame half-back Nick Eddy. For me to be recognized as the best college football player in the country that season was an honor I've cherished throughout my life.

My Heisman Trophy sits in my office at the University of South Carolina, along with seven footballs that commemorate the South-eastern Conference championships our teams won at the University of Florida.

In high school, I had no idea where I wanted to go to college until Coach Ray Graves from the University of Florida began recruiting me. We threw the ball quite a bit at Science Hill High School, and I wanted to pitch it around in college. That's what Gators coach Ray Graves assured me we would do if I went to Florida. I came back home after our visit down there, and then signed with Florida. I loved Coach Graves and appreciated that he was the son of a preacher, just like me. I also thought that I could end up living in Florida after my playing career was over.

After my NFL career ended I went into coaching and was very fortunate to have one of my players win the Heisman Trophy. Florida quarterback Danny Wuerffel won the award in 1996 and then he led us to a 52–50 victory over FSU in the Sugar Bowl for the national championship.

It is fitting that this honor is named for Coach John Heisman, one of the great early American football coaches and a true innovator for the sport. After reading *Heisman: The Man Behind the Trophy*, I was surprised to learn how much John Heisman contributed to the sport that I love so much. Among other innovations, Heisman introduced the center snap, audible "hike" signal, hidden ball trick, and lateral passes. Much of what Heisman invented nearly one hundred years ago is still very much a part of the game today, which is quite remarkable.

But what impressed me more than anything else about John Heisman was that he embraced the characteristics of what being a coach is all about. He cared deeply about the young men who played for him and required them to attend classes and graduate with degrees. John Heisman knew his influence over his players would have a lasting effect on them long after they had left his teams to become husbands and fathers while earning a living.

As I am one of the very few Heisman winners to become a coach, I consider it a huge privilege to represent the coaching profession and the Heisman Trophy. The award is named for one of the very best college football coaches ever to pace the sidelines, John Heisman.

Steve Spurrier
University of South Carolina

Introduction

I grew up in the Midwest in the small town of Curtice, Ohio, some twelve miles east of Toledo. My father was an ironworker and member of Union Local 55. My mother was a registered nurse and later postmaster of the town's class II post office. I played baseball, caught crawdads and carp in the creek, and hung out with the Shields kids most every spare hour of summer vacations. One September Saturday afternoon, I sat on the living room floor playing with my green army men while my dad watched the Big Ten game of the week. The curtains were drawn to dim the glare on the black-and-white Zenith, and thick cigar smoke hung in the air as Pop relaxed in his recliner. On the television Wisconsin was playing at Ohio State and the Buckeyes were moving the ball down the field. Dad suddenly gave my shoulder a shake and said, "That running back is going to get a trophy that's named for our family!" I thought that sounded interesting so I looked up to pay attention. The announcer was calling the play: ". . . Cassady takes the handoff, he sweeps left, picks up a block, sidesteps. . . . He's past the line to the twenty-five to the twenty. . . . He's got one man to beat . . . to the ten . . . five . . . TOUCHDOWN OHIO STATE! Howard 'Hopalong' Cassady puts the Buckeyes into the lead!" Now this really caught the attention of this eight-year-old. I was fascinated. Hopalong Cassady was on TV Saturday mornings after Gene Autry and before Roy Rogers, so how did he get from the Wild West to Ohio State and change into football clothes so fast? Did all cowboys play football?

I asked my dad about this. He smiled and said that it was another Hopalong and that he was going to win the Heisman Trophy. I took this in without comment and continued to watch the game. Dad made a few more observations about the trophy and something about his uncle and a couch. I went back to playing with my army men and rolled these things over in my mind.

Antsy and bored from being cooped up in the house on a sunny September day, I asked to go next door to the Shieldses' house to play. As I walked down Reiman Road and into their driveway, I kept thinking about what Dad had said. I tapped on the side door and went in. Rich Shields, head of the clan, was watching the game too, and Mike and Rick were getting out a deck of cards to start a game. Tina had a bunch of curlers in her hair, and little Mark sat with his dad in front of the TV. Doris, my second mom, plopped a yellow-mustarded bologna sandwich on a paper plate in front of me and I was dealt a hand of rummy. What had tumbled about in my brain finally came out, "So what kind of award does your family give out?" I asked, and received blank stares. It was a guileless, innocent question; one that I had no clue would begin to reveal so much, for so long, in my lifetime. Rich turned to me and replied, "So your dad told you about that did he?" I nodded. "Well, John, you'll learn more about that soon enough." I took that at face value and went back to trying to draw another 5 for rummy. Rich's words were and would continue to unfold all too true.

The years passed and I noticed our name more often in the sports pages. This would prompt from me more questions to my dad. He responded with wonderful stories of Uncle Bill, officially known to the sporting public as Coach John W. Heisman. The *W* in his name stood for William and our family affectionately called him Uncle Bill. Dad would begin a story with "Uncle Bill this" and "Uncle Bill that," or, "One time Uncle Bill . . ." With each telling, I began to understand more and more the rich history of my family. Later, as a father raising four of my own children, I saw the value of passing on the heritage my father had instilled in me. When Dad wanted to give a lesson in character, I heard a story about Uncle Bill. When he wanted to impart a picture of manhood, I heard a story about Uncle Bill. When he wanted me to understand good sportsmanship, scholastic effort, or gentlemanly behavior, I heard an Uncle Bill story. These stories were effective, entertaining, and always hit the mark.

John W. Heisman was the middle of three sons, Dan the eldest, John, and the youngest, Mike, my grandfather. Mike had one son, William Lee, my father and the conveyor of the family stories. My dad, born in 1909, knew his uncle Bill in the first twenty-seven years of his life, until 1936, when Uncle Bill died of pneumonia. Uncle Bill's widow, Edith, survived him by some twenty-eight years, and I remember her visit to us in Curtice one summer in the early 1960s. She was a kind and stately lady who left a wonderful impression on me even to this day. Upon her passing we were notified of some family articles left to us through her estate. We collected a couple chests from Rheinlander, Wisconsin, and brought them back to Ohio.

Here, indeed, was a treasure: the memoirs of Coach John W. Heisman, his original writings, and other memorabilia. I found in these volumes not only football history but written verification that all my uncle Bill stories were not only true but amazingly accurate.

I hope you will enjoy this account of an American legend: the flesh and blood man whose name in football is well known but whose life is not. In my words, my father's words, and in places, Uncle Bill's words, here is the story of Coach John William Heisman and how he shaped America's great passion: football!

Prologue

Early in 1935, the officers of the Downtown Athletic Club of New York proposed an idea to name one football player the best in the country. The club would honor that player at a formal banquet hosted by the Downtown Athletic Club with great pomp and circumstance. It seemed like such a grand notion that they took the idea to the club's college football authority, John Heisman.

"Why?" Heisman asked.

Heisman had been hired as the club's first athletic director in May 1930. He was an obvious choice for the position, having been one of college football's most successful early coaches and innovators, as well as having worked in similar capacities at the Atlanta Athletic Club and the Houston Athletic Club. For the position in New York, Heisman received recommendations from legendary University of Chicago head coach Amos Alonzo Stagg; another legend, sportswriter Grantland Rice; and world-famous golfer Robert Jones Jr., among others. Heisman argued that since the Touchdown Club of New York's annual banquet was already in place for December, having another ceremony to honor a player of the year would be redundant. Besides, how could an individual be found or judged as the best in the country? Football is and always has been a team sport, Heisman argued, so where exactly is the merit in creating this type of an award?

As to how the player of the year would be determined, Jack Prince, a prominent member of the Downtown Athletic Club, proposed that a system of voting should be implemented. Sportswriters, whose jobs required them to have a degree of objectivity in reporting on football players and teams, would be the likely voters. Their qualifications would need to include the breadth of their reporting, both in the number of teams they covered and in the number of regional conferences attended. The player of the year would be determined by a consensus vote, weighted by opinions across many regions. Ignoring Heisman's objections, the officers continued to press the issue, maintaining that the new award would enhance the reputation of the Touchdown Club and become a driving force for new membership.

Heisman, then sixty-five—and eight years removed from his last coaching job—had worked arduously in his position as athletic director and supervisor of physical facilities at the Downtown Athletic Club. Heisman and his wife, Edith, had moved in 1927 to New York, where he worked with a sporting goods company and continued his writing career. His role at the Downtown Athletic Club was to attract new membership, host social events, and bring a wholehearted physical fitness program to the business community of lower Manhattan. Heisman's constant admonishments for fitness and overall health maintenance had not been ignored. When one of his *Downtown Athletic Club Journal* articles proclaimed how fitness promoted a good digestive tract, one of the members jibed, "Heis, I knew you were a coach and a lawyer, I didn't know you were a doctor, too!" The moniker stuck. "Doc" Heisman roamed the club and carried a well-earned yet unpretentious air of authority. "Doc" simply seemed fitting, and the moniker was used with respect, affection, and appreciation.

Undoubtedly, in his second-floor office at the Downtown Athletic Club, Heisman debated for hours the merits of awarding a national player-of-the-year trophy. It was his favorite method of mulling over a problem and devising its solution. Heisman's stepson from his first marriage, Colonel Carlisle Cox, a retired US Cavalry officer, recalled in the December 1964 issue of *Atlanta Magazine* how his stepfather used to pace the floor of his study. "And at times, I must confess he was the perfect absent-minded professor. In our study—this was in a home coach had bought on Ponce de Leon [Avenue in Atlanta]—he would pace the floor and talk out his problems aloud. In this room, and God knows why it was permitted to remain, there was a chandelier, which hung just low enough to hit his bald spot. For one entire season his head never got well. He would walk under that chandelier, it would clip him, he would cuss a little, move off to one side and four minutes later he would walk under it and bust his head again."[1]

Finally, Heisman admitted there were some merits in a trophy. Maybe the idea would work if the correct qualifications were in place, as well as a proper voting system. It might even make for a nice luncheon for a handful of players and a few dignitaries. After much thought, Heisman finally gave his support to the idea and embraced Prince's proposal of a voting system. With great enthusiasm, the officers encouraged him to draw up the qualifications[2] and give the award a proper name. Heisman was put in charge of awarding the first Downtown Athletic Club Award. One can almost hear his sigh across the decades.

The trophy would initially be awarded by a simple majority vote from sportswriters. Jack Prince's voting system would later include a matrix of regions, with each voter giving weighted first-, second-, and third-place votes. The initial voting region was simply "east of the Mississippi River," as Heisman still wasn't convinced great football was being played out West.

More than anything else, Heisman wanted the award to reflect his own ideals of a football player. The individual needed to be of good character, someone who always presented himself as a gentleman. The player's attitude should be selfless—with his team's best interests in mind—not self-aggrandizing. After jotting down about half a dozen qualifications, Heisman sent the requirements to the club's executive committee, which approved them as written.

Next came the issue of what the trophy would look like. In searching for a unique design, the Downtown Athletic Club commissioned Frank Eliscu, a twenty-three-year-old recent graduate of Pratt Institute in Brooklyn, New York, to design the trophy. Eliscu had recently won a National Academy prize for his sculptures and was now looking for a job that actually paid. He decided to cast the trophy by an artistic method known as the lost wax process of bronze medal molding. He asked his friend Ed Smith, a running back at New York University, to pose for the design of the sculpture. Eliscu decided to go with a football player sidestepping and straight-arming a would-be tackler. The Downtown Athletic Club officers approved Eliscu's initial design, and he molded a clay sculpture. Eliscu took the model to Fordham University, and Rams head coach Jim Crowley, one of Notre Dame's famed Four Horsemen, had his players take various positions to illustrate the football sidestep. Eliscu shaped the model's arms and legs while watching, to depict a player's movements accurately.

Once Eliscu finished the model, he showed it to Notre Dame head coach Elmer Layden, another of the Four Horsemen, at a dinner in New York. Layden and his players loved the sculpture, and Eliscu moved forward with his bronze molding. His finished product weighed 25 pounds and was 14 inches long, 13½ inches high, and 6½ inches wide.

Over the next seventy-six years, it would become the most valued and coveted trophy in American sports.

On December 9, 1935, University of Chicago halfback Jay Berwanger, the legendary "one-man gang," was presented the first Downtown Athletic Club Award during a noon luncheon at the club. The *New York Times* reported, "the luncheon gathering was large enough to fill two dining rooms of the club and overflow into a third."[3] Because Berwanger's nose had been broken twice, he played wearing a helmet mounted with a face mask made of spring steel. Because of the helmet, Berwanger was also known as "the man in the iron mask." He was an excellent student, and his athletic abilities won the respect of his peers. Of the 107 opponents he faced, 104 of them named him the best halfback they had ever seen. Berwanger was a gentleman and would become a very successful businessman later in life. Heisman heartily approved of the first selection for the Downtown Athletic Club Award. Heisman didn't have a large role in the first Downtown Athletic Club presentation, but he did preside over a Touchdown Club of New York meeting at the Hotel Martinique, where Berwanger was honored again.

It was the last time Heisman would meet a winner. It was also the last time the Downtown Athletic Club Trophy would be presented.

CHAPTER ONE

American Dream

Is it or is it not a matter of importance that a young
man starts out in life with an ability to shut his jaw hard
and say, "I will," or "I will not," and mean it?
—JOHN WILLIAM HEISMAN, *PRINCIPLES OF FOOTBALL*

The air split with loud, clattering crashes. Voices bellowed quick and raw—a chorus of shouts not trained in finery. Sharp, cracking slaps of noise reached the ears of men walking home from work. Men with faces layered in heavy soot, hands toughened like leather, and bodies exhausted from ten-hour workdays stopped to watch the tumbling mass of young men. They watched the boys' arms and legs flailing to capture a round ball. They shook their heads and could only smile, sometimes wishing for their youth again so they might join the fray of this fascinating game that looked like soccer, was played like rugby, and had rules waiting to be broken. This was the infancy of American football in the early 1880s.

Older men watched the mass of boyhood, plunging, running, shoving, tripping, kicking, and falling over one another. Their legs and arms were intertwined, struggling, wrestling, and fighting for an underinflated ball. These wildcats and riggers of Titusville, Pennsylvania, who walked home late in the afternoon knew it for what it was—the daily scrimmage behind Michael Heisman's cooper shop. They also knew that Heisman's sons were always in the thick of it.

Only one thing would interrupt the mayhem, only one sound would pierce the din and bring it all to a stop. It always came from the front porch of 126 East Spring Street. It was Sarah Heisman's nightly call to supper: "Daniel! John! Come and eat before cold it gets! Bring Michael! Be quick!"

As soon as the call was heard, three players were immediately removed from the pile. Sarah Heisman was not one to be trifled with or kept waiting. Stern as she was, her knowing glance graciously ignored busted lips, bruised cheeks, or torn clothing when her boys scurried into the house. Raising boys is more art than science, and domesticating those three wild rascals into refined gentlemen was her undertaking. She did so without a second's hesitation. To sit at Sarah Heisman's table and expect to eat required a clean face, neck, and hands, as well as proper restraint while grace was offered before their meal. When the last "amen" was reverently uttered, excited discussions erupted—sometimes about the afternoon scrimmage and sometimes about events in town, such as the unpredictable antics of the colorful workers at Papa Heisman's shop.

According to widely accepted legend and a family tale that has been passed from generation to generation of Heisman descendants, Michael Heisman was a German immigrant and son of nobility. His father, Baron von Bogart, disapproved of his son marrying a peasant girl from Alsace-Lorraine, a French region that abuts the western border of Germany and was often the booty for the winning side after great wars between the countries. Disinherited by his family, Michael took "Heisman," the surname of his wife, Sarah, and sailed with her to America, leaving his family's fortune and royalty behind in the name of love.

The tale of Michael Heisman's humble beginnings has been widely publicized and generally accepted ever since Heisman became the most familiar name in all of American sports. The story is included in John W. Heisman's biographies at universities where he coached, and in profiles of him published in *Sports Illustrated*[1] and the *Philadelphia Inquirer*.[2] The story became widely known when Heisman's stepson from his first marriage, Colonel Carlisle Cox, relayed the tale to a Georgia Tech alumni group in Atlanta in the spring of 1964. "Cox dropped a bombshell with his disclosure that Heisman was not the true family name," *Atlanta Magazine* reported in 1964. "The fact that this surprised the assemblage—surprised the Colonel. He had believed the information common knowledge. National wire services nevertheless blared the story throughout the world."[3] Cox even went as far as telling the alumni group that Michael Heisman's father attempted to reconcile their relationship after his son struck it rich in America. "By this time, the old barony apparently had grown rather barren," Cox reportedly told the group. "But Coach's father would have no part of it. The name Heisman stuck."[4]

But the story of Heisman's German nobility was actually nothing more than a tall tale, one that Michael Heisman might have told others as he began to strike it rich in his new country. German birth records reveal that Michael Heisman was actually born Johann Michael Heissmann around midday on January 1, 1835, in Vorra, Germany, about forty-two kilometers east of Nuremberg, in the German state of Bavaria.[5] According to Protestant parish records there, Heissmann's mother was Anna Heissmann, the eldest daughter of the farmer Johann Michael Heissmann and his wife, Magdalena Steif. The elder Johann Heissmann is identified as his grandson's godfather, but a biological father's name is not included in the records. The younger Johann Michael Heissmann was baptized in a Protestant church the day after he was born. Anna Heissmann, who was twenty-three when her only son was born, died of dysentery—inflammation of the intestines, which was often fatal when untreated—on September 2, 1836.[6] The young Johann Michael Heissmann, who wasn't yet two years old at the time of his mother's death, was raised by his grandparents on their farm in Vorra, which his grandmother's family had cropped since 1618.

When the young Johann Michael Heissmann was twenty-three, he boarded the steamship *Borussia* to seek a new life in America.[7] The ship left Hamburg, Germany, in June 1858 and after sailing a day through the North Sea and the English Channel, it was briefly docked in Southampton, England, where it picked up additional passengers and cargo. Heissmann was one of 304 passengers aboard the ship, most of whom were German immigrants and third-class passengers. Heissmann was listed as passenger No. 222 on the ship manifest sworn to and signed by Captain N. Troutman and which was given to customs officials when the *Borussia* arrived in New York on July 1, 1858.[8] Heissmann probably spent more than two weeks sailing through the North Atlantic from Southampton to New York. The *Borussia*, a 2,349-gross-ton ship, was nearly 280 feet long, single-screwed, and was equipped with overhead oscillating engines, iron hull, clipper stem, one funnel, and three masts. It traveled at speeds of about ten knots. According to a March 7, 1857, report in the *Times* of London, the *Borussia* arrived in Hamburg, Germany, from New York after a run of "16 days and 9 hours, and averaging 9½ knots the hour throughout her trip."[9]

The *Borussia*, which started its first Hamburg–New York voyage on January 1, 1856, and sailed its last on April 30, 1870, was one of several steamships that carried German immigrants to the United States during the second half of the nineteenth century. Because of political unrest, religious persecution, and a shrinking economy in Germany, immigrants were attracted to the promises of free land and better financial opportunities in America. News of the settlers' experiences in America had been widely circulated in Germany through letters from relatives and in newspapers throughout the country. For a young man such as Heissmann, there was little to risk in going to America and so much to gain. The US National Archives and Records Administration has documented more than four million passengers arriving at US ports from Germany between 1850 and 1897. About 90 percent of those immigrants identified their country of origin or nationality as Germany or a German state, city, or region.

Johann Michael Heissmann, who changed his name to Michael Heisman shortly after arriving in America, was among them. He settled near Cleveland, Ohio, in 1858, three years before his new country would begin fighting the American Civil War. Fortunately for Michael Heisman, most of the fighting occurred to the east and south of Ohio, and he avoided having to join a Union Army regiment. After the Civil War ended in 1865, German immigrants began flocking to America once again. Cleveland became a popular destination for German immigrants after the Ohio and Erie Canal was constructed in the 1820s. Before the canal was dredged to link the Cuyahoga River with the Ohio River and other canal systems, it was easier for immigrants to reach Cincinnati or St. Louis via railways or the National Road, the first highway constructed by the US government, which was supposed to link Cumberland, Pennsylvania, with St. Louis. After the Panic of 1837, however, federal funding vanished and the road stopped in Vandalia, Illinois.

By 1850, after immigrants could reach Cleveland via railroads, the city's German-born residents had swelled to 33 percent of the population, more than even the native-born residents.[10] By the start of the twentieth century, more than forty thousand Germans lived in Cleveland. They worked as butchers, jewelers, tailors, cabinetmakers, and mechanics. They were widely known for constructing fine pianos and other musical instruments, and they introduced thirst-quenching beer and, of all things, the Christmas tree. German churches—there were more than 130 in Cleveland at the height of immigration—founded three hospitals and sponsored German-speaking schools. The German Concert Orchestra, also known as the Germania, was an ensemble of German musicians and was one of the longest-lasting acts in early Cleveland. A German newspaper was published in 1846 and was printed until the 1980s.

Cleveland seemed like the perfect place for Michael Heisman to raise a family after leaving behind his ancestry in Germany. Eight years after arriving in America, Heisman married Sarah Lehr, a twenty-two-year-old daughter of German immigrants, on July 21, 1866.[11] Like Heisman's grandfather, Sarah's father, Michael Lehr, was a farmer from the Bavaria region of Germany. He and his wife, Catherine, had eleven children. Sarah Ann Lehr, their second-oldest daughter, was born in Trenton, Ohio, on February 9, 1844.

It didn't take Michael and Sarah Heisman long to start their family. On April 10, 1867, their first son, Daniel, was born in Cleveland, and then John William came along on October 23, 1869. Their third son, Michael, was born in Erie, Pennsylvania, on February 25, 1872. An 1870 US Federal Census report revealed a bustling Heisman household on Cleveland's West Side. Along with Michael, Sarah, and their three sons, a domestic servant resided in their home at 59 Frankfort Avenue. The house was only a few blocks south of the Lake Erie shoreline. The location seemed convenient, since Michael Heisman spent his workdays at the shipyards, where his company produced wooden barrels used to transport beer, wine, and other liquids. The Heisman home wasn't far from the open-air West Side Market, where Sarah could purchase fresh vegetables, meat, and seafood for her family's meals. Streetlights, postal service, public libraries, and a police department were introduced in Cleveland in the 1860s.

For an immigrant who arrived in America with very little, life was good for Michael Heisman. Over the next couple of years, however, Heisman and his family would truly begin to live the American Dream, largely because of an unexpected discovery in the western Pennsylvania wilderness.

CHAPTER TWO

Titusville

America's first oil boom didn't occur until Edwin L. Drake successfully drilled the world's first flowing petroleum well in 1859 near Oil Creek in Titusville, Pennsylvania. By the time the country's first oil rush had run its course, some of the most famous names in American history—Carnegie, Rockefeller, and even John Wilkes Booth—had staked their claim to land at the foothills of the Allegheny Mountains, hoping to get rich or, in some cases, even richer. Michael Heisman, the father of John W. Heisman, was among the pioneer oil "boomers," moving his family in 1874 from Cleveland to Titusville, where he transformed his small business into a prosperous enterprise that supplied wooden barrels to many of the world's first oil barons.

It is impossible to know how long petroleum has been seeping through the dark soil and floating in the creeks, streams, and rivers of northwestern Pennsylvania; geologists contend that oil probably first came to the earth's surface there shortly after the last glacial period approximately 110,000 to 10,000 years ago, when ice covered most of Canada and the upper Midwest of the United States, resulting in the formation of the Great Lakes.[1]

In 1750, during a scouting mission into the Pennsylvania wilderness, French army ensign Joseph Coulon de Villiers de Jumonville witnessed the Seneca Native Americans incorporating oil into their religious ceremonies. Jumonville, who was born in modern-day Québec and was the son of a French military officer, served at Fort Duquesne near Pittsburgh. Jumonville's capture by George Washington and his subsequent death at the hands of the Native American Half King sparked the Seven Years' War, or French and Indian War, from 1756 to 1763.[2] Before his death, Jumonville reported the following observations to his commanding officer, General Louis-Joseph de Montcalm:

> I would desire to assure you that this is a most delightful land. Some of the most astonishing natural wonders have been discovered by our people. While descending the Allegheny, fifteen leagues below the mouth of the Conewango and three above the Venango, we were invited by the chief of the Senecas to attend a religious ceremony of his tribe. We landed, and drew up our canoes on a point where a small stream entered the river. The tribe appeared unusually solemn. We marched up the stream about half a league, where the company, a large band, it appeared, had arrived some days before us. Gigantic hills begirt us on every side. The scene was really sublime. The great chief then recited the conquests and heroism of his ancestors. The surface of the stream was covered with a thick scum, which burst into complete conflagration. The oil had been gathered, and lighted with a torch. At the sight of the flames, the Indians gave forth a triumphant shout and made the hills and valleys re-echo again. Here, this is revived the ancient fire worship of the East; here, then are the children of the sun.[3]

Crude oil was not refined or marketed for everyday use to the public until 1850. Samuel W. Kier of Pittsburgh built a small refinery with a five-barrel still and converted petroleum into lamp oil. Petroleum was more abundant and a cheaper option than whale oil or animal fat, which were the most common lighting fuels of the day.

At about that time, during the summer of 1853, George H. Bissell of New Orleans, an 1845 graduate of Dartmouth College, was visiting his alma mater's campus. Professor Dixie Crosby showed Bissell a bottle of crude oil that had been procured from the farm of his nephew, Dr. B. F. Brewer, near Oil Creek in Titusville. Bissell and an associate visited Titusville the next year, convinced the oil could be utilized in manufacturing and heating. Bissell obtained the rights to lands on Oil Creek from Brewer & Watson Lumber Company for $5,000 on a ninety-nine-year lease.[4] A pump was attached to a working gear of a nearby sawmill, and surface oil and water were then pumped into large vats. The water eventually settled to the bottom, allowing oil to be extracted in its natural state. The pump initially yielded three hundred barrels of oil, which were shipped to Professor B. Silliman Jr. of Yale University, who had been appointed an original member of the National Academy of Sciences by the US Congress. Silliman was hired by Bissell to analyze the oil's worth and potential uses. In the fall of 1855, Silliman famously pronounced the crude oil's constituents as "promising," and his report was widely circulated in New England.

Bissell and his associates formed the Pennsylvania Rock Oil Company—the first petroleum company chartered in the United States—and it was the first enterprise to trench and gather surface oil around Oil Creek. But the venture yielded only modest results for the first couple of years; the oil was measured by the gallon and sold for a price as high as $1.50 per gallon.[5] After the Depression of 1857, the company was reorganized as Seneca Oil Company, with a capital stock of $300,000. Drake, a conductor on the New Haven Railroad, was hired to sink an artesian well near Oil Creek in the spring of 1858. He hired William "Uncle Billy" Smith, a blacksmith, who was experienced in making salt drilling tools, to assist him in the venture. Drake and Smith built a derrick and engine house and initially tried to dig the rock and curb a well, but their plan failed. After several months of futile results, the Seneca Oil Company ceased investing capital into the venture and abandoned Drake. He was forced to sink his own money into the seemingly hopeless cause. Drake's biggest obstacle was that the well became engulfed with water and collapsed every time he tried to drill through the rock with a steam engine. As a solution, Drake and Smith drove a four-inch pipe into the ground and drilled inside the casing, which allowed them to drill about three feet per day.

After reaching a depth of 69½ feet on August 27, 1859, Smith and his two sons decided to stop drilling for the day. The next afternoon, Smith checked on the well and saw a black substance inside the pipe. They'd struck oil! The oil was brought to the surface with a hand-pitcher pump and was collected in a bathtub. A pump was eventually rigged in the well and it produced about twenty barrels a day. It was the first successful oil well in the world. The great Pennsylvania oil rush—the first oil boom in US history—was on.

Michael Heisman co-owned and operated the Stephens & Heisman Cooper Shop, along with George Stephens, at the corner of East Spring and Kerr Streets. Shortly after Drake struck oil at his pioneer well, wooden barrels became almost as valuable as the petroleum itself. Drake managed to secure every barrel in Titusville—they had previously stored everything from wine to beer to whiskey to fish—and then he managed to find twenty-eight barrels in nearby Meadville, Pennsylvania.[6] In 1859, the pioneer wells of Titusville produced about two thousand barrels of oil; by the end of 1860 there were seventy-four producing wells churning up about two hundred thousand barrels per year.[7]

Heisman apparently struggled initially to make his way into the oil business. On October 27, 1879, he filed for bankruptcy in US District Court in western Pennsylvania.[8] But once the oil really started flowing, it didn't take him long to recover financially. At the height of oil production, Heisman employed about thirty-five workers. Barrel-making was considered an art form, and coopers were considered very skilled laborers. The barrel's staves were made of prime white oak, and the hoops were hickory (which were eventually replaced by iron hoops). According to oil historian Sir Boverton Redwood, the forty-two-gallon oil barrel was manufactured as follows: "staves were assembled in a circle and held in position by an iron ring; the infant barrel was steamed in an iron cylinder, thus softening the wood; the staves were bent into shape and drawn together by a circle of wire rope run by an engine; an iron hoop was slipped over the upper end to hold the staves in position; the barrel was fired inside by burning shavings or some other easily fired material; thick temporary hoops were slipped over the barrel and drawn together by machinery; the rough ends of the staves were pared off in a lathe and grooves for the heads were cut in the barrel; six iron hoops were driven over the barrel by a steam engine; and hot glue, glycerin or soluble glass was poured into the barrel and the barrel was rotated to make it tight."[9]

Among Heisman's customers were Andrew Carnegie and John D. Rockefeller. Carnegie was one of the principal stockholders in Columbia Oil Company, which financed twelve wells at Blood Farm, and his earnings helped him build his first steel mills (Carnegie later sold his steel company for $480 million to J. P. Morgan in 1901). John D. Rockefeller, a produce merchant from Cleveland, visited Titusville in 1860 to explore the oil industry, but he wasn't convinced the petroleum supply would sustain so many producers. Five years later, after oil was struck in nearby Pithole, Pennsylvania, Rockefeller became a major investor in petroleum. He formed Standard Oil of Ohio in 1870, which quickly became the country's most profitable refinery. By 1872, Standard Oil Company had purchased twenty-two of the twenty-six oil refineries in Cleveland and was the largest producer of oil and kerosene in the world. With a net worth of $1.4 billion at the time of his death in 1937, Rockefeller is widely considered the richest man in US history, and much of his early wealth was the result of his speculation in Titusville.

Not every oil speculator struck it rich in Titusville. In 1863, a well-known Shakespearean actor named John Wilkes Booth formed an oil partnership with members of his theater group after reading about the oil boom in newspapers while performing in Cleveland. Booth called the venture the "Dramatic Oil Company," and he acquired a lease to drill a well at a farm near Franklin, Pennsylvania. After drillers started working on the Wilhelmina No. 1 well in May 1864, Booth was so confident he would become rich from oil that he gave up stage acting altogether and traveled to the Allegheny region to watch the well's progress. Alas, the well went dry after explosives were detonated inside it. Less than a year later, and only five days after Confederate army general Robert E. Lee surrendered to Union army general Ulysses S. Grant in Appomattox Court House, Virginia, ending the American Civil War, Booth shot US president Abraham Lincoln at Ford's Theater in Washington, DC, on April 14, 1865; Lincoln died the following day. If Booth's oil well had flourished, American history might have been different.

In July 1891, Michael Heisman used the small fortune earned from his cooperage to buy interest in American Oil Works, which was founded by a group of German-speaking immigrants in 1885 on South Brown Street. Along with Frank Von Tacky, Louis Walz, and William Teege, Heisman was one of the company's largest shareholders. It wasn't an expansive operation; American Oil Works primarily refined kerosene and lubrication oil and was later sold to Pennsylvania Refining Company (now the Penreco Division of Pennzoil) in 1926. According to Titusville researcher David Weber, Heisman also had working oil leases in the Church Run field north of Titusville. Heisman became involved in local politics and was a local beer distributor, offering customers Toledo Beer and Ale in quantities of "1½, ¾ or ½ barrels."[10] He still managed to have fun in Titusville's numerous saloons. On July 19, 1886, Heisman pled guilty and was fined $3.00 for his role in an altercation after a night of drinking. "On Saturday night last, M. Heisman and John Meising had an argument and altercation which wound up with Heisman giving John a little one behind the ear to remember him by," the *Titusville Morning*

Herald reported. "John thought his memory needed no such incentive and after reducing the bump with frequent applications of ointment, had a warrant sworn out."[11]

Inside the shop, Mr. Heisman's three sons loved to watch the scruffy coopers working in their blackened aprons. A good cooper could take a rod of iron, still red-hot from the forge, and weld it into a hoop with a single strike of his hammer. The iron was bent around a loop form, its ends were put into the forge until white-hot, and then they were welded together on an anvil. The cooper quickly plunged the new hoop into a vat of water to draw a modest temper on the iron, and then he tightly fastened the hoops over the beveled planks to complete the barrels.

Curled shavings left by long stokes from the adze covered the floor and had to be swept several times a day to prevent any spark from catching fire. The cooperage actually burned to the ground in December 1885, but was rebuilt in less than a month.[12] Daniel usually drew the job of sweeping the shavings as Heisman's eldest son, and he quickly became the boy most likely to take over the family business. Learning from the ground up was the way Papa Heisman wanted his son to mature. If Daniel didn't know all of the operations of the cooper shop, how could he run it one day? Sadly, Daniel Heisman didn't live long enough to take over his father's company. On May 21, 1892, five years after younger brother John left Titusville for college and two years after his father sold his interest in the cooperage and returned to Cleveland, Daniel Heisman, who was still working at the cooper shop operated by the Stephens family, was killed while unloading two rail car loads of oak staves.

According to a May 22, 1892, story in the *Titusville Morning Herald*, "Heisman was employed at the works and had been detailed, together with Foreman H. S. Edwards, Ed Millner, Thomas O'Hare, William O'Hare and Adam Schultz, to unload two carloads of staves standing on the adjacent track. It was necessary to run the cars down toward the works. They were uncoupled and the six men put their shoulders to the rear of the leading car and were slowly moving it along the track, which is slightly down grade at this point. They had previously, as they supposed, blocked and braked the other car, which was heavily loaded. Heisman and his companions were unaware of their danger before the runaway car from behind was on them. Heisman was walking directly between the bumpers when the cars came together, and when they broke apart he fell forward on his face with the exclamation, 'My God, boys, I'm killed.' " [13]

According to the article, Daniel Heisman's coworkers carried him to his home after he was fatally injured. Doctors were summoned to the house, but "an examination showed that the unfortunate man had sustained internal injuries that must prove fatal in a few short hours at the most. Death came to his relief at 5:10 o'clock in the afternoon, and probably resulted from internal hemorrhage. Consciousness did not desert him, and he talked rationally before death and did not suffer great pain. Reverend John Lusher was with the young man during his last hours." [14] Daniel Heisman was twenty-five years old when he died and left behind his wife, the former Annabel McGarvie, and their three young children.

Even after his brother's death, Michael Heisman decided to remain in the oil business. As a young boy, he loved to go to the oil fields with his father to deliver the barrels. The towering oil derricks fascinated him, and in time the oil field would lure him into the operations industry. John William, the middle son, enjoyed talking with the men in the shop and learning about the nature of people. Regardless of their station in life, John could draw out stories from each worker. The young man had a gift in being able to listen, read, and comprehend people. The oil town of Titusville taught the Heisman boys lessons of life that each would take and build upon: personal responsibility; hard, persevering work; and honest dealings.

The people of Titusville could have never known where John William Heisman would take those lessons.

CHAPTER THREE

Brown University

Baseball might be America's pastime, but football is America's sporting passion. Many American males have strapped on the pads and tried out for a football team. From high school to college to the National Football League, the talent rises; the game intensifies; the competition grows fierce; and eventually size, speed, and strength separate the gifted from the average. Even after hanging up their cleats and realizing they will not play the organized game again, former players continue to have a fascination with football, a game of human chess played with twenty-two athletic pieces on a hundred-yard board. At some point everyone retires to the sideline to watch and cheer, knowing how intense the game is and appreciating those who play it. Football fans pour over sports pages and the Internet with continued obsessions for their favorite teams, players, and coaches. How did this football fetish begin? Where did the game originate? Though the game played by young John Heisman was called "football," the twenty-first-century observer would be hard-pressed to recognize it as football. By 1880 the game had not even progressed to the state of rugby. In 1928, after Heisman had retired from coaching, he wrote of his boyhood football days for *Collier's Weekly*:

> The memory of those shin-breaking afternoons of Association
> football wherein active brains were secondary to durable legs

is still bright. Actually, the game we played in Titusville was only a species of Association football. Of rules we observed few, having few. Signals we had none—needed none, wanted none. We butted the ball, punched it, elbowed it and kicked it. Incidentally, many were the butts, punches, kicks and assorted socks that fell short of the ball and found lodging on us. Fine, uncomplicated, two-fisted days those. Yale, Harvard, Princeton and several other Eastern colleges were playing Walter Camp rules, still very much a mystery to us of the inland schools although Mr. Camp had evolved them seven years before the free and easy American interpretation of old English Rugby. He had abolished the stupid, bull-headed scrum and had invented the faster and more spectacular scrimmage. Also he had reduced the number of players on a side from 15 to 11. Bah! What cared we in Titusville and innumerable points west and south for all this fuzz-buzz. We were having the times of our lives assaulting a round, black rubber ball up and down expansive fields. We had fifteen men on a side and in the game that we played, the ball belonged to him or them strong enough and fleet enough to take it. What did we want with signals? Let Yale and Harvard have their signals— whatever they were. *They* would have signals. Our simple attitude toward all that nonsense was that of the relatively recent and highly successful fullback who, five yards from the enemy's goal line, silenced his quarterback's chatter with: "Ah, t'hell with these signals; gimme the ball."[1]

Heisman's ancient game of football, like the daily contests played behind his father's cooper shop in Titusville, was not yet rugby as played on the college grounds. It looked at best to be soccer, without the finesse and less than half the rules. In these contests, mass pile-ups were common and referees less so. To be caught in the middle of a scrum was to realize that kicking, squeezing, hitting, and biting would go on until the ball worked itself free. Holding on to life and limb was of prime importance to continued play. Given the frequent games behind the cooperage, the Titusville squad, which always seemed to include the three Heisman boys, had worked its way into "a fair bunch of kickers that won all their games." Football became the driving passion of young John Heisman, a determination that would carry him to the next levels of football as well as into the evolution of the game itself.

Heisman was both an exceptional intellect and an exemplary athlete. He was captain of Titusville High School's baseball team and a champion gymnast. Though Heisman was smallish for a football player, outweighed by fifteen pounds in high school and later by as much as fifty pounds in college, he played on the line at the position of guard. Heisman competed on the school's varsity teams in 1884, 1885, and 1886. Michael Heisman, a short man of about five feet four inches, refused to watch his son play what he believed was a barbaric game. "I have never known a man more stubbornly opposed to the game," John Heisman once recalled. "It was brutal. It was a waste of time. It should be prohibited."[2] John Heisman graduated as salutatorian of his senior class at Titusville High School in 1887. His father hoped he would attend Brown University in Providence, Rhode Island, and pursue a law career. Fascinated by the writings of Shakespeare and other classics, Heisman was already a great speaker and writer. On June 17, 1887, Heisman delivered a commencement speech at his graduation ceremony at Titusville Presbyterian Church.

"The church was crowded almost to suffocation, and many were unable to obtain admittance," the *Titusville Morning Herald* reported the next day. "The programme [sic] began with the Hallelujah chorus by Handel, a powerful composition which was rendered with precision and effect. After prayer by the Reverend Robert Murray the class sang 'Our Father' following this with the chorus 'Tramp, Tramp o'er Moss and Fell' by Sir Henry R. Bishop. John W. Heisman's oration— 'The Dramatist, A Sermonizer'—was full of dramatic emphasis and fire, and showed how the masterpieces of Shakespeare depicted the end of unchecked passion. Sermons are not confined to the pulpit, and as the plays of the great bard teach lessons of divine truth, it is no error in regarding him as a servant of the master, and so a sermonizer. Mr. Heisman's effort was greeted with well-merited applause."[3]

As Heisman approached his senior year at Titusville High School, three former teammates returned home after their college courses broke for the summer in 1886. William Perrin had been the captain of his team at Andover University (now Phillips, Andover Academy in Andover, Massachusetts, about twenty-five miles north of Boston); Will Johnston had played at the University of Pennsylvania; and Frank Payne was a member of the Princeton squad. How exciting it was to have college men home in Titusville, explaining football as it was played by the educated (football at this level was still American rugby). Johnston, Payne, and Perrin labored long in explaining the rules and gave demonstrations of the rugby game. Heisman later wrote, "Then and there the old game lost its savor. From that moment nothing of football, which did not permit of running with the ball, appealed to me. I bought a rules book for ten cents and retired to seclusion, which I labored over such puzzling terminology as: touchdown, touchback, touch-in-goal, safety, punch-out, drop kick, on side, off side. They meant nothing to me."[4]

In September 1887, at age seventeen, Heisman left Titusville for Brown University. Brown was founded in 1764, prior to America's independence from the British Empire. The Baptist Church founded the school, but it was the first American university to accept students regardless of religious affiliation. At the time Heisman enrolled at Brown, it was still an all-male school. Brown didn't become coeducational until a women's college was established in 1891. Because Heisman's career aspirations—or at least those of his father—were to attend law school and become an attorney, it's unclear why he chose to attend Brown. To this day, Brown is one of only two Ivy

League schools (Princeton is the other) that have neither a business school nor a law school.

Regardless, Heisman was excited about making his first solo adventure and living for the first time on his own. "I was seventeen and football mad," Heisman recalled. "Likewise, I was making my first momentous journey. Believe me, it was just a trifle too much for me to handle calmly. I missed trains right and left."[5] One of the missed connections led to a long layover of several hours in Albany, New York. With time on his hands, young Heisman walked about town and, at its edge, found a large field where a bunch of boys were playing football. Here for the first time, Heisman beheld an oval, tan leather football. Up until that point in his life, all his football was played with a round, black rubber ball that had been kicked and elbowed toward the goal. The Albany chaps not only had an oval ball but also uniforms and verbal signals! "But best of all they ran with the ball," Heisman wrote. "I missed another train."[6]

The hundreds of miles of railway track sped by as Heisman contemplated what he had seen: oval ball, uniforms, and signals. A new world was appearing to him, and his excitement was now barely containable. The ball would have no predictable bounce. Just imagine what that would mean! Kicking blindly at it might not give the desired and expected results. The ball was made to be carried in one's arms. Could he dare think it? And uniforms on a town team, no less! Heisman's eyes were opened to a new universe of tight-fitting jackets and matching knee shorts. How much easier it would be to identify teammates from the opponent! The Albany boys had looked smart in distinct team colors, and their uniforms looked quite stylish and right full of dirt! At least he could relate to the dirt. Bucking, assaulting, and punching your own teammate in the midst of battle was not uncommon, though sometimes embarrassing. Uniforms would cure that problem, or at least greatly reduce the number of occurrences.

And signals! Maybe Yale and its blokes weren't so pretentious after all! If you can direct your lads to go a certain way just before putting the ball in play, oh, my stars and garters! Heisman's thoughts revolved around football the rest of his trip. Even when the conductor called out his station at Providence, he barely took notice until the train whistle broke his daydreams to announce their arrival. What a red carpet before him! On the grounds of Brown University, a game of football was already in progress. Heisman recalled: "Was I impressed with the ivy-clad halls? Did the enchantment which clothes the college vistas for the wide-eyed freshman grip me? Ah, no, no chance, no chance. I do not remember that I gave more than a fleeting glance at the buildings because, dear reader, there at my feet on the campus a game of football was in progress. On one side were freshmen who had caught their trains and had arrived in good order and according to schedule. Opposed to them were the town boys. And as I stood there watching all this magnificence, luck tapped me. One of the freshmen had quit."[7]

Dressed in a tailor-made black suit, quite possibly made for him at J. J. Carter's Tailor Shop or Lammer's Store on Spring Street in Titusville, Heisman quickly jumped into the fray. "With sagging jaw and popping eyes I stood there, 144 pounds stripped, the only available player. 'Hey, want to play?' For me the Gates of Paradise had been opened." Inserted into the game at left tackle, Heisman's responsibilities were to block, render, charge, and otherwise assault the other team's right tackle to clear the way for the ball carrier. At this point in football's evolution, the general expectation was to assume that the runner was coming your way. Whether on offense or defense, the lineman must clear or stop the progress of the ball carrier. So here Heisman was, fresh off the train, suitcases and trunks piled at the side of the field and suddenly called to battle. He ran onto the field with only his stylish, hand-tailored Titusville suit as his padding and uniform. Buttoning his beautiful coat and hitching up his trousers, Heisman bent over into an approximation of a sprinter's crouch as the quarterback called signals. The ball was heeled back and in a blink young Heisman was buried under the huge opposing tackle.[8]

The game raged on with the big tackle making a meal of Heisman, but nothing would deter his enthusiasm. Nothing would daunt his passion. Football had consumed him since Albany, New York, and now he was in his element. Near the end of the contest a unique opportunity presented itself to Heisman. The opposing runner had been hitting the tackle positions in what was becoming a predictable pattern. Heisman noticed the regularity of the pattern: right side, left side, right, left. He also noticed a difference in his opponent's stance when the ball was coming his way, indicating the way the tackle intended to block him. Heisman, in fact, thought he had picked up on the signal that the ball was coming his way. Now he was certain, as the tackle was tensing. When the ball was heeled, Heisman sidestepped the block as the runner received the ball. Simultaneously, the defending guard pushed through to knock the play off-kilter and the runner lost his stride and began to stumble. It was now or never, so Heisman grabbed the ball from the runner's hands in midstumble.

Heisman didn't recall how long the game lasted or even which team won. When the game was over, Heisman was left with a black eye and a bloody nose. The Titusville suit, which he had spent previous hours brushing and flecking to remove coal particles and lint, was covered in blood and dirt. "That suit, that gallant effort of Titusville's best tailor, was an unqualified ruin," Heisman recalled years later. "But I was happy. *I had run with the ball.* Somewhere near the close of hostilities I had snatched the ball from an opponent's arms and had run like a mad thing 30 yards before being fetched to earth with a crash that loosened a number of teeth."[9]

Now imagine Heisman's disappointment the next day when he learned that Brown had dropped its intercollegiate football team. The Brown administration had been slow to embrace the sport, which was already flourishing at other future Ivy League schools such as Harvard and Yale. Football was banned by Brown University president Barnas Sears in 1862 because of its violent nature, and then was reinstated as an intramural sport between freshmen and sophomores in 1866. A football association was formed in 1874, but Brown didn't play its first intercollegiate football game until four years later, when Brown played against Amherst College in Amherst, Massachusetts, on November 13, 1878—nine years to the day after Rutgers and Princeton played the first intercollegiate game, in Piscataway, New Jersey. Brown arrived at its inaugural game wearing new white canvas uniforms and brown stockings, which they had purchased two days earlier for a $50 down payment and the security deposit of Brown Football Association president George Malcolm's watch.[10] Amherst won the game by a score of one goal and four touchdowns to nothing. Brown played its second game in 1880 (Yale won) and its third in 1886 (Brown finally defeated Providence High School by a 70–0 score). The 1886 Brown team finished the season with a 1-1 record, also losing to Boston University, 10–6. Because of the school's lack of interest in football and lack of funding to support it, the team was dropped for two seasons and picked up again in 1889. "I had chosen my college badly," Heisman wrote. "Brown had played such a rotten game during the several preceding seasons that the authorities had decided, in defense of the fair name of the college, to abandon intercollegiate competition. For a while, I was in revolt against the world."[11]

Heisman, still weighing only about 148 pounds, was forced to make do playing for a local club team. Bert Meador, a fellow freshman from Pawtucket, Rhode Island, was impressed with Heisman's play and effort during his first scrimmage on campus and invited him to play on a Pawtucket team that was scheduled to play a team from Taunton, Massachusetts, the following week. It was still another opportunity to play football, and that was good enough for Heisman. He was given his first football uniform, complete with shorts, jersey, and jacket. Heisman's chest puffed with pride as he donned the garb of contest. Kingly robes, Heisman thought, as he strutted about. Then he spotted the team's gigantic center, the behemoth who anchored his opponents, wearing a haircloth jacket. "Have you ever seen the stuff, black shiny stuff, which years and years ago they used to cover sofas?" Heisman wrote. "That was it. To this day I have never seen any material that compared with that football garment. You could never get a handful of that stuff, or if you did you'd bend every nail on your hand. I was shot with envy for that jacket." [12]

For whatever reason, the team's captains wouldn't share their signals with him. "Meador was a firm believer in keeping them from linemen," Heisman wrote. "Perhaps it was quite as well. The lad opposing me was 25 pounds my superior physically. I was far too busy to be bothered with signals." [13]

Heisman returned to the club team the following year, after he was invited to come back by manager George Walker, another Brown classmate, whose parents had forbidden him from playing the rugged game. Heisman played left guard for the team; the right guard, Fatty Williams, weighed about 210 pounds. Another teammate was Fred Hovey, who was a national tennis champion and the best athlete on campus. The signals that had thoroughly fascinated Heisman were actually nothing more than shouts of encouragement from the team's quarterback. For instance, if the quarterback shouted, "Boys, we must play better," it was the signal for Heisman to take the ball from the quarterback and hit the opponent's right tackle. "Line up Brown" meant for the left tackle to run through right tackle, and "Charge hard now" was a signal for the left end to run to the right. [14] The archaic signals were a far cry from the those used by NFL teams in later years (For instance, New York Giants quarterback Eli Manning called "seventy-six Union Y Sail" before throwing a thirty-two-yard pass to David Tyree in the closing minutes of the Giants' 17–14 upset of the New England Patriots in Super Bowl XLII on February 3, 2008), but they were groundbreaking in Heisman's mind nonetheless.

"If the quarterback elected to take the ball on an excursion himself he served notice by cussing out the center," Heisman wrote. "We had no signal for our regular right tackle, he being an earnest and oversubstantial youth who was far too unwieldy to run. Clever? But wait. Messer, one of our gifted halfbacks, was a master of a number of forms of entertainment, among them being the ability to sneeze at will. We were quick to make use of his accomplishments. A sneeze from Messer meant that Fred Hovey, our fullback, was to punt. And all went well until, alas, one day immediately following our quarterback's call to the other halfback to take the ball Messer turned loose an involuntary sneeze. Hovey punted and simultaneously Messer's running mate ran to take the ball. He took it between the shoulders, fresh from Hovey's swift foot. It rebounded 30 yards into our territory and a Fall River [High School] man fell on it within one short plunge of our goal."[15]

By all accounts, Heisman flourished at Brown University, where he was an articulate student, popular among his classmates, and a budding athlete. In two years at the school, he flourished academically. According to a transcript found in Brown University's archives, Heisman took twenty-one courses in four academic terms at the school. He scored no lower than 17.6 (the low mark came in analytical geometry) on a grading scale, which was based on a scoring range of 1 to 20. Perhaps not surprising to anyone who knew him, Heisman aced English literature and astronomy.

But after two years at Brown, Heisman transferred to the University of Pennsylvania. He informed his father that he wanted to pursue a law degree, which Brown didn't offer its students, and desired to be closer to his parents' home.

But it wasn't a coincidence that Penn had something else Brown couldn't offer Heisman—an intercollegiate football team.

CHAPTER FOUR

University of Pennsylvania

hile Heisman's father might have never approved of him playing the unrefined game of football, his ambitions for John accomplishing something in life had to be galvanized when his middle son transferred to the University of Pennsylvania to attend law school in 1890. Penn is one of America's oldest institutions; it was founded by Benjamin Franklin in the fall of 1749 and was the first school in the English colonies to educate the new land's children. Harvard, Princeton, William and Mary, and Yale came along sooner than Penn, but each of those schools was established to educate the clergy, rather than preparing America's children for careers in business and public service. Penn, which was first known as the Academy of Philadelphia and later the College of Philadelphia, was also the first American college to introduce a curriculum that included both the classics and more practical sciences.

After the Pennsylvania state government seized the College of Philadelphia in 1779 because of its faculty's perceived antirevolutionary views (despite nine signers of the Declaration of Independence and eleven signers of the Constitution having been associated with the college), the school was transformed into the University of the State of Pennsylvania, thus becoming America's first state school and the country's first university.[1] Once the school became public, Penn's Board of Trustees included members of every religious denomination, and its faculty was strictly nonsectarian. A medical school—the first one established in the English colonies—was organized in 1765, and law lectures were first given to Penn students in 1790. By the middle of the nineteenth century, Penn founded a law school and a school of engineering and applied sciences. Schools of dentistry, finance and commerce, veterinary medicine, and fine arts were established over the next four decades. Minority students were admitted for the first time in 1879, and Penn became coeducational when women enrolled in its graduate school in 1882 and then in its school of education in 1914.

When Heisman enrolled in law classes in the fall of 1890, Penn was considered one of America's preeminent institutions of higher learning. Of course, Heisman's primary concern when he arrived on the Penn campus, near the Schuylkill River in West Philadelphia, was his quest to join the Quakers' intercollegiate football team. Heisman asked the first undergraduate he saw about the team and promptly joined the practice warm-ups. Large numbers of young men turned out for football at Penn. Heisman, now twenty and still weighing only 158 pounds, was faced with competing for a position for the first time.

Football on the University of Pennsylvania campus dates back to at least 1872, when teams of students from each class played the game among themselves. In 1873, the newly formed University Athletic Association sponsored football games between classes during the fall athletics games. Penn's first intercollegiate game was played against Princeton on November 1, 1876, with the Tigers defeating the overmatched Quakers by a score of six goals to zero. Penn won its first intercollegiate game only sixteen days later, beating an All-Philadelphia team by a score of four goals to nothing. Football's rules and scoring system were still rather archaic, and the game still closely resembled rugby, with more emphasis on kicking than tackling. Teams had twenty players per side, and no one wore helmets or padding. Penn played an average of about four intercollegiate games per season from 1876 to 1882 and, as its results suggest, wasn't very competitive against its northeastern rivals. The Quakers scored only one goal in five games during an 0-5 season in 1881 and were embarrassed by Princeton in two games the next season.

A point-scoring system was introduced in 1883, and football's new rules seemed to suit the Quakers. Penn went 6-2 in 1883 and scored a milestone victory in its opener the next season, defeating Harvard 4–0 at Jarvis baseball field in Cambridge, Massachusetts. It was a monumental moment for the Quakers, who had never beaten more established teams such as Princeton (0-11), Harvard (0-2), and Yale (0-2) since first fielding a football team in 1876. The Quakers might have been the only ones not surprised by the game's outcome, according to the *Boston Daily Globe*:

> About 3.30 yesterday 300 or 400 students wended their way to Jarvis field to see what they thought would be an easy victory for the home team. But when they saw eleven stalwart youths clad in tights and jerseys, striped with orange and black, pitted against their own rather under-sized and motley-arrayed eleven their hearts began to sink. The youths from the City of Brotherly Love didn't show much of the said brotherly love to their opponents. Individual criticism of the teams would be useless. Harvard played poorly all round. The rush line is weak, the tackling poor, the running with one or two exceptions slow, the passing mediocre and the team play is scarce. In kicking alone did they excel yesterday. The University of Pennsylvania shone only by comparison.[2]

Because of the victory over Harvard more than anything else, Penn was invited in 1885 to join the Intercollegiate Football Association, which already included Harvard, Princeton, Wesleyan, and Yale. The Quakers hired Frank Sole as their first paid football coach, and the team began playing games on the newly constructed playing grounds at Thirty-Seventh and Spruce Streets near the Penn campus. By the time Heisman arrived at Penn, Sole had already been replaced as the Quakers' coach, after compiling a 23-19-1 record in three seasons. Under Sole's guidance, the Quakers beat up on smaller teams such as Haverford, Lehigh, and Swarthmore, but were completely overwhelmed by the stronger squads of Princeton and Yale. In fact, Penn played Princeton nine times from 1885 to 1887, losing every contest by a combined score of 511–35, including a 96–0 rout on November 5, 1887. So it probably wasn't a surprise that Penn officials hired a former Princeton player, Ellwood Otto Wagenhurst, as their new football coach in 1888. Wagenhurst, a native of Gouldsboro, Pennsylvania, had played on both the Princeton baseball and football teams. After graduating from Princeton, he debuted as a third baseman with the Philadelphia Quakers of the National League on June 8, 1888. But after only two games, Wagenhurst quit baseball and agreed to become Penn's football coach. He guided the Quakers to a 9-7 record in 1888 and a 7-6 campaign in 1889, working as the team's coach and trainer and even briefly playing left end, which was then still permitted under intercollegiate rules. In 1889, Wagenhurst enrolled in Penn's law school and was one of Heisman's classmates.

Heisman made his presence known on the Penn team as a center during the 1890 season, first as a backup and later on the varsity squad. It was at center where young Heisman learned some of his most valuable lessons in line play. The development of football in the late 1880s and early 1890s was still characterized by mass plays: hauling, pushing, and pulling the runner along by any device available. Some runners even had leather handles from old suitcases sewn onto their jerseys, so their teammates could haul them along at a more rapid pace. The progress of the ball was dependent on strong, heavy men, as was the stoppage of their progress. The larger interior linemen, especially centers and guards, were deemed indispensable, and their desired weight was two hundred pounds or more.

At less than 160 pounds, Heisman was much smaller than Penn's other linemen. And while not the ideal for a center, he made up for it with strong will and determined fight. His flanking guards weighed 212 and 243 pounds, respectively, making for an interior average of just over 204 pounds, not bad on paper. The Quakers won their first two games in 1890, defeating Swarthmore 10–0 and Rutgers 16–4. Heisman saw his first real action against rival Penn State on October 11, 1890. But when he took the field in front of a home crowd, he quickly realized that he was in for a long afternoon. The Penn State interior averaged 218 pounds per man. He later recalled, "The five of them towered over me like a herd of pachyderms."[3] But Heisman gave a credible account of himself in the middle of the line, keeping the Penn State middle guard from penetrating the Quakers' backfield. There came a lesson of playing with your head as well as your muscle. "They all took a notion to fall on me at one and the same time," Heisman recalled. "With what was left of my flattened brain, I figured the whole firmament of heaven must have fallen and pinned me against an up-heaved earthquake. They never lured me under them again."[4]

The battle between the Quakers and the Nittany Lions raged on, with the game's outcome in doubt until the very end. Late in the contest, Penn State had the ball and set up to punt. Nittany Lions halfback Charles Atherton went back to kick. At this time in football's development, the ball wasn't hiked with a long snap directly to the punter, as it is today. Hiking wouldn't occur in any manner until its invention in another five years. The ball was pawed back by the center to the quarterback, who took it from the ground, spun around, and passed it back underhanded to the designated kicker. The method was obviously time-consuming and allowed opportunity for some creative defensive strategies. Heisman's earlier days as a gymnast would now play to an advantage. He saw Atherton go back to punt and sized up his opponent:

How was I to break through and block that punt? The opposing center was as wide as Gibraltar, but when he bent down he was not as high as wide. I got back a couple of feet, figured the exact instant he would snap, guessed it to a nicety and, in that instant, vaulted over him in a leap frog spread. Their quarter was just relaying the ball to Atherton. I chased after it like a hungry houn'dog yelping at the heels of a jackrabbit. I saw the ball flutter from Atherton's hands, saw his foot swing back, then forward. High in the air I leaped with both hands upraised. Did I block it with my hands? No! The durned thing found a hole between them just big enough to wiggle through, but it wouldn't get past my nose! Holy Kitty Cats of Isis! How it did smart! Another bloody nose for me and my eyes running tears as big as 'taters. But I took after that black comet as fast as I could, and, of course, along went Atherton. Neck and neck we ran until he took a sudden dive at something I couldn't see well. He must have missed it, but dimly seeing something round and dark on the ground, I pounced on it like a duck on a June bug. The thing wiggled out from under my clutch, and a harsh voice snarled, "What t'hell yah tryin' to do?!" It was Atherton's voice. I had mistaken his head for the ball. I wished then I had given it a swift kick! Meanwhile, [Penn teammate R. R.] Ammerman had fallen on the ball for us and a touchdown.[5]

Heisman's sacrifice helped the Quakers defeat the Nittany Lions by a 20–0 score, but he was left with a battle scar that would remain with him for the rest of his life. Whether it was this play or a later one, Heisman's profile would sport a slight downward deviation in the bridge of what had previously been a straight nose. Noseguard equipment was just coming into use, after Harvard's Arthur Crumnock invented one in 1890 for teammate John Cranston, who was said to have a soft nose that tended to bleed profusely. Nonetheless, Heisman and his teammates had pridefully shunned noseguards.

In 1888, football's rules were changed to allow tackling down to the knees. Until then a tackle was permitted only from the waist up to and below the head. From his play at Brown and then Penn, Heisman was a confirmed "high tackler," but something would happen that would change him for the better, though at a cost. In practice one day, Bob Hill, a teammate on the Penn squad, broke loose for a long run, with Heisman in hot pursuit. Catching Hill with "a crazy leap on his back and neck," Heisman stressed his teammate's leg too much and it broke.[6] Hill's injury put him out for the rest of the season, and Heisman recalled, "I grieved mightily over the accident and determined never again to make a high tackle."[7]

From that day forward, Heisman vowed to work on the fundamentals of sound, sure tackles. Over and over again, he would hit the runner where he bends, collapse with his grip, and then with a hard, snappy lift, roll him backward or to the side. Over and over again, studying the momentum of the runner, the angle of attack or pursuit, bend, grip, drive, and roll became a study for Heisman that he would practice to perfection. His dogged pursuit of sound fundamental execution would mark his future teams. "That didn't help Bob's leg any, but I am sure it resulted in my making varsity the next two years," Heisman recalled.[8]

Penn's teams were known for their rugged style of play under Wagenhurst, which was exactly the way Heisman had learned to play the game behind his father's cooperage in Titusville, Pennsylvania. After an 18–0 loss to Princeton on October 15, 1890, a reporter with the *New York World* described the Quakers as "probably the strongest team Princeton will meet before the game with Yale. The visitors' team was made up of some very heavy men. Their play was plucky and aggressive, showing hard training and desperate determination in at least score if not win."[9] While Heisman probably wasn't pleased with the game's outcome, he had likely been in heaven over the clean, loutish play. "Throughout the game the imported umpire took little cognizance of unnecessary roughness, and bad temper was exhibited on both sides in several private encounters," the *Boston Daily Globe* reported. "The game, on the whole, was a desperately fought contest. Nothing like it had been seen here since the Harvard game of 1885."[10] A week later, after Penn routed Columbia by a score of 18–0 at Brotherhood Park in New York, which was the home of professional baseball's Giants and later renamed Polo Grounds III, a journalist from the *Boston Daily Globe* wasn't nearly as impressed with the Quakers' relentless effort or that of their opponents: "The Pennsylvania men have a reputation of playing an unnecessary rough game this fall, and it is well deserved, if today's game is a sample of their work. The Columbias clawed the hair of her opponents in tackling, and when they found the umpire from Pennsylvania enjoyed slugging they used their feet freely."[11]

Slowly but surely, college football was catching on as a spectator sport in the Northeast. When the Quakers played their nemesis, Princeton, in New Jersey on November 8, 1890, more than eight thousand fans crammed the stands surrounding the field on Princeton's lush grounds. The Tigers, who were led by All-America end Ralph Warren, guard Jesse Riggs, and fullback Sheppard Homans, were considered one of the country's strongest college teams. By their second meeting against Princeton during the 1890 season, Penn had dropped twenty-six consecutive games to the Tigers and all but one of the outcomes hadn't even been close, with the Quakers losing by an average of nearly forty-six points after the point-scoring system was put in place in 1883. This time, though, the Quakers put forth quite an effort, according to the *Boston Daily Globe*: "Pennsylvania lost, to be sure, but only by the score of 6–0, and as any judge of football would have agreed, she outplayed her opponent at almost every point. Why she lost is a hard question, but much can be laid to the want of judgment. At the most critical points, where a little head-work would have enabled the university to have scored, that same headwork was wanting."[12]

Much like Heisman had been mesmerized by the audible signals during a pickup game in Albany, New York, when he was en route to Brown University, he was captivated by Wagenhurst's play-calling system. Heisman fondly recalled an incident during the Quakers' 28–0 victory over Franklin & Marshall of Lancaster, Pennsylvania, on October 25, 1890:

> Wagenhurst's system was most clever, I thought, yet simple enough too; certainly it drove none of us to bed with brain fever. We were to pay close attention to the first word uttered by the quarterback. If the first word of that sentence ended with "y" our right half was to carry the ball around left end—if possible. And if the first word concluded with "k" the left half went speeding toward the right end, e.g. "Hurry-Y up, men" or "Break-K through there, Johnny!" But even this excellent system seemed to have fault. You see, the quarter couldn't use the same first words all the time; he had to vary them quite often. Occasionally he'd be caught with a depleted vocabulary. I remember one game when we were playing against Franklin & Marshall. Our quarterback ran out of words ending in y. He was intimidated by the towering center, who looked like a gawk, but had the brain of an Aristotle, catching on to everything. Our quarterback was benumbed by a hard spill he'd taken the play before so pondered a long time and finally came out with: "Animated-ly now, fellows!" "What's that?" roared the Frank and Marshall lineman, clapping his hand to an imagined fevered brow. "For the love of Myrtle did you hear that?" he said. "A-N-I-M-A-T-E-D-L-Y now, f-e-l-l-o-w-s! Oh, my God!"[13]

Heisman recalled the Franklin & Marshall lineman falling to the ground, rolling over and over again, with the rest of the players on the field soon doing the same. After order was restored, Penn's quarterback shouted signals for the next play: "Watch diligent-ly!"

"We finally won, but he nearly laughed us out of the game," Heisman recalled.[14]

Heisman's self-discipline in academics and in strengthening his physique allowed him to play football for two seasons during his three years of law school at Penn. Stamina was important to play the game, as no substitutions were allowed except for injury, though some players would fake an injury to get out of the game. The Oscar-worthy acting was critical late in the second half of games, when fresh legs were often desperately needed. In fact, it wasn't unusual for a captain to whisper to one of his players suggesting that he "get your arm broke or something" in order to get much-needed speed and strength into the lineup. During an early fall game in 1890, Heisman once heard, "Get your neck broke, Heisman."[15] There is no record of how Heisman actually accomplished the feat.

Heisman's exceptional oratory skills and acting were also assets on the gridiron. Football wasn't yet played with ten-yard yard lines etched on the field, or with the benefit of a standard measure ten-yard chain gang.[16] A referee simply dropped a handkerchief as his best approximation of where the possession started. Of course, the game also entailed several of a team's best distracters engaging the referee in some dispute while their teammates kicked the hankie farther ahead or back as the strategy required. Also, no neutral zone existed at the line of scrimmage. Everyone on the line squared off across from his opponent and created general mayhem when the play commenced. This required a lineman to be a decent boxer and/or wrestler. He had no pads to speak of and would have been considered a sissy if he had any. The only helmet was the hair on his head. To prepare for football, a player started to let his hair grow out in June for the season in September. Many college men, usually seminarians, allowed their beards to grow out as well and were referred to as "go-rillas."[17] Heisman seemed to abstain from such practices, however, as photographs from this era and throughout his life always showed him wearing close-cropped, well-groomed hair.

In the course of a game, arguments followed nearly every umpire's decision, and everyone seemed to take part. The officials scarcely knew who the captains were because anybody with an opinion would talk for as long as they pleased with both referees and players of the opposition. The player who was a good spokesman was always a priceless resource to his team. Heisman proved his worth as an orator, both in football and his law studies. His dramatic, eloquent speech poured forth on the field as well as in the classroom. His keen perception of a situation, coupled with a piercing logic, would for-malize many future rule changes in years to come. Honed in the heat of battle, his quick wit and field generalship were hard-won. This development and much-practiced skill would save his college career.

At the end of the 1880s and evolving into the 1890s, two things happened to cause Heisman to study the development of line play even further. The first was the legalization of interference (block-ing) for the runner, a huge change to the game that would quickly lead to blocking schemes requiring more strategy on the line of scrimmage. This rule change forever separated American football from rugby. Not only could the linemen now block and push aside would-be tacklers, now also the other backs got into the mix by run-ning before the ball carrier to take out any defender whom the line missed. The development spurred worlds of strategy in Heisman's mind as he pictured blocking schemes, double-teaming, isolation, influence, cross-blocking, and invitations to misdirection.

The second development was young Heisman encountering ar-guably the best college lineman of the nineteenth century, William "Pudge" Heffelfinger of Yale. Heffelfinger, a stalwart guard from Minneapolis, Minnesota, played for the Bulldogs from 1888 to 1891, with his junior and senior seasons occurring at the same time Heis-

man played at Penn. Heisman went face-to-face with Heffelfinger
for two straight seasons and received a lesson in line play from the
very best. At six feet four inches and 201 pounds of steeled muscle,
Heffelfinger possessed a speed seldom seen in a back, let alone a lineman of his era. His strength and speed were perfect for the new rules
allowing interference for ball carriers. At the signal to go, Heffelfinger pulled out of the line and tore around the left or right end with
murderous intent, with the only question being how many defenders
he would lay waste. At halftime of one game against the Bulldogs, a
distraught Heisman asked one of his fellow linemen if he was able
to get through Heffelfinger. His teammate's response was, "Get
through him! Hell's bells I can't even get out of his way!" [18]

Heisman's first meeting with Heffelfinger occurred on November 15, 1890, at Yale Field in New Haven, Connecticut, where the
Bulldogs were heavy favorites to win the game, according to the
Boston Sunday Globe: "Such was the interest in the event that 2800
people surrounded the rectangle at the Yale field on which the game
was played, and Yale's supporters howled themselves hoarse in cheering their team on to victory. There was no betting. The U. of P. men,
of whom there were two hundred who accompanied their team to
this city, were not of the betting class. They did not care to bet on
the score even, and the only offer of money was made of eight to one,
and it was not accepted." [19]

While the Pennsylvania men might have lacked school spirit, they
certainly didn't lack brains. The Bulldogs, who were coached by the
legendary Walter Camp, won the game by a score of 60–0 and won
48–0 over the Quakers the next season. Despite the ugly defeats,
Heisman studied Heffelfinger's style and ability to lead a play. After
Heffelfinger graduated from Yale, he became the country's first professional football player when he was paid $500 by the Allegheny
Athletic Association to play in a game against rival Pittsburgh Athletic Club on November 12, 1892. Although Heffelfinger often got
the better of him, Heisman developed into a superb blocker and in-

terference man. Heisman's vision of speed and strength coming out of the line would be one of the blueprints that built his future teams. As Heisman once remembered Heffelfinger, "the black and blue spots where he dented me have long disappeared, but the memory of them I will take with me to the final Land of Nod."[20]

In Heisman's second season at Penn, in 1891, Wagenhurst decided to put greater size at center, leaving him to compete with nine other players for the only vacant position on the line—as well as the whole team—at left end. Charles Schoff, one of Heisman's closest friends, was the starting right end and knew how to play the position better than anyone, including the coaches. Schoff worked hard to teach Heisman how to play end, especially on defense. Schoff proved a good tutor and went to great lengths to run down backs from behind so none got by his star pupil. Heisman's other advantage was that Wagenhurst was familiar with his grit and determination in the midst of a struggle and knew he would figure out the surest advantage in the heat of a game. The more Wagenhurst thought about it, the more he liked having Heisman on the field and not on the sideline. Before the Quakers played at Lehigh in Bethlehem, Pennsylvania, on October 28, 1891, Wagenhurst informed Heisman that he had won a starting job.

"It was not until mid-October that I felt that I had the inside track," Heisman recalled. "Just before the Lehigh game our head coach said to me: 'Heisman, I believe you're the best man I've got for left end but nobody else seems to think so. Nevertheless, I'm coach and I'm sending you in against Lehigh today. Son, you and I stand or fall on what you do today. Get in there, boy. Play football.' I think that I'd have fought a battery of buzz-saws barehanded after that."[21]

Bolstered by his coach's vote of confidence and Schoff's never-ending assistance, Heisman played left end during his senior year at Penn, in 1891, and gave a credible account of himself. The Quakers went 11-3 during Heisman's first season in 1890, losing games only to Princeton (twice) and Yale. The Quakers went 11-2 the next

season, losing to the Tigers and Bulldogs again. Along with captain
E. M. Church and star center John Adams, Heisman helped lay the
foundation for a Pennsylvania program that would become one of
the best in the country near the end of the nineteenth century. The
Quakers finished 12-0 in 1894 under coach George Woodruff, defeating Princeton for only the second time in thirty meetings. Yale
went 16-0 and was widely recognized as the sport's national champion in 1894, although college football historian Parke H. Davis ret-
roactively named Penn national champion for that season in 1933.
The Quakers went 14-0 in 1895, 15-0 in 1897, and were consensus
national champions in both seasons. The Quakers also added national championships in 1904 and 1908 under coaches Carl Williams
and Sol Metzger, respectively.

Even though the sport was gaining popularity up and down the
East Coast, the rugged game of football still did not enjoy an auspi-
cious position in proper society. The young men participating on
the gridiron were viewed askance, as though pugilists at a county
fair prize fight. Many young college men had been strictly forbidden
by their fathers from playing football, much like George Walker at
Brown University. At Penn, which was then a school of many aspir-
ing lawyers and physicians, it was even more difficult to persuade
players to come out for the football team. One of Heisman's classmates, Tom Barker, was on the cusp of playing. Barker's father did
not like the idea of his son playing the rugged sport, but was fair
enough to withhold judgment, at least until he witnessed the game
himself. With Barker's father set to travel to Philadelphia to watch
the Quakers play, the Penn team put together a plan for Mr. Barker,
according to Heisman:

> On the day of the game, Mr. Barker arrived in a three-piece
> silk suit complete with tails, top hat, white spats, and white
> gloves. Never having attended a football contest, he assumed
> one dressed for such an occasion as one would to attend the

opera. He was properly escorted to the best fifty-yard-line seat and was flanked on both sides by two of the cleverest chaps from the school of law. At once the student body gave up a mighty cheer for the father of their "star" ball player, and the young legal beagles were abuzz about what a fine young man Tom Barker was on and off the field. "Why did you hear the incredible argument Tom gave forth in the ethics class last week?" "Yes, and did you see his heroic play last Saturday on the field at Dover? Why, we wouldn't have won without Barker! Tom has the ball now look at him go!" On and on they went. Everyone broke their necks that day to make Tom the hero and to let Dad Barker soak in the praise. In the third quarter, Tom broke loose into a long run for an apparent touchdown. By now a particular defensive back knew who had the ball and was getting tired of chasing down the same back. "There he goes again! Get Barker! Kill him! Don't let him score again! Kill him! Kill Barker!" he screamed as he was in hot pursuit. Aghast at this development, Dad Barker took off after the defensive back, top hat on head, cane in one hand, white spats awhirl, shaking a white-gloved fist in the air, and shouting, "Kill him, and I'll kill you!" All arrived in the end zone unscathed, as the players both explained with some amusement how certain expletives are not taken literally in the heat of competition. Mr. Barker enjoyed a good laugh at himself and returned home with Tom free to continue with the Penn football team.[22]

Near the end of the nineteenth century in America, a college education was still an opportunity seized by the precious few who could afford it through hard work and family sacrifice. When Heisman attended Penn's law school, his tuition was $305 for three years of courses, plus $180 per year for boarding and textbooks.[23] The students who graduated from what would later become the Ivy League schools normally went on to be heads of state or industry. Indeed, Heisman's teammates would go on to distinguish themselves in various arenas. Adams, who would become Penn's first All-American, in 1891, was a student in the veterinary school. T. F. Branson, Schoff, and S. M. Cone were medical students, and Everett Camp, Harry Mackey, and Howard Sypher were enrolled in law school with Heisman. Along with becoming the mayor of Philadelphia from 1928 to 1931, Mackey was later football coach at the University of Virginia in 1895. Henry Thornton, who was the Penn freshman class president in 1890, coached at Vanderbilt after graduation in 1894. He was later hired to modernize Great Britain's railway system and was elevated to the rank of major general of the Allied forces during World War I. In 1919 Thornton became a British subject and was knighted by King George V. Heisman also played against several young men who became prominent figures during the twentieth century, too. Riggs, the All-America guard from Princeton, was the son of Baltimore banker Lawrason Riggs, who financed Samuel Morse's invention of the telegraph in 1845 and loaned the US government $16 million to fight the Spanish-American War. Harvard quarterback Dudley Dean enlisted in Theodore Roosevelt's "Rough Riders" after graduation and was a hero at the Battle of San Juan Hill in Cuba during the Spanish-American War in 1898. Yale halfback Thomas "Bum" McClung was treasurer of the United States under President William Howard Taft, and his signature appeared on currency printed from 1909 to 1912.

Oddly enough, football, of all things, nearly ended Heisman's chances of graduating from law school. At the end of his junior season, the Quakers played against Rutgers at New York's Madison Square Garden on December 13, 1890. The Quakers won the game by a 13–10 score, and each of the Penn players was given a gold watch, although Heisman might have enjoyed his postgame bath even more. He later recalled the incident:

We played the game on a straight dirt floor, the earth being black loam as dry and as fine as powder. By the end of the game we were all as black as chimney sweeps. We raced below to the dressing rooms expecting to get a good shower somewhere. But no baths of any kind were to be found. I remembered seeing a horse trough a hundred yards around the circle. Saying nothing to anyone, I grabbed a towel and, as the lights were dim and no one down there, I sprinted "in the glooming" for the trough. Yes, there it was and full of nice, clear water nor anybody else in sight. In I plunged, rubbed and scrubbed briskly, then submerged. Ah, how cool and refreshing, how delicious! What wouldn't those other fellows give for a cleansing bath like this? [24]

But when Heisman pulled his head from the water, he was stunned at what he saw: "Holy popocatepetl! What a bellowing snort! What a stomping noise! What red, gleaming eyes were those glaring down at me! What frightful monsters were those cavorting about my improvised bathtub? With a bloodcurdling yell, I fairly hurled myself out of that trough and, with no further look, I fairly burnt up the landscape tearing back to the dressing room. So, after all there were some horses down there—and my tub was still a trough. Yes, I really was scared silly. To this day as I lie in my tub, I sometimes glance up nervously to see if there are any horses about." [25]

In the end, Pennsylvania's game against Rutgers at Madison Square Garden changed Heisman's life forever and altered the future of American football. The Garden's massive lighting system was hoisted on large carries by pulleys all the way to the top of the arena. To service and change elements the lights were lowered and worked on, fired up for testing, then hauled back up into position. While one of these units was being serviced and tested, Heisman ran by while chasing an errant ball. As Heisman retrieved the ball, the galvanic lighting system came on, emitting noxious and acrid fumes, which were normally not noticeable at the ceilings but quite strong at ground level. Heisman's eyes were immediately flashed and stung by the bright lights and hot fumes. Blinking back tears, he quickly returned to the team but with blurred vision. Heisman's condition continued throughout the game, though he hoped with each passing minute that his vision would clear up. When the team returned to the Pennsylvania campus it was apparent that there was a serious problem.[26]

After the accident in New York, Heisman couldn't see to read. Navigating to and from class proved no problem for him, but reading the volumes of books required in his law studies was impossible. In consulting a doctor, he was advised not to read for an extended time period, three to maybe six months. The doctor's prescription was unacceptable for Heisman, who was about to begin his final year of law school. But the doctor warned him to continue to read would strain his eyes possibly into blindness. How could this be remedied? The dilemma rolled over and over in Heisman's mind as he went to and from class, listening attentively and reviewing course material with his friends. Slowly Heisman began to formulate a plan.

Heisman enlisted the help of his classmates, both football players and others, including Mackey. There were agreeable benefits to oral review for all involved, and a review schedule began of fellow law students reading aloud their assignments to and with Heisman.[27] His keen perception and retentive mind would then argue back the case or create further discussion as the issues warranted. The early study groups would hone the skills of many young legal minds and, in this case, be the salvation of Heisman's college career.

The greatest hurdle came next. Heisman petitioned the faculty of Penn's law school to allow him to take all of his law exams orally rather than written. Heisman argued, as President Abraham Lincoln had once asserted, that a lawyer's knowledge was his stock and trade and the method of delivering that stock should not matter greatly, whether applying his knowledge in writing or through oral presentation. In fact, the oral tradition was more in keeping with an attorney's trade than the text from his own hand. The faculty was impressed enough to allow the waiver. The rhetorical elocution Heisman wielded produced victory in his opening argument, and now he would be allowed to apply it to his final exams. With an impressive command of the English language, Heisman stood before the law faculty. His exam wore on hour after hour. Afterward Heisman collapsed into his boardinghouse bed to rest and recoup his mental energies while he waited for his test results to be posted.

On June 6, 1892, during the University of Pennsylvania's 136th commencement ceremonies at the American Academy of Music, Heisman was one of thirty-seven students who received baccalaureate degrees in law. After the Reverend J. A. M. Chapman delivered an opening prayer, Beale's Orchestra played "The Antrim County Ball" from *Cleopatra*. William Duane delivered the valedictory address, and then Heisman walked onstage to receive his diploma. A few days later, Heisman packed his belongings, leaving the Penn campus with still blurred vision.

At age twenty-two, Heisman wasn't quite sure what his future held.

CHAPTER FIVE

Oberlin College

After Heisman graduated from the University of Pennsylvania's law school, the summer of 1892 passed slowly. Heisman now held a law degree, yet was undecided about what to do with it. Heisman's indecision came from his slowly improving vision. Everyday work and commerce did not present problems, but reading for any length of time did. Now left with no "readers," Heisman began to ponder the challenges of the massive reading required by his chosen profession. After all, reading was the very activity that doctors forbade to him in order to fully recover his sight. Could Heisman enter his career and, if so, when? The doctors continued to urge his patience, but the wait became unbearable. Anything was better than this medically authorized, unproductive, professional loitering!

For a short time, Heisman tried his luck selling kitchen utensils door-to-door, although buyers were difficult to find, as the prelude to the Panic of 1893 began to cripple the American economy. Early that autumn, Heisman received notice of a position open at Oberlin College, a rapidly growing Presbyterian school about thirty-five miles southwest of Cleveland. The school desperately needed a coach for its fledgling football team but didn't have much money to pay him. It might not have been a legal practice, but the opportunity certainly suited Heisman's passions. After boarding another train and going west this time, Heisman headed for Oberlin, Ohio. A Presbyterian minister, the Reverend John J. Shipherd, and missionary Philo P. Stewart founded Oberlin Collegiate Institute in December 1833. They wanted to establish a college and colony based on their religious beliefs and incorporated many of the ideals of Alsatian pastor John Frederick Oberlin, who had established schools and improved roads and living conditions in poor communities in France. At first, Oberlin Collegiate Institute exchanged free tuition for labor from its students, but the practice was eventually discontinued. Oberlin Collegiate Institute was the first American college to admit women, and in 1835 it became the first to admit African American students as well. In 1850, Oberlin Collegiate Institute became Oberlin College, and the school shifted its curriculum from theology-based studies to formal instruction in the classics, sciences, fine arts, and music. In the 1850s, Oberlin College was even a major hub along the Underground Railroad, an informal network of safe houses and routes used to help escaped slaves reach freedom before the American Civil War. The escaped fugitives were often sheltered at Oberlin College—even in the university president's home—and then ferried north across nearby Lake Erie to Canada.

When Heisman arrived on the Oberlin College campus in October 1892, it was the largest college in Ohio, with an enrollment of 1,492 students. The Yeomen had started playing intercollegiate football the previous year, losing 26–6 at the University of Michigan on October 24, 1891, in their first game. The Yeomen finished with a 2-2 record in their first season, defeating Western Reserve 12–6 and Case Technical 10–0 before losing a rematch against Western Reserve 18–8 in their 1891 finale. Even though much of Oberlin's faculty still objected to the sport, football had struck a chord with its students, and the general sentiment among them was that the school needed to get serious about fielding a team. "We have learned a great deal this year but we can not learn as much or more next year without a coach," the *Oberlin Review*, the student newspaper, reported in the spring of 1892. "We must have a man here next fall who has played on one of the great eastern teams. He must be on hand when school opens to perfect 'tackling and falling on the ball' and to lay out a definite plan of play toward the perfection of which all his and the captain's efforts shall be bent."[1]

Bert Hogen, the varsity team's manager, started the search for a new football coach. Oberlin's history suggests that Yale coach Walter Camp, who might have been impressed with Heisman's play in his earlier matchups against the Bulldogs' All-America Pudge Heffelfinger, recommended Heisman for the Oberlin job. Regardless, Oberlin's athletics department, which was still being run by students, didn't have money to pay him a salary. Heisman was allowed to enroll as a postgraduate student in the arts department, although "he never, so far as it is known, attended a single class, and never, it *is* known, earned a single mark or grade."[2] Perhaps most important, as a postgraduate student, Heisman was allowed to play on the Yeomen's varsity football team, allowing him one more opportunity to continue his playing career.

Oberlin College and its quaint setting galvanized Heisman immediately. Physical education instruction became rigorous under his tutelage. At the beginning of the 1892–93 school year, Heisman posted a no-nonsense notice—more like a command—announcing tryouts for the football team. In what would become his annual custom, the announcement read: "All men reasonably fit and hardy are to report to the campus square Friday at 2 p.m. to represent their school on the football field."[3]

From the mass of men who responded, Heisman molded his first football team. Many of the players from the 1891 varsity team returned to the squad, including half of Oberlin's so-called Four Horsemen. Halfbacks Carl "Cap" Williams and Charles "Fred" Savage were back, but the Yeomen would be without quarterback Carl Semple and fullback Howard "Howie" Regal. Semple and a group of other boys had stolen a chicken from a local coop and were caught by the farmers while roasting it. An argument ensued and one of the farmers was seriously hurt. Semple eventually confessed his actions to Oberlin's administration, but he was allowed to remain in school. Shortly thereafter, Semple was caught visiting a saloon and later participating in a poker game. He quit Oberlin and transferred to Kenyon College in Gambier, Ohio.[4]

At twenty-two years old, Heisman was older than many of his Oberlin College players. There were a few exceptions. Josiah Teeters, who had played at Purdue University and helped the Boilermakers win an Indiana state championship, was twenty-nine years old. Miles Marsh, the Yeomen's heaviest lineman at 180 pounds, was twenty-six years old. But Heisman, who had been coached by his law school classmate Ellwood Wagenhurst at Pennsylvania, was unfazed by his youth. In many ways, Heisman believed his youth and inexperience were assets because he had only recently experienced what his players were now going through.

"You must remember that the coach is dealing with youth," Heisman later wrote. "He is talking to and handling boys whose ideals are very real and frequently very high. They haven't lived long enough nor hard enough to be honestly cynical. Their college is very dear to many of them and personally I wouldn't give last year's straw hat for a dozen of them who weren't sentimental. What a coach says to his men can break them as quickly as it can make them. He has to be something of an orator. He must know his men individually as well as collectively. He can't be soft. He daren't be bitterly sarcastic. He must be a leader in football thought as well as football tactics."[5]

Heisman's long, hard-fought lessons learned on the line at Penn began to pay off as a young coach. The memories of Heffelfinger's impressive swift, powerful blocks, the center play at Penn State, well-executed tackling, the tactical play at end, and, of course, guards—his favorite position—came to life in drilling his new recruits. Heisman searched for a couple of fast, quick, young men to fill the critical guard positions and found them in Teeters and John Henry Wise, a strong half German, half Hawaiian. Swift of foot and eager for contact, the pair of meteors enthusiastically caught on to pulling and leading end runs. But Heisman knew that his guards' mettle wouldn't truly be tested until live action. "The true test of a player's value to a team is revealed in the practice scrimmage," he later recalled. "There's where the coach picks his men. This is where he selected the 150-pounder with the baby face and rejects the 200-pound husky whose fighting qualities are all over the surface."[6]

Of course, Heisman wasn't going to miss his chance to install his own system of audible signals, and he might have actually been the first coach to implement audibles at the line of scrimmage and a script for his team's plays. Heisman instituted a system in which the quarterback called a signal for the next six plays. Savage, the Yeomen's speedy halfback, carried a typed copy of them, which the author Nat Brandt discovered in Oberlin College's archives while researching the school's football history. It was paramount that players memorize the signals because at the time coaches weren't allowed to, well, coach from the sideline. Only team captains were able to give players instructions on the field. Heisman's signals looked like this:

Vowels a, e, i, o, u, y—Right half back.
Consonants b, c, d, f, g, h, j, etc.—Left half back.
Vowel followed by any number under 100 [such as] "a45"—right half back takes the ball and goes straight ahead on his own side through the tackle.
If this signal be followed by any letters whatsoever, the right half back cuts across to the left, as, "a 53 lmn[.]"
Consonants followed by any number under 100, as "b 62," left half back takes the ball and goes straight ahead. If followed by letters, as "b 62 adg," cut across.
Vowel followed by any number between 100 and 200, as ["]e 139" full back goes between center and right guard.—If followed by any letter, as "e 172 abc," he goes around the right end.

On signal "m128" (m128) full back between center and left
guard. On "P 128 def"—he goes around the left end.

Right guard number is "1" third figure mentioned, as "6, 5,
1, 4, 9. Left guard is "2" third figure mentioned—["]7, 3, 2, 4,
9." Right tackle is "3"—4, 8, 3, 6, 0,—left tackle "4"—5, 9, 4,
1, 8,—

Any number between 100 and 200 not preceded but followed
by any letters, as 187 efg, full back kicks the ball.

The word "OBERLIN" after a signal has been given means
that the signal is to be changed, and the right signal is given
after the word—"Oberlin."[7]

While Heisman's system might have seemed rather confusing,
the signals were constantly drilled into his players' brains. Heisman demanded that his players spend as much time focusing on the
mental aspects of the game as the physical ones, which is why Savage
probably carried a typed sheet of the signals in his pockets as he
walked to and from class. Though the young coach believed he had
created a starting eleven that held much promise, the young Yeomen
had yet to play a real game. Their first test came against Ohio State
on October 15, 1892. Ohio State wasn't yet the football power it
became in later years. In fact, Ohio State, which had been founded
in 1870 as the Ohio Agricultural and Mechanical College, was still a
relatively small school, with 770 students, which was about half the
size of Oberlin's student body. Football didn't become a varsity sport
at Ohio State until 1890, and the Buckeyes didn't produce a winning
record in their first two seasons.

Heisman was eager to coach his first game and, of course, he
planned to play in the contest, too. "For our first game the team
dressed in the training house," Heisman recalled. Hogen had arranged for the team to arrive at Oberlin's Athletic Park via an old,
weather-beaten bus. Heisman later recalled a comical conversation
among coeds in the grandstand:

"What's the yell for?" a fair co-ed asked of her escort.

"Why, for the team and the new coach. See, over there."

"Oh, yes, I see them now. Don't they look fine? Where's the new coach?"

"Why, right over there, too—alongside the team."

"That's new? Why, they've been coming out to games with that crazy thing for the last twenty years!"

"Twenty years! You're off your trolley, Ethel! I've been at Oberlin seven years myself and I never saw the man in my life till a few days ago."

"Man? What man are you talking about?"

"About Heisman-man, the new coach. That fellow with the new sweater on!"

"Oh, the coach! Is that what you call him? Humph! I thought you meant that rickety bus—the old stage coach!"[8]

Heisman's first game as a coach got under way, and he had to be proud of the results. The Yeomen lined up, toed the ball back, and off to the races they went, with their guards pulling right and then left, doing just what Heisman had told them to do. Oberlin's quick guards led the backfield around either end and destroyed everything in their way. Ohio State was coached by Oberlin native Jack Ryder, who was later a respected sportswriter for the *Cincinnati Enquirer*. But Ryder could only watch helplessly as the Yeomen ran up and down the field. Williams, who had moved to quarterback and was team captain, scored Oberlin's first touchdown, and then Teeters carried Thomas Johnson and Lynds Jones to scores. The Yeomen had a 28–0 lead at halftime and won the game in a 40–0 rout. The *Oberlin Review* declared Heisman's first game a complete success: "A new phase of the football question has been developed. Our team showed plainly the result of training. Their work was far more systematic, more scientific, than last year."[9]

The Yeomen played their second game six days later against

Adelbert College, a Presbyterian school from Cleveland that was founded as Western Reserve College in 1860. The second game was overshadowed on campus by a visit from Ohio governor William McKinley, who visited Oberlin to lead a Republican rally at First Congressional Church. With many of Oberlin's students attending the political rally, Adelbert had nearly as many fans at the game as the Yeomen did. Heisman might have been a bit anxious before the game because his father, Michael Heisman Sr., and John's younger brother Mike, were standing on the sideline watching. The elder Heisman, who was never a fan of the sport, apparently wanted to find out why his son had sacrificed a law career for coaching. Since he and his wife, Sarah, had by then returned to Cleveland from Titusville, Pennsylvania, it was only a short train ride to the Oberlin campus.

"I caught Father in a weak moment when I went to Oberlin to coach," Heisman recalled. "After an evening's argument, and much to my surprise, he was at the field on the following afternoon prepared to see what all the nonsense was about. He had decided that inasmuch as I had rejected the practice of law and had dedicated my life to the game, there must be something to football. Anyway he'd see. He watched my Oberlin team speed through signal practice. His eyes popped a bit when he saw the ball soar in towering punts."[10]

Before the Yeomen kicked off, Heisman's father approached him on the sideline.

"The crowd seems to be for the other fellows. Do you think you'll win?" Heisman's father asked.

"Yes," Heisman told him. "I think so."

"You think so?" Heisman's father repeated. "Pretty sure of it? Your team's small. The crowd doesn't think much of your chances."

At this point, Heisman questioned his father's motives.

"What's the matter with you?" Heisman demanded. "You're not a football fan, are you? What do you care who wins?"

"Oh, nothing," Heisman's father answered. "But I don't like this partiality. I'd like to see the big fellows licked."

A short time later, Heisman's brother approached him.

"Say," Mike said. "If you ain't pretty sure you're going to take this game you'd better let me head Dad off."

"Dad? What's he doing now?" Heisman asked.

"Oh, nothing," Mike replied. "Except walking up and down in front of Western Reserve's cheering section waving hundred-dollar bills and daring them to back their team."

With a pocketful of newly won currency, Papa Heisman might have actually left Oberlin College as a college football fan. Oberlin's Will Merriam recovered a muffed return for a touchdown the first time the Yeomen had to kick, and Savage ran for two touchdowns behind his speedy guards. After Oberlin led 24–4 at the half, the umpire that Adelbert provided gave up his whistle for a jersey, only to fumble on his second carry. After the umpire was injured on a hard tackle, the play turned rough, with multiple personal fouls from both sides.[11] Oberlin College won the game in a 38–8 rout.

The Yeomen won their next three games in convincing fashion too, walloping Ohio Wesleyan 56–0, Ohio State 50–0, and Kenyon College 38–0. For the rematch against Ohio State, the Buckeyes incorporated rail yard workers into their ranks to bolster their side. It seemed that Ohio State certainly wanted revenge. Heisman and his team traveled to Columbus to play on a polo field. Early in the game, Ohio State's extra "hired muscle" pushed the much lighter Oberlin line around, but then the systematic and disciplined execution of Heisman's team took over. The Oberlin guards pulled, and to add to it so did the backside tackle and end, creating a seven-man interference for its runners. It might have been the first "student body right" or "student body left" sweeps ever seen. Ohio State's rail yard workers could only watch and try to catch their wind.

For whatever reason, Heisman didn't coach the Yeomen in the victory over Kenyon. According to Brandt, Heisman might have actually been injured at the time, because the school's athletic association had reimbursed him 15 cents for an "ear bandage."[12] Much of

Oberlin's success was credited to Heisman's coaching. Along with the flying interference of his swift guards, Heisman created a wedge that would break into a smaller V and continue play after the larger one was stopped.[13] His players had the presence of mind to re-create the formation, usually under Savage's leadership, leaving those players entangled and occupied with opponents to press the attack farther down the field.

With the new challenge of coaching came the respect of a new position of authority that Heisman held in the lives of his young team. Almost a father, more than an older brother, and always an authority, Heisman defined, on the fly, what a coach should look like. The position of "coach," though not unheard of, was not yet an established entity, as it has since grown to be in American culture. A few of the more established football programs, such as at Harvard, Princeton, and Yale, had paid coaches near the end of the nineteenth century, but most other schools were still relying on team captains, who also served as managers and instructors. In 1892, Heisman was the first professionally paid coach in the state of Ohio, even if Oberlin's student-run athletics association could afford to pay him only a per diem for his boarding and meals, as well as covering his football-related expenses.

One incident early in the 1892 season affirmed to Heisman that his lessons of sacrifice, teamwork, and unselfishness were actually getting through to his players. Miles "Joe" Marsh and Ellsworth "Bill" Westcott had battled for the starting center position since the first days of preseason practice. Both were good players, but Westcott was a more natural athlete, with superior speed, aggressiveness, and instinct. Barring an injury, Westcott seemed destined to win the job. But during practice one day, Westcott was pulled from the action by one of his professors for having low marks in one of his courses. Heisman was considering what to do about the situation when Marsh pulled at his sleeve.

"Coach," Marsh whispered diffidently, "I'm in the same class with Bill, and math is my long suit. I fear that Bill resents me, that is, from our competition, but I believe I could tutor him so they'd let him back inside of a week, if he'd like to try."

Heisman was beside himself after hearing Marsh's offer. "With his own starting chances in sight, Marsh's proposal means nothing less than varsity suicide. Can't you just feel the gut wrench such an offer would cost any man? I try to say something but my tongue has grown too thick. So I give Joe a hard slap on the back and walk over to Bill, who sits on a nearby log, the portrait of despair. I tell Bill about it and he jumps up, crying, 'Why, how can Joe think I resent him? Try? You bet I'll try! Just watch my smoke."

With Marsh's tutoring, Westcott was able to raise his grade and return to practice. He became a dominant player at one of the most important positions on the field. Later in the season, Heisman walked up to Marsh on the sideline. Heisman was appreciative that Marsh was "scuttling his own ambition with every equation he drives through Bill's math-less cranium."

"Joe, all the credit of what Bill is doing for Oberlin goes to you," Heisman told him.

"Well, I'm satisfied," Marsh said. "Yeah, Bill's great!"[14]

Heisman knew he would need all of his men for Oberlin's final game of the season, at the University of Michigan on November 19, 1892. The Wolverines had soundly defeated the Yeomen in their first intercollegiate game the year before and were in the germinal stages of building one of the country's strongest football programs. The Wolverines finished the 1891 season with a 4-5 record and were off to a 6-4 start in 1892 under new coach Frank Barbour, who had played on Yale's national championship squad the previous year. Only a week earlier, Michigan defeated the University of Chicago, which was being coached by Amos Alonzo Stagg for the first time, by an 18–10 score in Toledo, Ohio. Even more impressively, Michigan had lost only one of its previous seventeen home games over the past ten seasons, and Heisman and his Yeomen were about to find out why. As Heisman's team made its way to Ann Arbor, Michigan, a blizzard threatened the region. It was a bone-chilling cold day, and a couple of inches of snow already covered the playing field.

Heisman was confident that his team's swarming interference would test Michigan's "mastodon team." Lining up to the ball would be a tricky business because of the snow. Football's rules prohibited any lineman, including the center, from extending past the ball. Usually the rule was relaxed so that the center could do his job properly, but that wasn't the case in the Michigan game. The hometown referee, Horace Prettyman, seemed intent on neutralizing Oberlin's swift offense. Heisman recalled, "We bumped into a referee there who didn't believe in special privileges to our center, Bill Westcott, or anybody else. Three times he called our halves back after long runs and stated that, in snapping, Bill's head had been offside. Thus we had to play those downs over, but were not able to 'encore' the long runs." [15]

Westcott and his teammates found other ways to overcome Prettyman's favoritism toward the Wolverines. With Oberlin holding an 18–10 lead, Michigan drove to the Yeomen's twenty-yard line and threatened to score. Oberlin didn't have an answer for Michigan left tackle William Pearson—until Merriam devised a way to stop him. Heisman later recalled, "With Michigan driving on Oberlin's twenty-yard line, this huge tackle took the ball and plowed fifteen yards toward the goal. It took us all, like a pack of timber wolves, to bring him down. He struck the ground at the five-yard line and rolled onto his back while his jersey pulled up exposing his abdomen. Quicker than a flash our end, Merriam, scooped up a double handful of the 'fleecy' [snow] and plopped it down on his bare tummy. Suffering wildcats! What a roar he let out, while simultaneously he dropped the ball and swung at Merriam's head. Instantly Carl Williams recovered the ball for us. The umpire saw the big tackle swing but not his provocation, so put him out of the game. Merriam's 'cold-hearted' trick perhaps saved us the game." [16]

Before the game, the team captains had agreed to shorten the second half. The game needed to end at 4:50 P.M. so Oberlin's players could return to their hotel to shower and then catch a train back to Ohio. Since the game was being played on a Saturday, Oberlin's players were under strict orders to return to campus that night, so they wouldn't miss Sabbath services the next morning. With less than two minutes left in the game, and Oberlin now trailing 22–18, the Wolverines drove to Oberlin's five-yard line. But the Yeomen defense buckled down and wouldn't let Michigan score, taking over possession on downs. Shortly thereafter, Savage broke through the line of scrimmage and ran ninety yards to the Michigan five, where Wolverines halfback George Jewett caught him from behind. Jewett, the son of an Ann Arbor blacksmith, was the first African American player at Michigan and later Northwestern University in Evanston, Illinois.

After Prettyman penalized Oberlin twice for intentional delay of the game and then for being offside, Heisman gained five yards to put the Yeomen back in position to score. On the next play, Thomas Johnson ran across the Michigan goal for a touchdown. Since touchdowns were still worth four points, the Yeomen had only tied the score at 22. With only a few seconds left in the agreed-upon time, Louis Hart kicked a ball over the crossbar to give Oberlin a 24–22 lead. For more than a century, Michigan and Oberlin would argue about what happened next. The Oberlin timekeeper said the game was over because the clock read 4:50 and it was time for the Yeomen to catch a train. But Michigan argued that four minutes were still left in the game because of earlier delays of game. As Oberlin's players celebrated and prepared to head for their hotel, the Wolverines lined up and Jewett walked into the end zone with no defense on the field. Michigan insisted it won the game by a 26–24 score, and its record books still reflect that outcome today.

"Oberlin compromised herself by leaving the field before time was up," the *Michigan Daily* reported two days after the game. "Referee Ensworth, an Oberlin substitute, lost all tab of time, and called the game at fourteen minutes to five, while the captain of each team had agreed to play until ten minutes of that hour. Time-keeper Spangler also verifies this. Captain Williams called his men off the field and they immediately got into the bus and were driven to their hotel. All expostulations with the Oberlin captain and manager were of no avail."[17]

Remarkably, the *Ann Arbor Courier*'s account of the game was a little more balanced toward the Yeomen: "Oberlin won because she outplayed Ann Arbor at every point offensive and defensive. Oberlin tackled low and hard, Ann Arbor high and loose. Oberlin played as a team; Ann Arbor did not. In short, Ann Arbor was outgeneraled, and outfought."[18]

The *Ann Arbor Courier*'s game coverage read as though the reporter were a participant on the field. In fact, Heisman was the writer of the article. Heisman probably penned it aboard the returning train to Oberlin, with his fresh recollection of the game's events fueling his ire as he recalled Prettyman's condescending arrogance. The final score had served justice. The young attorney now exacted justice with one of his weapons, the written word. Writing for the public would mark his developing career, supplying sports commentary and feature columns in the local community news and college press.

When word of the game's outcome reached Oberlin's campus by telegram, its students "raided every pile of boxes and barrels outside of every building and soon a 'monstrous bonfire' lit up the campus and attracted a cheering crowd of onlookers that included both students and professors. There were speeches, and then, when the fire burned low, a band led the spirited throng in a march to call out other faculty members, including the school's president, from their homes. The excited celebrants gave three cheers for every member of the starting team, for the team's substitutes, for Hogen its manager, for Heisman, and even for Prettyman. After all, Oberlin had won."[19]

The week after the game, Oberlin's football team was celebrated with an oyster dinner at an insurance agent's house and during a party at mayor A. G. Comings's home, where the glee club sang several songs and Heisman spoke "plainly and seriously, on the future of our athletics."[20] Heisman was presented with a collection of money raised by students and the Glee Club, as a gesture of payment for the joy, success, and exposure he had brought to Oberlin.

With some snow on the belly, a perfect season was secured.

CHAPTER SIX

Buchtel College

For all the exposure and success Heisman helped bring Oberlin College in 1892, the school's athletics department was still a sinking ship financially. According to financial records discovered by the historian Nat Brandt, Oberlin College actually lost money on its football venture during the 1892 season. The school spent $5.00 for each football and $1.00 for each inflator. Board at the team's training table cost about $6.00 per player, and $90 was spent to outfit the team in uniforms and cleated shoes. Oberlin College paid $75 for Ohio State's football team to travel to and from Columbus, Ohio, to play a game, and the Yeomen lost more than $80 after traveling to Ann Arbor, Michigan, to play the Wolverines at the end of the 1892 season.[1] Attendance at Oberlin College's home games was still sporadic, as the Panic of 1893 was beginning to cripple the American economy. Many Oberlin residents simply couldn't afford to spend 35 cents for admission to college football games.

Oberlin College's student body was able to raise enough money to pay Heisman a small stipend at the end of the 1892 season, but the school couldn't justify paying him a more suitable salary at a time when its enrollment was actually decreasing. Just when Oberlin's football team was becoming one of the most successful in the Midwest, Heisman left to become athletic director, football coach, and baseball manager at Buchtel College, about sixty miles southeast of Oberlin, in Akron, Ohio. Buchtel College was founded by the Ohio Universalist Convention in 1870 and is today the University of Akron. Among other things, Universalists believed that God would not create a person knowing that she or he would be destined for eternal damnation. Instead, Universalists believed that all people were destined for salvation. The Ohio Universalist Convention voted in January 1870 to establish a school based on its religious principles in whatever city could provide $60,000 and land for construction. John R. Buchtel, a wealthy industrialist and philanthropist in Akron, helped raise money and acquired land to build the school. The school was built on a hilltop site that was actually earmarked for a cemetery, but the soil was declared too rocky for proper burial. Once the interred bodies were transferred to another location, construction of a schoolhouse started on July 4, 1871.[2]

Over the next twenty-seven years, nearly all of Buchtel College's academic and social activities took place in a five-story building that was fondly called "Old Buchtel." The school's first class included forty-six students. Tuition was $30, rent was $10 per year, and board was $5.00 per week.[3] Old Buchtel included classrooms, a library, a dining room, and labs, as well as dormitories for men and women and unmarried faculty members. Buchtel College first fielded an intercollegiate baseball team in 1873, and a football squad followed in 1891. The first Buchtel College football team didn't have a coach and finished its maiden season with a 1-3 record. Frank Cook was hired as coach in 1892, but he lasted only one season after a 3-4 record. Buchtel's students besieged the college's president, the Reverend Orello Cone, to persuade the school's board of trustees to hire a full-time coach. The trustees agreed, but only if the students would raise $300 to pay a portion of the coach's salary and buy out the contract of the former gymnasium director. Heisman visited the Buchtel campus in January 1893 to inspect its facilities and meet with the faculty. On January 28, 1893, Buchtel College's trustees extended Heisman a one-year contract as gymnasium director and special teacher of gymnastics in baseball and football. Buchtel College agreed to pay Heisman a salary of $900 annually, and his only demand was that a batting cage be built for the baseball team. Shortly after Heisman was hired, the student newspaper, *Buchtelite*, published the headline "Heisman! Heisman! Rah! Rah! Rah!" There was little doubt that the student body believed Heisman would deliver a winner, if you believed their newspaper: "Everybody get out and yell. If you can't yell, get a bunch of firecrackers and make some noise, or steal a box and have an Indian war dance. What for? Why, because 'Old Buchtel' is going to stand at the head in athletics, as she does in everything else. We have secured both cage and coach, and we are going to make things hum when the base ball season opens."[4]

Heisman put forth as much effort in coaching Buchtel College's baseball team as he did in coaching football. Heisman spent the early part of 1893 molding a group of about thirty-five candidates into a baseball team. The *Akron Daily Beacon* reported that the players were required to spend four hours a week in the gymnasium until the weather improved, lifting weights and running under Heisman's watch. After the batting cage was built, players were required to spend six hours per week in training. "The candidates will be pitted against the best pitchers and every man will be kept at the bat until he has had five good raps at the ball," the *Daily Beacon* reported. "The number of strikeouts will be tallied and the standing of the candidates for the team will be published every week in the college paper. In this way the spirit of competition will be maintained."[5]

Buchtel College's baseball team had only modest success under Heisman, finishing 10-8-1 in 1893 and 8-5 in 1894. After a 12–7 loss to Denison College near the end of the 1893 season, a reporter from the *Newark (Ohio) Daily Advocate* even accused Heisman of loading his roster with "ringers," or former professional players, which was a common practice in college athletics at the time. "Buchtel, who has expended considerable money for this base ball season, and who, some time since, was confident of winning the pennant, has been defeated by every team of the association," the *Daily Advocate* reported. "Her discomfiture over repeated defeats had been aggravated until, in self defense, she robbed Kenyon [College] of a victory by villainous umpiring. This, assisted by several other misdemeanors, led to her expulsion from the association. Buchtel was resolved to steal the game from Denison, if she could not win it fairly. To this end she imported a twirler named Joe Neal, an old favorite of the St. Louis Browns. They expected his powerful delivery to win the game. It didn't."[6] The reporter might have been referring to Joe Neale, a native of Wadsworth, Ohio, who was an outfielder and pitcher for the Louisville Colonels and the St. Louis Browns from 1886 to 1891. Neale died at age forty-seven in Akron in 1913.

If nothing else, Heisman was able to identify a quarterback for his Buchtel College football team by coaching baseball, and that experience led to one of his early football innovations. Harry W. Clark was a standout pitcher, and Heisman was convinced that his athleticism could be transferred to the gridiron as well. In an interview with the *Arkon Daily Beacon* after his playing days, Clark, who later became a prosecuting attorney in Chardon, Ohio, said he won Buchtel College's quarterback job by default. "In the fall when the call came out for football candidates no one seemed to be on hand for the position of quarterback," Clark said. "After trying out different members of the team I was finally prevailed up by 'Heis' to come out. He assured me he would personally attend to any parental objections that had kept me away from football activities. I was given a six-piece uniform, consisting of a pair of shoes, a pair of stockings, a pair of pants and a jersey. And that, by the way, was all I ever wore upon the football field, sans headgear, nose piece, shin guards and what not."[7]

There was only one problem: Clark was six feet four inches and had problems bending over to pick up the football off the ground after it was pawed to him by the center. In an article Heisman wrote for *Collier's Weekly* in October 1928, he recalled, "A good quarterback he was, altho a bit too long in the legs. Leaning over to receive the ball from center was something of a contortionist's trick for Harry. His legs were so long one got the impression he was leaning from a roof to take the ball. He was missing quite a few flips on this particular afternoon."[8]

Clark told the *Akron Daily Beacon* he missed "what seemed like a thousand fumbles" before Heisman came up with a solution for his lanky quarterback.

"Throw the ball up to him," Heisman told his center. "Try that and be sure to throw it *up*."

It worked.

"Clark soon wore a star's halo and within the season all the colleges were using this method of transferring the ball," Heisman recalled. "And it's still being used, as you know."[9]

Clark won enough of Heisman's confidence to start at quarterback in Buchtel College's first game of the 1893 season, against Hiram College of Hiram, Ohio. It was the first game on the new Buchtel Field.

"It had been plowed, dragged and rolled for the occasion," Clark said. "Dust was so thick it required occasional application of water to tell friend from foe. The mercury in the thermometer was flirting with 90 [degrees]. Twelve times we drove the ball across Hiram's goal line and 12 times I added points from goal. We thought we were great and it was a happy gang of boys who swaggered into the dressing room after the game, expecting to be praised."[10]

Even though Buchtel College had won the game by a whopping 54–2 score, Heisman saw plenty wrong in their performance.

"Our mutual admiration society was just getting well under way when in stalked Mr. Heisman himself," Clark recalled. "He proceeded to unleash the most vitriolic abuse on the team and individuals thereof I have ever had the displeasure of hearing. I thought the other boys were getting it rather hard, but when it came to [halfback] Jimmy Gardner and myself we knew his words to the other lads had been in the nature of a warm-up. How he threw it on us! Before

Heisman was half finished tears were streaming down Jimmy's face and he threw his uniform at the coach and told the world in general and Heisman in particular that he was through." [11]

Heisman had learned a lesson from his first season at Oberlin College in 1892, when he praised his team for its fine work in the first half of a game. The Yeomen responded with lackluster play in the second half of a narrow victory. After dressing down his Buchtel College players following their first game together, Heisman visited Clark and Gardner in their dormitory rooms that night. Clark recalled, "Heisman came to our rooms and assured us, Jimmy and me, that what Heisman the coach had told the boys that afternoon was merely to prevent them from becoming over-confident. From that time on Jimmy wore his uniform to classes for fear someone else might wear it. He was a great coach and every man on the squad is proud to have learned his lessons under such a sterling leader." [12]

With Clark playing quarterback, Heisman guided Buchtel College to a 5-2 record, with their only losses in 1893 coming against Case Tech and Ohio State. At about the time Buchtel College's season was ending, Heisman was somehow able to persuade the Buchtel College administration to allow him to assist Oberlin College in its preparations for a rigorous two-game road trip at the University of Chicago and the University of Illinois. Such a practice would be unheard of today—can you imagine University of Alabama coach Nick Saban assisting Auburn's football team? But it apparently wasn't out of the ordinary in 1893.

When Heisman left for Buchtel College the previous spring, the Yeomen hired E. B. "Jake" Camp as their new coach. Camp had played halfback for four seasons at Lafayette College in Easton, Pennsylvania, and then played two more seasons at the University of Pennsylvania. Heisman might have even recommended Camp for his old job. Camp didn't inherit the team Heisman guided to an unblemished record the season before. Quarterback Carl Williams, a star player in 1892, transferred to the University of Pennsylvania on Heisman's recommendation, and six other players graduated. Despite the heavy personnel losses, big things were still expected of the Yeomen in 1893. "They must play up to last year's record," the *Oberlin Review* said. "Surrounding colleges assume from last year's record that we have the strongest team in Ohio, and expect our team to equal, even surpass last year's standards."[13]

Imagine the *Oberlin Review*'s disappointment after the Yeomen limped to a 6–0 victory over Kenyon College in the opener. The Yeomen rebounded to flatten Ohio State 38–10 on the road two weeks later, and then won 30–8 at Kenyon College in a rematch on October 23, 1893. But after a 40–0 shutout of Adelbert College on October 28, 1893, Camp resigned as Oberlin's coach. According to Brandt's records, the Oberlin Athletic Association paid Camp $250 in salary in four installments, the last of which came on the day he coached his last game.[14] Apparently Camp had reason to believe that the Yeomen were out of money. With the blessing of Buchtel College, Heisman returned to Oberlin's campus to oversee the Yeomen's preparations for the two biggest games of their young football existence. On November 3, 1893, Heisman boarded a train for Chicago with his football team.

Amos Alonzo Stagg, who had played end at Yale University and was a member of the first All-America team in 1889, was in his second season of coaching at the University of Chicago. Stagg began his coaching career at the YMCA in Springfield, Massachusetts, which is now Springfield College, and he organized the school's first football team in 1889. James Naismith, who invented basketball, was one of his football players. Stagg was hired as football coach and director of the department of physical culture at the University of Chicago in 1892 by new university president William Rainey Harper, who was his divinity professor at Yale. Stagg coached at Chicago for forty-one years and, along with Heisman, was considered one of the great innovators of the game. Among the innovations credited to Stagg are the huddle, the reverse and man-in-motion plays, tackling dummies, lateral passes, uniform numbers, and the tradition of awarding varsity letters. But the Maroons weren't yet a great team under Stagg, who would eventually lead them to 242 victories and seven Big Ten Conference championships during his career.

The Maroons limped to a 1-4-2 mark in 1892, and the Yeomen easily handed them a 33–12 loss in what would be Chicago's 6-4-2 campaign in 1893. Ernest Boothman, the Yeomen's speedy left halfback, ran for two touchdowns, and so did fullback Howard Regal. Near the end of the first half, Regal kicked a field goal, "a splendid play and one seldom seen, even in the Eastern college games,"[15] according to the *Chicago Tribune*. The second half was shortened by fifteen minutes because of darkness or the score might have been even worse. "Stagg's pet Chicago University eleven was trampled in the dust yesterday, and soundly thrashed by the red clad team from Oberlin," the *Chicago Tribune* reported. "From start to finish the Ohio men outplayed and outscored their opponents. Their rush line was powerful, their backs ran well and made no fumbles, and the team interference was perfect. Oberlin's only weakness was in defensive play, Chicago occasionally bursting through the line. The home team played game ball, but was so clearly outclassed that the result of the game was never doubtful."[16]

Despite the lopsided outcome, the Chicago game still took a physical toll on the Yeomen. Halfback Lee Tolly suffered a "broken nerve" in his thigh and was left to heal in a Chicago hospital. Right end Ed Fitch would need days to recover from the beating he took from one of the Maroons' most imposing linemen. Heisman recalled, "In my pre-game pep talk to the Oberlin team, I urged them not to stall around—no 'beginning to get ready to commence to make preparation to get started'— but to jump into Chicago and take the heart out of them right off the bat."[17]

As the Yeomen prepared to kick off, Fitch shouted encouragement to his teammates.

"Now remember what Coach said, fellows," Fitch yelled. "Let's pile in and give 'em hell right from the start."

Fitch weighed only 157 pounds and was clearly overmatched by Maroons tackle John Lemay. "A mist came into my eyes as I thought of that weight and his proven valor," Heisman recalled. "I looked to see what kind of adversary he would draw on the Chicago eleven. Angels of Shasta! [It was] a raw-boned giant, [as] hard as a steel bridge, and as tall as a Norway pine. At that moment I would have liked to recall my 'Siccum, Tiger'—at least as far as Ed was concerned. On the first down, Fitch sailed in to the colossal Swede 'full steam ahead' with a shower of fists, which suggested a bantam rooster attacking an ostrich. In evident surprise the Norseman drew back. The next down was a repetition of the first. A hard look came over the face of the Swedish Samson. Third snap and Ed cyclones into the huge fellow more savagely than ever. POW! There lay his inert form."

Heisman revived Fitch and advised him to use a little more tact against Lemay. When the game was over, Fitch's teammates had to help him off the field, according to Heisman.

"Struck a pretty good man, didn't you, Ed?" asked one of the Oberlin players.

"Good man?" Fitch muttered. "Say, what I struck was a cross between a wolverine, a boa constrictor, a hippopotamus, and a buzz saw." [18]

Only two days later, the Yeomen lined up to play the University of Illinois in Champaign, Illinois, on November 6, 1893. Because of injuries, Oberlin was down to only fourteen players, including just two halfbacks. Since the Yeomen were playing a rare Monday afternoon game on the road, captains of both squads agreed that the contest would end at 5:10 P.M., no matter how much time was left on the clock. The Yeomen were slow out of the gate, falling behind Illinois 12–10 early in the first half. But then Oberlin scored four consecutive touchdowns. By the start of the second half, Oberlin's players

were completely out of gas, and Heisman emptied what was left of
his bench. Then he started watching a nearby clock tower, hoping its
arms would move to 5:10 P.M. as quickly as possible. Heisman later
wrote of the final anxious moments of the Illinois game:

> Aching in every muscle, suppressing a groan with every
> tackle, the boys hobble back to one line up after another. Il-
> linois scores a touchdown and cuts down our lead. We flick
> many an anxious glance toward a tall tower clock visible in
> the distance. A new and dreadful thought: What if the train
> is late and we have to play the full 45 minutes? I dare not even
> think such a thing. Faltering fast, the boys line up again, and
> again Illinois goes through us like a prairie fire. We are pow-
> erless to stop them. Again, they score and cut our lead still
> more. Are those clock hands frozen fast? Will that snail train
> never come? Illinois is romping over us as though we were
> Lilliputians. They are past midfield again—now on our forty,
> thirty, twenty, ten-yard line! In one more minute they will
> tear the tortured hearts right out of us. But behold! Those
> snail-like clock hands point at last to ten after five. Thank
> heaven, we are saved![19]

The Yeomen had pulled out a 34–24 victory, but much like when
Oberlin played at Michigan in Heisman's first season, Illinois's
captain disputed whether the game was supposed to end prematurely.
The Illini manager admitted he had agreed to such a deal prior to
the contest, but his captain insisted that the Yeomen finish the game.
Heisman knew his team couldn't miss its train back to Ohio, but they
also couldn't leave without their share of the gate earnings.

"That's nothing to me," snarled the Illinois captain. "In another
minute we can tie the score and in five more we'll win the game.
We're playing for the whole game and a whole game they'll play."

Before the captain could say anything else, the Illinois manager reached into his pocket and presented Oberlin manager Charlie Bracken a roll of bills "big enough to choke a cow."

"There's your guarantee, Mr. Bracken," the manager told him. "Thank you for the licking, and I hope you'll come again. And now you'll all have to run like hell. Good-bye." [20]

It was a long train ride back to Oberlin. The Yeomen had to change trains in Toledo, Ohio, and by the time they reached the station, many of the players were covered in black-and-blue bruises.

"That night I had the blood-bruised ears of three of them lanced and bound up, and at least eight of them required surgical and medical attention, though fortunately none seriously," Heisman recalled. "The boys slept mighty little. They stumbled through the Toledo station gates, some on crutches, some with arms in slings, many with bound heads and all with scars and court plastering on their faces. Even the manager came off on a stretcher with acute indigestion. Many people seemed to be awaiting us. I heard them saying, 'Oh, it must have been terrible,' and, 'Just look at that one!' [Then] comes a fellow running up to me with, 'All right, sir, ambulances are this way.' I looked around and saw people offering my boys food, cake, fruit, helping them with their grips and luggage." [21]

At about that time, a young newsboy yelled, "Here's your extra! All about the tur'ble wreck on the Clover Leaf."

"They had taken us for train wreck survivors," Heisman recalled. "We looked the part."

Oberlin College lost its final game of the 1893 season (two other games had been canceled), falling to Cass Tech 22–8 without Heisman on the sideline. Over a two-year period, Heisman helped the Yeomen compile a 13-1 record. After the 1893 season, the *Chicago Tribune* considered Oberlin among the best teams in the country. "One more college should receive special praise," the *Tribune* reported. "Oberlin, far down in Ohio, has sent forth a magnificent eleven, and Chicago and Champaign have already been met and vanquished. The backs of Oberlin are of the winning sort, and the team interference is the best this side of the Alleghanies [sic]. Oberlin could give Purdue or Minnesota a hard tussle, and the other colleges mentioned in this article would be easy prey for the red-legged tribe from Ohio. A series of games between Purdue, Oberlin, and Minnesota would bring out the best football in the West and would be worth a long journey to see. But such a series, unfortunately, is hardly possible and certainly cannot be played this year."[22]

Heisman returned to Buchtel College to coach one more game, against Ohio State, on the grounds of the Ohio State Fair and Industrial Exposition on September 5, 1894. The contest was part of a three-day tournament that also included teams from Denison University, Miami (Ohio) University, and Wittenburg College of Springfield, Ohio.[23] It was a blisteringly hot day, and Buchtel's players weren't in top physical condition because it was so early in the season. Early in the game, the heat began to take its toll on Heisman's players, he later recalled:

> To make matters worse, [the game] befell at exactly noon of the horridest, torridest, humidist, darned day I almost ever saw. At the end of the first half each team had garnered six points and a dozen "all-in" players. My captain, Frank Fisher, whose yeoman line plunging, coupled with the heat, had resulted in a bad attack of "sun-staggers," had to be led off the field to the shade of a nearby tree. While bathing Frank's eyes with cool water and wondering how I could start the second half without him, we were approached by Captain Wood of the O.S.U. team. I greeted him, and we shortly settled a ground rule that had given us some trouble in the first half. As he was about to return to his own team he caught sight of Fisher, still out of combat, and asked, "Anything the matter with that chap? Can I get you a doctor?" I thanked him, told him the trouble, and said I would keep Frank out of the lineup for the second half.[24]

"That would be a real pity," Wood replied. "He seems to be your best back. I tell you what. You take more time, say twenty minutes, and maybe he'll come around all right."

Fisher recovered in time to play in the second half, which is when Heisman's hatred for fumbles was born. Heisman was playing quarterback on the squad, and the unthinkable happened in the flick of an instant, when he took his eye from the ball as it came back. "It took us nine minutes to get that ball to their goal line, and then I made the first fumble of the day, the rolled snap going crazy in the wheat stubble," Heisman recalled. "They secured the ball and punted it back to midfield, and we had to do it all over again. I could have committed hari-kari!"[25]

With time running out, Butchel's players began another march toward Ohio State's goal line. Hot as they were and near dehydration, again and again they plunged the line. Several minutes later, they were on Ohio State's three-yard line. Heisman rallied his troops: "Fellows, we're here again. Last time I had a dratted fumble, but I'm not going to fumble now. So every man get into this play and let's make it the last."[26]

Heisman took the snap and handed the ball to Fisher, his fullback. Heisman and the rest of Buchtel's team "dragged, pulled, and pushed till we practically tore all his clothes off as we yanked the ball across the line, won the game 12–6, and called it a day."[27] It would also be the end of Heisman's coaching career at Buchtel College. The Ohio State game was the only contest Buchtel College played in the 1894 season. The school's faculty had never warmed up to athletics like the professors at Oberlin College had, and there was even some resentment among the faculty over Heisman's salary. "Too much emphasis on athletics!" professors cried. "An unhealthy sway, detracting from academic endeavor, this football game would ruin the good standing and reputation of this institute of higher learning!"[28] Heisman, of course, disagreed and argued that a strong, well-fit body was a sound foundation to strong will, mind, and character.

He argued that competition in the field strengthened young men to the rigors of scholarly pursuits and professional life, and, primarily, it trained a young man's volitional resolve in the face of opposition. His arguments were to no avail.

Fortunately for Heisman, he was able to return to Oberlin College for a full season in 1894. Heisman's assurances that a proper emphasis on academics would be maintained helped pave the way for his welcomed return. By now Heisman was three years into his hiatus from pursuing a law career, and his father was still growing impatient and wondering when his college-educated son was going to embark on his calling as an attorney. But Heisman was enjoying his situation. Having started as a college athletic director and football coach, and being paid quite fairly, he decided to stick with it. His eyes had healed considerably and he could see with only minor blurriness, although he still needed glasses to read. Heisman could see well enough to take part in games, when desired or necessary, and without the demands of continued heavy legal reading his vision was no longer in jeopardy. He also was aware of the influence a coach held over his players and felt a certain responsibility to them. A great good could be done in their lives with a timely spoken word of encouragement, directions, or corrections that would build the character of the players. Heisman recognized his opportunity to help build future leaders and saw its far-reaching value. Until something better came along, Heisman decided he would continue to coach.

Heisman guided Oberlin College to a 4-3-1 record in 1894, after the Yeomen lost three of their last four games. The Yeomen played Washington & Jefferson to a 0–0 tie in Washington, Pennsylvania, in their first road trip east and lost to Penn State 9–6 at home after a controversial ending. After completing the 1894 season, Heisman returned to his apartment in Cleveland. At the time, he had developed a very close relationship with Edith Maora Cole, a student at Buchtel College. Cole and Heisman seemed to be very much in love and were engaged to be married. In November 1894 there were published reports that Heisman had married an Oberlin College student named Dorothy Emerson Fairfax Brown in Buffalo, New York, but the reports were never substantiated.[29] Cole, the daughter of a farmer from Norwalk, Ohio, was the target of Heisman's affection. Her father, Sterry Cole, had served as a second lieutenant with Company B of the 166th Regiment, Ohio Volunteer Infantry, during the Civil War. Sterry Cole died when Edith was seven years old in 1876, leaving her mother, Ascha, to raise their three children.

By now Heisman was drawing attention from around the country as someone who knew the game of football. But coaching at Oberlin College and his impending marriage to Cole were all he could foresee in the near future. But then Cole, who had been plagued by asthma throughout her life, became seriously ill sometime in late 1894. At first her illness seemed like only a bad cold that wouldn't go away, but eventually it left her weak and frail. Cole's mother summoned a doctor as a precaution. After an examination, the physician made a devastating prognosis: Edith had consumption (tuberculosis). The doctor said her condition would probably become terminal and that she would slowly weaken until dying. In 1900, tuberculosis was the third-leading cause of death in the United States, behind only heart disease and influenza. In fact, Americans were three times more likely to die from tuberculosis than any form of cancer at the start of the twentieth century.[30] Tuberculosis was often called "consumption" because the disease consumed a person's body, severely damaging or even destroying lungs and other organs.

Heisman listened to the doctor's prognosis in disbelief, and Edith's family was stricken with grief. Heisman attended to Edith daily, encouraging her, reading to her, and wooing her anew. He still asked Mrs. Cole for Edith's hand in marriage and wanted to marry her quickly. Cole's mother consented, but what followed shocked everyone. In a magnanimous act of selflessness, Edith refused marriage and released Heisman from his pledge to her. She did not wish to be a burden or leave him as a widower.[31]

Heisman fought her decision. Day after day he came to Edith's bedside and restated his love, but despite his keen intellect, eloquence, and powers of persuasion, Heisman had met his match. Edith's strength of character and volition met his desperate appeals with calm certainty and courage. Mrs. Cole intervened with a gentle yet firm hand, requesting Heisman to say good-bye and not return, as his attempts were becoming too heartbreaking to witness. The Cole family was heartstricken for Edith and became very concerned for Heisman. The young attorney had lost his first case. With the greatest reluctance, Heisman relented and said his good-byes. He left the Cole home sick at heart.

A crisis of heart and spirit rolled through Heisman. Staying in Ohio represented all the potential of life with Edith. The familiar college landmarks and memories would be lived and relived but without her. The football season would dredge up memories of a beautiful young lady waving from the stands, someone who loved the game nearly as much as he did. With a broken heart, Heisman made a decision for a new vocation and a new location. After gathering his assets and resigning as Oberlin College's coach, he headed to the South, where he would begin a new life and try a completely new venture.

CHAPTER SEVEN

Auburn

I t might be thought of as luck, good fortune, or perhaps even des-
tiny. More than anything else, it was a rescue. Early in 1895, after
Heisman had walked away from the stricken Edith Cole's bedside
and fled Cleveland with a broken heart, he invested most of his life's
savings in growing tomatoes in East Texas. Apparently Heisman
wasn't much of a farmer. While there is scarce information available
about this failed venture—there are no property deeds, financial records, or personal recollections of any kind—it is clear that Heisman
wasn't in East Texas for very long.

Walter Riggs, manager of the fledgling football team at the Agricultural and Mechanical College of Alabama, probably saved Heisman from financial ruin. The sweltering Texas sun had taken its
toll, and all Heisman could do was watch helplessly as his enterprise
cooked away. When Riggs went searching for a new football coach
in 1895, he wrote to Pennsylvania captain Carl Williams, who had
played for Heisman at Oberlin College. Williams advised Riggs to
find Heisman. Riggs's search took a few weeks, as Heisman was labor-
ing in fields of withering, sunbaked tomato plants. Riggs, a native of
Orangeburg, South Carolina, who earned engineering degrees from
Agricultural and Mechanical College of Alabama in 1892 and played
on the school's first football team, could sense Heisman's plight immediately. But Riggs graciously ignored comment and refrained

from pressing any advantage in Heisman's unfortunate state. Riggs simply presented his team's need for a coach and its desire to acquire Heisman's services for the coming fall. Heisman at once keenly appreciated Riggs's well-managed regard and was won over by his gracious approach. They came to a gentleman's agreement quickly, and their early interactions commenced a lifelong friendship.

Prior to Heisman arriving at Agricultural and Mechanical College of Alabama in 1895—the school later became known as Alabama Polytechnic Institute and then Auburn University—the Tigers had gone through four coaches in as many seasons. George Petrie, an Auburn history professor, introduced football to the school after witnessing the rugged game while earning his PhD in modern languages at Johns Hopkins University in Baltimore, Maryland. After accepting a teaching position at Auburn in 1891, Petrie organized and coached the school's first football team. The Tigers played their first game against the University of Georgia in Atlanta on February 20, 1892, defeating the Bulldogs, 10–0. Petrie resigned as Auburn's coach after the 1892 season to concentrate on his teaching duties. D. M. Balliet, a former Princeton player, coached Auburn for one game during the 1893 season, guiding the Tigers to their first victory, over the University of Alabama. Former Cornell University player G. H. Harvey coached Auburn for the final four games of the 1893 season, and then F. M. Hall, a Princeton graduate, coached the Tigers to a 1-3 record in 1894.

The Deep South's entanglement with intercollegiate football was just beginning when Heisman arrived at Auburn. The sport's roots were ingrained in the Northeast, but football was beginning to become very popular among male students at southern schools such as Alabama, Auburn, Georgia, Sewanee, and Vanderbilt. Heisman was encouraged by his players' desire to absorb everything he knew about the sport. Heisman threw himself into his work with a will and, most likely, a purpose to heal the heart he left in Ohio. It was a fit match, and Heisman began to build a fine team. The Auburn student newspaper, the *Orange and Blue*, didn't wait long to endorse Heisman's hiring: "He is just the man we were looking for and if we had searched the country over again we could not have done better. He is a perfect gentleman and has won himself into the hearts of all the boys, as well as members of the faculty, by his hard, earnest, conscientious work. He is always ready, be it night or day, to work for the success of the team. He is certainly doing his work well and he is the best coach we have ever had. Let the boys obey him in all points and I am sure his reputation will be fully sustained."[1]

While eager to play, many of the young men who came out for football at Auburn in 1895 had never seen a football before, let alone played the game. Heisman had much to explain and had to go over the fundamentals and formations in step-by-step fashion and with endless patience. Heisman later recalled an example of how unfamiliar football was for many of his players: "On this team played a strong country boy named Jackson. The first day he ever came out for football—he had never seen the spheroid ball—he heard us speaking of the first half and the second half. Wanting to—and I had told him to ask when he did not understand—he now came through with, 'How many of them halves is there in a game?'"[2]

Heisman had his hands full, but the sheer enthusiasm of his young players lent him the forbearing strength of a father. In Oberlin College's 1893 game with the University of Chicago, Heisman remembered watching Amos Alonzo Stagg's offense pull his ends back from the line of scrimmage a yard or two and then run them around the other end like halfbacks. At Auburn, Heisman found the right place to copy and modify the "end-around" play and made it a devastating weapon. With a renewed passion for coaching, ideas and innovations seemed to come to Heisman in clusters. His mind worked quickly to assess what would work on the field, picking up one idea and discarding another. So fertile was Heisman's mind that one fall evening he retired to bed and woke up with a full-blown play! Heisman later wrote:

I was coaching at Alabama Poly in 1895 and I dreamed this play—the only one I ever dreamed that worked! After dreaming this play in action, I woke up. I could hardly wait till morning to get hold of the fellows one by one and instruct them in the details. That afternoon we pulled it on the scrub [team]. The [quarterback] simply gave the ball to the right end, who came running for it. The right half and [fullback] crossed rapidly in front of the left half, who stood in his tracks and took the ball from the right end as the latter passed him. The quarter acted as trailblazer, and straight through the center they both shot like bullets. There was simply nobody there. It went for a touchdown. That play yielded me thousands of yards and dozens of touchdowns in the next fifteen years. It was the forerunner of practically all delayed bucks.[3]

Heisman saw another opportunity with his eager squad of neophytes. At the time, most teams were concentrating on running the ball with as much interference as could be mustered at the point of attack. Lateral passing had been one of the features of the early game of rugby, and its use was in rapid decline. By 1892, lateral passes were all but extinct. But Heisman reasoned that with so much defensive emphasis on stopping the run, the time to revive lateral passing was now. Auburn easily wrapped around opposing ends with long lateral passes to halfbacks hiding out near the sideline. Heisman found the perfect back to run those long passes, George Mitcham, who would become an Auburn hero. Catching defenses asleep, Mitcham ripped off long gains with blazing speed game after game. Mitcham's immediate success clearly showed that inside of ten years, players and coaches alike had forgotten there was such a play or that there were backs fast enough to take advantage of it. Heisman wrote:

The invention of many wonderful new formations and running plays gave such a fillip to the development of offense that, for the time, no coaches could find ways and means to stop all the new plays. Defense was not so alluring a subject then, and it was not being studied intensively. This comparative weakness of defense was a significant fact that I was fortunate enough to recognize early in my coaching career. Forthwith, I concentrated in my coaching on interference and variety of attack, sure that if my teams mastered these two elements, no team would have a good enough defense to stop us.[4]

Armed with an ever-expanding playbook, Heisman prepared to coach his first season at Auburn in 1895. At the time, the Tigers were permitted by the school's faculty and board of trustees to play only three or four games per season. The school's governing bodies had grown to tolerate the sport but weren't quite ready to embrace it. In a June 10, 1895, meeting, the Auburn board of trustees approved a resolution that prohibited the football team from playing games at neutral sites off campus. The board apparently wanted to keep the players away from the temptations of large cities. The following passage was recorded in the minutes of the meeting: "Athletic exercises are worthy of encouragement in every college, and when judiciously practised [sic] promote the well being of the students both physically and morally. But it is the duty of those in authority not to place students in the way of temptation but to remove as far as possible all influences of evil tendency. For these reasons intercollegiate football games in cities, are, by action of the faculty, prohibited in the future, save one next season."[5]

Heisman lost his first game as Auburn's coach, a 9–6 defeat at Vanderbilt University in Nashville, Tennessee, on November 9, 1895, a game that was played in "mud ankle-deep."[6] During that game, Heisman revealed his "hidden ball" trick for the first time. He actually devised the play while sitting in team captain Walter Shafer's room, where Heisman was discussing football strategy with quarterback Reynolds Tichenor.

"You know, boys, I had a kid ask me once if it was against the rules to hide the ball," Heisman told them. "I don't see anything against it, but honestly I don't see how you could work a trick like that."[7]

There was a long, thoughtful silence in the room.

"I've got it, Heisman!" Shafer shouted. "Why not just stick the ball under Tick's jersey?"

Tichenor hurried to the room next to Shafer's, grabbed a jersey from an undergrad, and then slipped a football underneath it. Once all three men could see that the ball would easily fit, they set to creating a formation to conceal the deception. Heisman later recalled how the play worked against Vanderbilt:

In those days we were all enamored of the cleverness of tricks and plays of deception. All's fair in war, and football comes close to being war. Also, the rules did not explicitly forbid it. A concealed ball trick [was now unleashed] by Alabama Poly on Vanderbilt. Early in the second half, the Alabama boys wheeled from scrimmage formation into a swirling ring. This "revolving wedge" held the quarterback, Reynolds Tichenor, in the middle, with the ball. While they revolved and obscured him, he stuffed the ball up under the front of his jersey. Next he dropped one knee and pretended to nurse a sprained ankle, while the circling mass sloughed away from him—likewise the Bandy tacklers who still strove to tear up our wedge. With the leap of a cat arose now the crouching Tichenor and "pussyfooted" 35 yards to a touchdown. The officials, the Vandy players and coaches, and their college paper The Hustler all thought the game most clever. They never dreamed of it as unsportsmanlike any more than we had.[8]

After losing at Vanderbilt, the Tigers rebounded two weeks later to blast rival Alabama 48–0 in Tuscaloosa, Alabama. According to a November 24, 1895, report in the *Atlanta Constitution*, "it was apparent to spectators as soon as the two teams came in the field that Auburn greatly out-classed the university team in size, and when play began it was soon seen that it was a battle of fresh recruits against veterans. The university boys put up a plucky game, but it was no avail against the heavy-weight of Auburn's seasoned veterans, who went through the university line for touch-down after touch-down."[9] The Alabama-Auburn series had obviously not yet become one of the most intense rivalries in all of sports. After the game, Alabama's players hosted "a brilliant hop in the famous old 'Mess' hall in honor of their victorious rivals. In the elaborate decorations of the hall the orange and blue of the visitors was as much in evidence as the crimson and white of the home team."[10]

While the Crimson Tide would eventually grow to become Auburn's most bitter rival, Georgia was actually the team Tigers fans and players really cared about defeating in the late nineteenth century. The proximity of the schools was the root of much of the intensity: Auburn's campus is only thirty miles from the Georgia state line. Still known as the "Deep South's Oldest Rivalry," Auburn and Georgia have played each other nearly every season since 1892. The 1895 contest unfolded on the grounds of the Cotton States and International Exposition in Atlanta on Thanksgiving Day 1895. The teams met on a field that had been plowed for "Buffalo Bill's Wild West Show," and exposition planners promised a postgame fireworks show that would be the "finest Pyrotechnic display ever seen, the likes of which may never occur again in the South."[11] The *Atlanta Constitution* reported on the day of the game: "Thousands of people will see this great interstate championship game, this being the last of the season. There has always been a world of interest in these games and the people who come from Athens [Georgia] and from Auburn today will find themselves surrounded by thousands who will cheer them with equal vigor to victory."[12]

Glenn Scobey "Pop" Warner was in his first season coaching the Bulldogs, after finishing his playing career at Cornell Univer-

sity. Warner would go on to coach his alma mater, as well as the
Carlisle Indian Industrial School in Carlisle, Pennsylvania, where he
coached the immortal Jim Thorpe from 1907 to 1912. Like Heisman
and Stagg, Warner was an innovator in the early days of football,
introducing the practice of numbering plays, spiral punts, huddles,
and the double-wing formation. Early in their careers, Heisman and
Warner developed a budding rivalry, and Heisman won the first
round, with Auburn defeating Georgia 16–6 in 1895. The *Atlanta
Constitution* reported the following day, "It was a game of greater
interest to the people of Atlanta and Georgia than any other football contest ever seen on her soil. From start to finish it was full
of exciting features. Athens was downed by fair, hard playing. The
avoirdupois of the Auburn men was just a little too much for her. The
game was marked for the hard, steady play on both sides, the absence
of individual plays, the heavy rush work of Auburn, and the quick,
snappy but unsuccessful tackles of Athens." [13]

The Tigers went 2-1 in their first season under Heisman and
then won their first three games in 1896, defeating Mercer 46–0 in
Macon, Georgia; Georgia Tech 45–0 at home; and Sewanee 38–6 in
Montgomery, Alabama. The only game that stood in Auburn's way
of posting an undefeated season in 1896 was its annual Thanksgiving Day game against Georgia, in Atlanta. A week before the game,
Heisman sent an update of his squad to the *Atlanta Constitution* that
might have made even the most poor-mouthing coaches blush:

> The students here are much worried over the fact that three
> or four of the best men on the team are crippled so that they
> can at best do inferior work. Never in Auburn's history has
> she suffered such hard luck from accidents. The accident to
> Stokes's ankle was a blow to the Alabamians that they will feel
> very keenly on Thanksgiving Day, for Stokes [was] one of the
> fastest men and the best ground gainers on the team before
> his ankle was hurt. One of the best men behind the line that

ever wore a canvas suit for Auburn has been knocked up, and when he enters the game Thursday, if he enters it at all, he will be at great disadvantage. Tichenor has worked so hard to put his men in shape for the big game that he is quite thin and looks as if he were over-trained. He says that he is all right, but the students are anxious about him and fear that he will not be up to his usual form.[14]

Of course, Tichenor and the halfback Stokes were ready to play when the Tigers met the Bulldogs on Thanksgiving Day 1896. A crowd of more than eight thousand fans showed up to watch Georgia defeat Auburn by a 12–6 score at Brisbane Park, which was the home of Atlanta's professional baseball team. "Small boys who did not have enough money to buy tickets began to climb up on the roofs of the houses [and] looked like black birds squatted on the top of houses and perched up on the limbs of the trees," the *Constitution* reported. "It was unquestionably the best exhibition of scientific football playing ever seen in the south. The Alabamians contested every inch of ground and worked with splendid spirit in face of defeat. The Georgians played with real old-fashioned Georgia grit. They went into the game determined to win, and they did it."[15]

According to the report, Auburn might have been confused by Georgia's quick offense, which "ordered a series of plays which are played as fast as the men can line up without any signals whatever. Every man on the Georgia eleven knew just what play was to be put in practice. Without a word they hammered into Alabama's line, skirted around Alabama's ends, bucked between Alabama's guard and tackle and carried the ball eight and ten yards at a time toward Auburn's goal."[16]

Afterward, Heisman told the *Constitution* that he was proud of his team's effort, even in defeat.

"We are well satisfied with our team's work, even if they were defeated," Heisman said. "We played the best game we were capable of, and our men stood to their work from beginning to end. We did not prophecy that we were going to win, and have no excuse to make now that the game is over. We labored under many difficulties at Auburn this year and the work of the team throughout the season has been in the nature of the revelations to its adherents. I consider the Auburn teamwork superior to that of Georgia. As it is, we fought the finest up-hill football game, in my opinion that has ever been waged in the south. Our men never gave up until the referee's whistle blew, ending the game. We have nothing to be ashamed of, while Georgia is to be congratulated upon the finest team she has ever turned out."

Even though Heisman might have stretched the truth about his team's health in his pregame scouting report to the *Constitution*, the Tigers were dealing with quite a few injuries when they traveled to Atlanta. In practice two days before the Georgia game, Auburn's fullback and guard collided, knocking the fullback out of the lineup. Heisman lost not only his best interference man but also his only punter. It didn't take long for the news to reach Charles Nelson, who had played end for Auburn the previous season, but left the team after struggling in the victory over Georgia in 1895. "Charlie and I never had an argument over the matter, but I think he felt he was not to blame for the gains of the opposition," Heisman wrote. "And perhaps he wasn't—maybe I made an error. Who shall say? The next year Charlie did not come out for the team. I hunted him up and he told me his schedule was so heavy he could not afford the time. He did have a tough schedule, but I felt badly over the thought that, possibly, he was sore over the last game."

But when Heisman's team was depleted by injury the next year, Nelson was there when the Tigers needed him most.

"As I left the field house, there stands before me Charlie Nelson— *the best punter by far* in college," Heisman recalled.

"Coach," Nelson said, "I've just heard. Mighty tough luck. I know Pete's your only punter and I wonder whether there is any way I can help out. I thought maybe I could take a stab at guard in Jim's place and punt for you. I've been punting off and on for exercise, so I'm all right there."

As Heisman extended his hand to Nelson, he said, "Charlie, I was just fixing up a little prayer for a punter. No doubt you are heaven's answer—some service, I'll say."

Two days later, with no practice or conditioning, Nelson played left guard, never missed a signal, and punted spectacularly.

"Through all these years—and all that remain for me—that man Nelson has stood, and will stand, as one honest to goodness real and all-around man," Heisman later wrote.[17]

Before the next season at Auburn, in 1897, Heisman was shown the fiber of another young man, whose nerve and strength of character the coach could but stand back and admire. His name was John Penton, who transferred to Auburn after playing guard for three seasons at the University of Virginia from 1893 to 1895. Graduation had depleted Heisman's roster, and Tichenor, his star quarterback, had transferred to Georgia to attend law school. Heisman also desperately needed a fullback, and Penton stepped up to fill the void. The Tigers opened the 1897 season with two easy victories, 26–0 over Mercer at Central City Park in Macon, Georgia, and 14–4 over the University of Nashville. Then the Tigers played Sewanee to a 0–0 tie on the road the day after playing in Nashville. Heisman later recalled his team's two-day trip through Tennessee:

> I kept Penton out of the starting line-up for he had torn a muscle in his thigh the day before. But our sub at fullback sprained an ankle, and I was forced to put John in after the second half. As he came on the field, he was recognized by the Sewanee players, who sent up a blood-curdling shout. Each had a snappy wisecrack for him. Claiborne's, an opposing guard, was typical: "Well, well, well," yells he. "Look who's here! Old Rip Van Penton, the grandfather of football. Where's your cane, grandpa?" But they were barking up the

wrong tree, for here was a man who couldn't be "razzed." He grinned broadly and came right back with: "Grandpappy is right, thank'ye. Now just hand me that ball and let me show the chillums haw this little game is played." He took the ball, lowered his head and went into the line like a hawk among chickadees. Fully twelve yards he tore leaving a trail of cyclone wreckage behind. To give him his due, I would like to say that in 42 years of football I have never seen the player I thought had more iron nerve than he.[18]

On the same day Auburn played Sewanee, an event occurred in Atlanta that threatened the very existence of intercollegiate football. While the University of Georgia was playing Virginia at Brisbane Park on October 30, 1897, Bulldogs fullback Richard Von Gammon was seriously injured in the early part of the second half. According to a report in the *Atlanta Constitution* on October 31, 1897, "Gammon was in the crowd and he made a lunge at the player who had the ball. He missed his tackle and was thrown violently to the ground. He fell with a thud, and the strong, heavy men tumbled over on top of him. Some say Gammon's head hit his shoe as he almost doubled when he was thrown. Others claim his head struck the hard ground. The fearful fall stunned Gammon, and he was picked up dazed and half unconscious. He quickly commenced to vomit, and it was seen by those who ran to his assistance that he was badly hurt. He turned white and the color left his features entirely."[19]

According to the report, a physician was summoned from the grandstand, and the doctor "injected morphine into the injured man's chest in the hope that he could be revived and saved from the pain." Von Gammon was rushed to nearby Grady Hospital, where he died at 3:45 A.M. the next day, according to the *Constitution*.[20]

News of Von Gammon's death spread throughout the South quickly. Football programs at Georgia, Georgia Tech, and Mercer voluntarily disbanded, and Auburn's team did the same on November 2, 1897. Within days, the Georgia state legislature introduced a bill that would outlaw playing football in the state. A newspaper headline from the *Atlanta Journal* read "DEATH KNELL OF FOOTBALL," and the *Atlanta Constitution* reported, "the end of football playing in Georgia seems to be in sight. Its death knell has been sounded. The arch enemies of football have turned upon it, and from all sides come bitter denunciation of the game."[21] A Georgia state representative introduced a resolution on November 1, 1897, that "the game of football should be prohibited from all schools and colleges receiving financial aid from the state"; it passed by a vote of 91–3. Several days later, the Georgia Senate passed a bill by a 31–4 vote that prohibited "the playing of football in Georgia and to provide a penalty for the violation of the same."[22] The Senate bill needed only the signature of Georgia governor William Y. Atkinson to become law. But then Rosalind Burns Gammon, the fallen player's mother, wrote the following letter to her local state representative:

> It would be the greatest favor to the family of Von Gammon if your influence could prevent his death being used for an argument detrimental to the athletic cause and its advancement at the University. His love for his college and his interest in all manly sports, without which he deemed the highest type of manhood impossible, is well known by his classmates and friends, and it would be inexpressibly sad to have the cause he held so dear injured by his sacrifice. Grant me the right to request that my boy's death should not be used to defeat the most cherished object of his life.[23]

After hearing of Rosalind Burns Gammon's request, Atkinson, on December 7, 1897, vetoed the bill outlawing football. Auburn reassembled its team within a few weeks, but the Tigers had already been forced to cancel the rest of their games during the 1897 season, including the Thanksgiving Day game against Georgia. Heisman later recalled: "In '97 we had a great aggregation of players; but the untimely death of one of Georgia's star players in mid season led to the cancellation of the Thanksgiving Day game; and without that we could not worry through the financial end of the work, so we also had to disband."[24]

On December 18, 1897, representatives from the schools that were charter members of the Southern Intercollegiate Athletic Association met at a hotel in Birmingham, Alabama, to discuss ideas of how to make football less violent. Some members discussed seven-men-on-line rules and the prohibition of mass play. Heisman believed he had the answer for opening up the game of football that would put less emphasis on the line of scrimmage, where rough play and serious injuries usually occurred. Heisman didn't actually invent the forward pass, the play that would change football forever, but he ended up being its biggest proponent after witnessing a pass while scouting a game between North Carolina and Georgia on October 26, 1895, in Atlanta. The play evolved because of the desperation of North Carolina fullback Joel Whitaker, who threw the ball forward to teammate George Stephens while trying to punt out of his team's end zone:

> Instead of punting straight into the leaping bodies of these on-rushing Georgians he ran a few mincing steps to the right. Raising the ball to his shoulder he tossed it. Luck was with the boy. The ball was caught by a North Carolinian. Now as we today know forward passes it was not much. It traveled a few yards, and laterally as well as forward. It may have appeared to the spectators that it had been knocked from that fullback's hands. At any rate that lad who caught it ran 70 yards for a touchdown! Georgia was stunned, not quite realizing what had happened there beneath North Carolina's goal. But Glenn Warner, then coaching Georgia, had not missed a moment of it. And neither had I. I had been standing not more than eight

yards from North Carolina's fullback. I had seen the first forward pass in football. It was illegal, of course. Already Warner was storming at the referee. But the referee had not seen the North Carolina lad, goaded to desperation, toss the ball. And he refused to recall the ball. A touchdown had been made, and a touchdown it remained.[25]

An October 27, 1895, article in the *Atlanta Constitution* verified Heisman's account of the play: "The defensive work of the Georgians was good and they succeeded in holding their opponents down to small gains until Stevens [sic], of the Carolina team, got the ball on a fumble pass and made the first touchdown, within four minutes. This was clearly a fluke, but then they count for just as much as hard-earned plays."

Over the next several years, Heisman campaigned for the legalization of the forward pass, believing its inclusion would open the game up and eliminate many of the sport's serious injuries. Heisman wrote many times to Walter Camp, head of the football rules committee, about legalizing the forward pass, which was finally approved in 1906.

Heisman coached for two more seasons at Auburn, with the Tigers finishing 2-1 in 1898 and 3-1-1 in 1899. Both seasons ended in controversy against Georgia, including the Tigers' 18–17 victory over the Bulldogs in Atlanta on Thanksgiving Day 1898. After the Tigers fell behind 13–4 in the first half, Heisman instructed Mitcham to start pounding Georgia's line with bullish runs. Auburn scored the game's next three touchdowns and had an 18–13 lead in the second half (touchdowns still counted as only four points). Georgia scored a touchdown with about eight minutes left in the game, but then missed the extra point to make the score 18–17. Georgia argued that Auburn's players were offside on the missed extra point, but the officials didn't agree. Inexplicably, Georgia's players walked off the field in protest. The *Atlanta Constitution* reported the next day, "The Auburn rooters claim that the victory of their team would have been more decided, and the Georgia men assert with equal vehemence that the red and black would have scored one and possibly two more touchdowns. Many, even of the Georgia men, criticized Captain [P. H.] Walden for ordering his men off the field at that stage of the game."[26]

Heisman told the *Constitution* that the better team won the game: "My men were just in better condition than Georgia's, and that tells the whole story. The longer Auburn played the better the men took to their work, and while Georgia had three or four men laid out during the play, Auburn did not have one."[27]

The next season, when Heisman might have assembled his best team at Auburn, the Tigers were on the wrong end of two officiating controversies that ended up sullying their season. Auburn opened the 1899 season by running over its first three opponents: 63–0 over Georgia Tech, 41–0 over Montgomery, and 34–0 over Clemson. The Tigers had an 11–6 lead over Georgia in Atlanta on November 18, 1899. But with only "thirty seconds of play left, [and] with darkness already at hand and a wild, excited crowd surging over the field, Referee Rowbotham called the game and under the rules of the Southern Intercollegiate Association declared the score 0 to 0."[28] Heisman was incensed afterward, telling the *Constitution*, "We had worked hard for the game, and by good football had it won. I feel very badly that the game was called. There was only one-half of a minute to play, and it was taking victory from between our teeth before we could enjoy it. Georgia played hard ball, but we had the game won, and it should have been given to us."[29] More than a year later, the Southern Intercollegiate Athletic Association reversed the official's ruling and awarded an 11–6 victory to Auburn.

Nearly two weeks after the controversial ending against Georgia, Auburn played Sewanee in Montgomery, Alabama, with the winner moving on to play the University of North Carolina for the southern championship. Sewanee hadn't been scored upon all season, but

Auburn scored two quick touchdowns to a take a 10–0 lead (touch-downs were now worth five points each). Sewanee scored to cut its deficit to 10–5, and then a controversial finish once again took vic-tory from Auburn's teeth. According to the *Constitution*, "The second touchdown made by Sewanee was almost a gift from Referee Martin. Auburn had held Sewanee for downs on her five-yard line, and se-cured the ball [on a fumble]. But Referee Martin could not see it that way, and gave the ball to Sewanee inside of Auburn's ten-yard line, and it was taken over for a touchdown in a few plays. The decision was clearly wrong, as it was clearly Auburn's ball."[30]

Sewanee defeated North Carolina 5–0 in Atlanta to win its first southern championship. Heisman was so outraged by the official's error that he wrote a lengthy letter to the sports editor of the *Bir-mingham Age-Herald* on December 4, 1899: "I think we completely outplayed Sewanee from start to finish, both offensively and defen-sively; and it was only outrageous work of the officials that made it possible for Sewanee to score at all. I think the work of both officials was, by all odds, the worst I ever saw, and I don't mind proclaiming it from the housetops."[31] Heisman also wrote that "what [the referee] didn't know about the rules would make the entire game of football, and what he did know wouldn't even spell the word."

William P. Taylor, a boys' school headmaster who worked as the umpire in Auburn's loss to Sewanee, wrote a rebuttal to Heis-man's claims the very next day: "The plain truth of the matter is that Coach Heisman has proved a failure in producing winning teams at Auburn; he wishes to retain his position as football coach and hopes to be retained also as professor of elocution and oratory. Is it not most likely that he must keep in Auburn's good graces by ascribing his defeats to the officials?"[32]

For whatever reason, Taylor also took exception to Heisman's stage acting skills, to which Heisman replied in the *Birmingham Age-Herald*: "I have said nothing of Mr. Taylor's work or ability as a school teacher; but he will do well to remember that acting and coaching are my regular means of making a livelihood and that there is a law in the land on the subject of libel. My position, however, is too firmly fixed in the hearts of all Auburn men to imagine Mr. Taylor could ever unseat me. Should he go whining to the Auburn faculty I know what answer he will get. I know he will be told that, instead of making 'lurid appeals,' Mr. Heisman and the faculty all had difficulty in preventing the outraged spectators from deliberately going into the field of play and taking both officials out bodily." [33]

Clearly, Heisman had proven his coaching skills during his five seasons at Auburn, and, in a couple of long-winded letters to the sports editor, had once again proved his exceptional debate and elocution skills. The ragtag scrappers of Auburn had grown before Heisman's eyes and won some renown in the South. The sport's popularity was growing as well. Youngsters off the farm and heading to college all wanted to try their stuff at playing football. Some would learn the game and play well making the team; others simply wouldn't or couldn't catch on and so ended up as spectators. These boys would go to great lengths to get the coaches' attention and earn a chance to play. Gently and objectively, Heisman would have to deal with not only the enthusiasts before him, but also the budding men of letters he represented.

As the 1899 season came to a close, Heisman would be hired at another school with a budding football team and hungry alumni base. And it was an old friend who would once again lure him there.

CHAPTER EIGHT

Clemson College

Walter Riggs brought Heisman to Auburn but didn't stay around long enough to watch his new coach transform the Tigers into one of the South's most dominant college football teams. In 1896, Riggs left Auburn for Clemson College in South Carolina to continue his postgraduate studies and work as an assistant in the mechanical and electrical engineering department. Clemson didn't have a football team when Riggs arrived, but it didn't take him long to help organize one. During a meeting in the military school's barracks in September 1896, the first Clemson football association was formed and the cadets asked Riggs to coach the team. He guided the Tigers to a 14–6 victory over Furman in their first game, on October 31, 1896, and a 2-1 record in their first season.

Riggs resigned as coach after only one season to concentrate on his studies, but was persuaded to return to the sideline in 1899 because the athletic association didn't have money to hire a full-time coach. Shortly before Riggs was named head of Clemson's engineering department (he was also its president from 1911 until his death in 1924), he helped the Tigers hire Heisman as their new coach. How much money Heisman was paid in his first season at Clemson in 1900 isn't exactly known. But given his salaries in future seasons, Heisman was probably initially paid about $1,000 to coach baseball and football at Clemson. According to documents found in Clemson's archives, Heisman was paid $350 to coach Clemson's baseball team in 1901 (the contract was handwritten on stationery from the Central Hotel in Charlotte, North Carolina) and $815.11 to coach its football team in 1902, according to a typed contract signed by Heisman and Riggs on November 28, 1901.[1]

It didn't take Heisman long to prove he was well worth the investment. At the start of the twentieth century, the greening of America's football game continued, and Heisman played his part by transforming young men who had little or no football experience into fine-tuned, well-oiled teams. Direct snaps from the center to backs—a Heisman creation—were now standard in the game, though how they were accomplished and what manner of harassment a center had to go through to put the ball in play continued to unfold. Football was still played without protective headgear—Samson-like hair was still the only padding on a player's head—and players wore tightly fitting, laced, leather jackets. Much like at Auburn, Heisman discovered that his Clemson players were quick studies, and as their overall athleticism improved, the results were obvious to anyone. Where the "Mighty Midgets" of Auburn had once ruled, the "Demons from South Carolina" quickly ascended to the throne of southern college football.

In his first season, Heisman led the Tigers to a perfect 6-0 record and a Southern Intercollegiate Athletic Association championship, outscoring their opponents 222–10. In its first game, Clemson blasted Davidson 64–0 on October 19, 1900; defeated Wollford 21–0 in Spartanburg, South Carolina; and then walloped rival South Carolina 51–0 at the state fair in Columbia, South Carolina. According to a November 2, 1900, report in the *State* newspaper, the Tigers' victory over South Carolina seemed even worse than the lopsided score: "It was a greater game than the score indicates. Not so great to the spectators from the grand stand, nor, in fact, to the casual observer from the side lines. Far from it. It was too one-sided to be great or even interesting for them. It simply had the appearance of big fellows running over smaller ones, and yet not so much smaller, either, for Carolina and Clemson came nearer being of like weight this year than in some time."[2]

About five thousand spectators watched the Tigers run over their rivals, a positive sign for Heisman that college football was beginning to take solid footing in his new home state.

"A score of counting machines and a score more could not register the crowds that were here yesterday," the *State* reported. "Everything else faded into insignificance beside the people. Everybody was here, and so was everybody's brother, sister, cousin and aunt. They came by the carload and the wagonload. There were stylish city ladies and ladies from the country whose attire was not so fashionable. There were rich men and poor men, city men and country men, handsome men and ugly men, sober men and drunk men, fat men and lean men. Such an aggregation!"[3]

Nine days after trouncing the Gamecocks, Clemson defeated Georgia 39–5 in Athens, Georgia, and the Tigers "played a trick game—fake passes, several variations of old cris-cross, fake bucks and fake kicks, followed in such rapid succession that red and black's ends lost their heads and were easily fooled. These tricks were faultlessly executed by a swift backfield and seldom failed to gain."[4] The Tigers won their toughest game over Virginia Tech, 12–5, in Charlotte two weeks later, and then shut out Alabama 35–0 in Birmingham, Alabama, to preserve a perfect season.

By now, Heisman was gaining notoriety for his trick plays and creativity. He never liked to run the same trick play twice and had no use for players who couldn't memorize his expanding playbook and adjust on the fly. In a 1903 essay in the *Oconeean*, Clemson's annual yearbook, Heisman described how revolutionary the Tigers' style of football was at the time:

It is hardly an exaggeration to say that the possibilities in the scientific development of the game of football are only beginning to be realized. Perfection was supposed to have been attained a dozen years ago; but each successive season since has witnessed the invention of new plays and improved systems of offense and defense, until now the game is as far ahead of what it was a decade ago as the electric car is ahead of the old-time stagecoach. Each college now aims to have a style of play of its own, and so many and various have these systems—particularly of offensive play—become, that no one defensive formation will suffice to meet the attack of all teams on a season's schedule, as was formerly the case.

At Clemson we have a style of football play radically different from any other on earth. Its notoriety and the fear and admiration of it have spread throughout the length and breadth of the entire Southern world of football and even further. There is not a single offensive play used that was ever learned from any other college, nor are the defensive formations any less different than those of other teams.[5]

The Tigers slipped to 3-1-1 in 1901, although, in their October 5 opener, they defeated Guilford College of North Carolina 122–0. It is still the most lopsided outcome in Clemson football history (although not nearly as bad as the most lopsided score in Heisman's history). Clemson opened the 1902 season by winning its first three games, including a 44–5 victory at Georgia Tech on October 18, 1902. That game involved perhaps Heisman's greatest act of deception. The day before the game, a train full of Clemson cadets arrived at the train station in Atlanta. Believing the young men were Clemson's football team, several Georgia Tech boosters proceeded to take them out on the town, inviting them to wild parties until the early morning hours. The Georgia Tech men saw the redness in the Clemson men's eyes and felt confident that a Yellow Jackets victory was "in the bag." Only after Clemson won the game so convincingly did the Georgia Tech men realize that Heisman had sent the equipment bags ahead with the scrubs, managers, and other Clemson underclassmen. It was a glorious trip for those youngsters, and they returned to campus with wonderful stories of hospitality in the "big city." Heisman and his varsity team had taken a later train and spent the night in Lula, Georgia, a small town about sixty-five miles northeast of Atlanta.[6]

During a 28–0 victory over Furman in "carnival week" in nearby Greenville on October 24, 1902, Heisman pulled out another memorable trick play after he noticed an unusual landmark on the playing field:

> Arriving at the field we observed a fine old oak tree growing right in the field of play, about on the fifty-yard line and midway, perhaps, between the center of that line and the boundary. When I saw this huge tree, I instantly grasped how this withheld pass play of ours should go like wildfire, and explained this in haste to the boys. How they chuckled! And how boys all love tricks and plays of deception! It must be the atavistic throwback of the race. Presently we had the ball just short of the midfield, with the magnificent tree on our right and slightly ahead. We started what looked like a short end run toward the tree. [John] Maxwell, [quarterback], passes the ball to [H. R. "Polly"] Pollitzer, left half. He swirled in a curving end run just inside the big tree, thereby drawing their left end and secondary right before the threatened spot. Meanwhile, [Vet] Sitton had come off the line with the snap of the ball, and crossed over behind Pollitzer, and was racing like a hunting cheetah, back of, yet going beyond the tree. Now, under the protection of the interference, which also turned down on the inner side of the tree, "Polly" flipped the ball back of the tree and out to Sitton. The latter scooped in the ball, kept on clear around the tree and went 40 yards to touchdown. Twice more in that game we played "Ring around the

Rosy" with that sturdy oak. Not long after that game, the Furman authorities consented to the removal of the Monarch primeval from the football field.[7]

In an interview with the *Atlanta Constitution* late in the 1903 season, Heisman explained his philosophy on running trick plays:

"I do not intend to give up these tricks," Heisman said. "Tricks help to run up the score and aid the team in many ways. I find that these tricks are just as successful against strong as weak elevens. All this talk, however, about our playing nothing but tricks is absurd. It is paradoxical in itself. Here one critic says Clemson plays nothing but tricks, and immediately adds that such tricks will not work against good teams. This is an absurd statement, for we have played good strong teams and won from them constantly. Therefore one of two things is certainly true, either that we do not play tricks, or that the tricks are successful."[8]

Heisman also told the *Atlanta Constitution* that he integrated several trick plays into his game plans because his players at Auburn and Clemson were so much smaller than their opponents:

> Many people have considered tricks an unworthy way of winning games, but I hold that it is the same as in war, where all kinds of tricks go by the name of strategy, and I prefer to call my style of playing strategical instead of trickery. Surely, when a college has only light material she should not announce to the football world that she will retire for this year and wait until she has eleven good, strong, heavy men, when she will be willing to play. This would not be sportsmanlike. Instead it is far better for her to take her light men and teach them to win by using their brains instead of crushing down all opposition by a display of brute strength. A team does not need to be composed of men as large as elephants to play successful ball.[9]

What was perhaps most remarkable about Clemson's efficiency under Heisman was the fact that the Tigers didn't have much time to practice. Because of the cadets' academic and military commitments, football practices typically didn't start until 5:30 P.M. To have longer practices in the dark, Heisman painted the footballs white.

Not all college coaches were amused with Heisman's coaching tactics. The *Atlanta Constitution* reported on November 3, 1903, that "many students at [Sewanee] are not in favor of playing Clemson just so long as she retains her present coach, because it is said that in one game when Heisman was coaching Auburn he ordered his men to slug. And Vanderbilt, after putting up a bluff, refuses to play Clemson."[10]

Six days after fooling the Paladins, Clemson played South Carolina again at the state fair in Columbia. Heisman had won his first contest against the Gamecocks in 1900, but the teams didn't play in 1901 for reasons that aren't exactly known. There was a boiling rivalry between the schools long before football was ever played. South Carolina College was founded in 1801; Clemson didn't come along until eighty-eight years later. South Carolina College was closed during the Civil War, and African Americans and women were admitted when it was reopened during Reconstruction. The school was closed again in 1877 and then reopened as the South Carolina College of Agriculture and Mechanic Arts. The college returned to its antebellum roots as South Carolina College in 1882, and its administration deemphasized agricultural education, which upset many of the state's farmers.

At about that time, future South Carolina governor "Pitchfork" Benjamin Tillman was emerging as a major political force in the state. He believed that South Carolina College needed to put more emphasis on agricultural education or a separate agricultural university would need to be opened in the state. In 1888, South Carolina statesman Thomas Green Clemson died and left most of his estate to the establishment of a state agricultural school. After lengthy legal and political battles, South Carolina governor John Peter Richardson III signed a bill establishing the Clemson Agricultural College of South Carolina in November 1889. Clemson College formally opened in July 1893 with an enrollment of 446 all-white, all-male students. Clemson didn't become a nonmilitary, coeducational institution until 1955, and Harvey Gantt, its first African American student, wasn't admitted until 1963. Gantt was elected mayor of Charlotte in 1983 and twice ran unsuccessfully for the US Senate.

The schools' football rivalry reached its climax in 1902. Under coach C. R. Williams, the Gamecocks had their best football team, winning their first three games by a combined score of 98–0. While the Tigers had played well in their first three games, the 1902 squad was one of Heisman's most inexperienced and smallest at Clemson. The Gamecocks had waited nearly two years to avenge their embarrassing 51–0 loss to Clemson in 1900, and excitement for the game was quickly building at the state fair, according to the *State* newspaper. "Never in the history of South Carolina football has such widespread and intense interest been manifested concerning any game in the Palmetto State as is this year shown over the rapidly approaching game between Clemson college and the South Carolina college," the *State* reported four days before the game. "Clemson has generally had a shade the better of the argument, but this year it looks as if the tables would be turned and the Tiger driven back to his jungle to ruminate for once on the pleasures of a defeat and how to be patient for a whole year till he can once more gird up his loins and swoop down with overwhelming might upon the Garnet and Black." [11]

The South Carolina State Fair was an extravagant event. According to the *State*, its events included cattle and horse contests, shotgun tournaments, ostrich and horse races, and vaudeville shows. At the corner of Main and Taylor Streets there was a "Hall of Fame," where "pretty effects [were] given with the aid of the electric stereopticon," and Lunetta, the flying lady, was just across the street. [12] There was an "oriental streets of India" display at the corner of Blanding and Main, and a high dive on Main Street, where "the champion high diver and bridge jumper will today thrill immense crowds with his plunge from an elevation higher than any store in the city into a basin of water eight feet square."[13]

Of course, the state fair's main attraction was the football game between the Gamecocks and the Tigers. When the teams took the field at 11:00 A.M. on Thursday, October 30, 1902, two open carriages "filled with beautiful young ladies wearing the Clemson colors and a carriage bearing the fair sponsors for Carolina drove into the grounds and occupied opposite sections of the side lines."[14] By game's end, the Carolina sponsors were thrilled with the results. With its cheering section shouting, "Heisman's day is at an end," and "We'll twist the tiger's tail," South Carolina defeated the Tigers 12–6 in front of a crowd of about three thousand people.

Then the real trouble began. Clemson officials leased a special coach for its corps of cadets and players to make the short train ride from Calhoun, South Carolina, to Columbia. The cadets and players arrived in Columbia the day before the game and were allowed to remain in town until Saturday morning to enjoy the festivities. The first sign of trouble came when a battery of Clemson cadets fought with a group of South Carolina students in the streets. During an Elks parade through downtown streets after the game, South Carolina's students displayed a transparency that "showed a crowing game cock, marked 'S.C.C.,' standing on the head of a dead tiger."[15] Clemson's cadets had warned South Carolina's students not to disparage their school by waving the transparency during the parade. But that's exactly what the South Carolina students did. Later that night, a large group of Clemson cadets marched to South Carolina's campus with swords and bayonets drawn. A smaller group of South Carolina students, armed with pistols and shotguns, barricaded themselves behind eight-foot walls.

Christie Benet, who would later become a US senator (when

Tillman died in office in 1918) and chairman of Clemson's board of trustees, was helping coach the Gamecocks in 1901 and witnessed the standoff at the campus walls. Benet told the *State* on November 2, 1902, "The Clemson cadets had swords and bayonets drawn. The Carolina men had armed themselves as well as they could and were prepared to do their best to prevent the cadets from entering the campus."[16] Before any blood was shed, Benet persuaded the student bodies to each present a three-man committee to negotiate a resolution. Both sides agreed that the transparency would be burned. "The burning of the transparency should be a pledge on the part of each student body that all trouble and animosity would be burned with it," Benet told them.[17]

If only it were that easy. South Carolina's faculty decided to discontinue its rivalry with Clemson the next year, and the teams didn't meet again until 1909. Clemson rebounded to win its last three games in 1902, shutting out Georgia 36–0, Auburn 16–0, and Tennessee 11–0. The Tennessee victory was memorable for Heisman because it was played in a snowstorm and he witnessed the longest punt he ever saw:

> The day was bitterly cold and a veritable typhoon was blowing straight down the field from one end to the other. We rushed the ball with more consistency than Tennessee, but throughout the entire first half they held us because of the superb punting of "Toots" Douglas, especially because, in that period he had the gale squarely with him. Going against that blizzard our labors were like unto those of Tantalus. Slowly, with infinite pains and a maximum of exertion, we pushed the ball from our territory to their 10-yard line. We figured we had another down to draw on, but the referee begged to differ. He handed the ball to Tennessee and the "tornado." Their general cheerfully chirped a signal—Saxe Crawford, it must have

been—and "Toots," with sprightly step, dropped back for another of his Milky Way punts. I visualize him still, standing on his own goal line and squarely between his uprights. One quick glance he cast overhead—no doubt to make sure that howling was still the same old hurricane.

I knew at once what he proposed to do. The snap was perfect. "Toots" caught the ball, took two smart steps and—BLAM!—away shot the ball as though from the throat of Big Bertha. And, say, in his palmiest mathematical mood, I don't believe Sir Isaac Newton himself could have figured a more perfect trajectory to fit with that cyclone. Onward and upward, upward and onward, the crazy thing flew like a brainchild of Jules Verne. I thought it would clear the Blue Ridge Mountains. Our safety man, the great Johnny Maxwell, was positioned 50 yards behind our rush line, yet the punt sailed over his head like a phantom aeroplane. Finally, it came down, but still uncured of its wanderlust it started in to roll—toward our goal, of course, with Maxwell chasing and damning it with every step and breath. Finally, it curled up and died on our one-foot line, after a bowstring journey of just 109 yards.[18]

With a victory at Tennessee, Heisman guided the Tigers to their second Southern Intercollegiate Athletic Association title. His good work wasn't going unnoticed. The University of Alabama attempted to hire Heisman as its new coach, offering to more than double his salary, to $2,500 annually.[19] Heisman eventually rebuffed Alabama's offer, but it wouldn't be the last time another school tried to lure him away from Clemson.

Clemson opened the 1903 season impressively, and Heisman believed it might have been his strongest team. The Tigers defeated Georgia, Georgia Tech, and North Carolina State by a combined score of 126–0. After the Tigers shut out the Bulldogs 29–0 and a week before they would play at Georgia Tech, the *Atlanta Constitution* commended Heisman's work:

> Clemson College realized that radical measures had to be taken before her football eleven would become a factor in the football of the south. Just at this time Auburn turned Heisman, her great coach, loose and Clemson seized the opportunity and engaged him as a coach. From this time Clemson's football can be dated. Heisman had good materials at hand and used it to the best advantage. He taught his men to work with their heads, their hands and every part of their bodies and he instilled into them the spirit which always wins games. Instantly, with his Heisman spirit and Heisman tactics, the South Carolina College began to win games.[20]

After Heisman had hoodwinked Georgia Tech's boosters so easily the previous season, they were understandably a bit more cautious when Clemson played the Yellow Jackets in Atlanta on October 17, 1903. Georgia Tech's boosters had read reports that Sitton, the Tigers' star halfback, was injured and wouldn't play in the game. The boosters were still guarded, though, believing Sitton could be holed up in Lula, only to be unveiled in Atlanta just before the game's kickoff. However, when Heisman confirmed that Sitton wouldn't play, Georgia Tech's confidence was bolstered.

What the Yellow Jackets didn't know was that Clemson substitute Gil Ellison, though not as fast as Sitton, was quite large and strong, ran great interference, and broke up runs as needed. Ellison ran all over Georgia Tech in Clemson's easy 73–0 victory.

Georgia Tech decided it wanted Heisman as its coach.

Chapter Nine

Heisman Onstage

Near the end of his tenure at Clemson, Heisman developed a relationship with a divorced woman named Evelyn McCollum Cox. She worked as an actress in a theater company with Heisman and had a young son, Carlisle Cox, from her previous marriage. Cox and Heisman were married in Columbia, South Carolina, on October 29, 1903, the day after he guided Clemson to a 24–0 victory over North Carolina State at the state fair (the Wolfpack replaced South Carolina College as the Tigers' opponent after the in-state rivals' ugly confrontation the previous year). Apparently Heisman's marriage caught his players and friends by much surprise.

"The many friends of Mr. John W. Heisman, the popular coach of the Clemson football team, were surprised to hear this morning of his marriage last night, the ceremony being performed by Dr. M. L. Carlisle, at the Washington Street Methodist church," the *Augusta (Georgia) Chronicle* reported on October 30, 1903. "The bride was Miss Evelyn Barksdale, a charming young lady of Atlanta. The engagement was announced some time ago, but only a few friends of the family were present at the ceremony. Mr. and Mrs. Heisman were the recipients of congratulations and best wishes this morning from his friends in the city."

Heisman's new wife used the stage name "Evelyn Barksdale," but her actual maiden name was McCollum. Her father, Benjamin

Franklin McCollum, was a notorious Confederate soldier during the Civil War. Evelyn McCollum grew up in Cherokee County, Georgia, north of Atlanta, and her father had already served in the Georgia volunteer infantry and cavalry when her mother, Rosa Lee Garrison, became pregnant with her. When Evelyn McCollum was born on September 25, 1863, her father was serving in Company C (the "Cherokee Dragoons") of the Phillips Legion Cavalry in Virginia. Benjamin McCollum's Confederate Army service records show he enlisted for three years in 1862 and his unit fought in the bloody battles at Chancellorsville, Virginia, and Gettysburg, Pennsylvania. Muster rolls for the Cherokee Dragoons show that McCollum was listed as absent without leave (AWOL) after August 16, 1864.

After abandoning the Confederate Army, McCollum led a group of renegade soldiers known as "McCollum's Scouts" in the North Georgia Mountains. This band of outlaw soldiers was widely feared and infamously known for robbing and killing Union loyalists as well as for terrorizing the families of Confederate soldiers who were off fighting in the war. Many of the crimes allegedly committed by McCollum's Scouts took place in 1864 and 1865, at about the time Major General William Tecumseh Sherman led the Union Army on its infamous "March to the Sea," in which his troops captured Atlanta and burned and destroyed nearly everything in its path of advance.

When the Civil War ended in 1865, Confederate soldiers who returned to Georgia began to hunt down members of McCollum's Scouts. On September 6, 1865, the *Macon Telegraph* reported that "a serious shooting affray took place at a church in Pickens county, Georgia, in which a man by the name of Collins, and another whose name we have not been able to learn, both formerly of McCollum's scouts, were killed, and three others wounded. The attack, we learn, was made by some returned Confederate soldiers, whose families had been badly treated by this notorious band of outlaws while the latter were absent in Virginia."

Benjamin McCollum, who worked as a blacksmith before the Civil War, studied law and became an attorney in the 1870s after moving his family to Fayette County, south of Atlanta. But McCollum was never able to escape his alleged war crimes. In May 1873, a group of nearly one dozen men surrounded McCollum's house and captured him so he could be tried for murder in Pickens County.

The *Atlanta Constitution* reported on May 24, 1873:

We learn from a friend just from Canton that a party of ten or a dozen men from Pickens county, led by one Jerry Warren, and armed with pistols and shot-guns, surrounded the house of Colonel Benjamin F. McCollum early on Friday morning of last week, called him to the door, presented a pistol at his breast, and ordered him to surrender. McCollum, being entirely unprepared to defend himself at the time, yielded to the demand, and sent for Col. James R. Brown and others, who examined the authority of the party for making the arrest, and found that it came from the Superior Court of Pickens county, based upon an indictment for a murder which McCollum was charged with committing during the war, and which had been stricken from the docket sometime ago, in accordance with an act of the Legislature, but which had again been recently revived.[1]

The newspaper report said the party refused to release McCollum, so he took matters into his own hands.

"Warren and his party refused to release McCollum on any condition whatever, and declared their intention of taking him to Pickens, dead or alive," the *Constitution* reported. "They accordingly procured a rope, intending to tie the prisoner after leaving town. He was marched before them for a short distance, when he suddenly made a thrust at Warren with his knife, making a considerable wound on his neck, but failing to sever the jugular vein, which was his intention to do, he then broke ranks, and a volley was fired at him, but he succeeded in making his escape unhurt."[2]

It wasn't McCollum's last gunfight. On October 27, 1877, the *Constitution* reported that McCollum "and three brothers named Brassell, waked up Brooks's station the other day by indulging in a regular war. Pistols were freely used until finally McCollum engaged one of the brothers in a rough and tumble tussel, coming out ahead of the game."[3] More than two years later, McCollum "attempted to assassinate Reverend John B. Caldwell at this place on the 8th instant," the *Atlanta Constitution* reported. "Mr. Caldwell, though seriously wounded, is doing as well as could be expected under the circumstances."[4]

Benjamin McCollum's life came to a violent end on May 27, 1880. While living in Hampton, Georgia, McCollum had complained about a brothel near his law office. When the city council failed to do anything about it, McCollum went to the brothel and "turned it over." The *Constitution* reported that Ben H. McKneely, the deputy town marshal, "had the building restored to its proper position, and when he heard threats that there would be a second effort to remove it, threatened to kill any man who dared to do so."[5]

A couple of days later, in the back of a general store, McCollum was in a dispute about the brothel. Someone drew a pistol, and McCollum took it, hoping to avoid a gunfight. McKneely entered the store and demanded the pistol.

"I would have given you the pistol but you are drinking," McCollum told him.

"If you say I'm drunk, then you're a damned liar," McKneely replied.

According to the *Constitution*, McCollum hit McKneely over the head two or three times. McKneely left the store and returned with a double-barrel shotgun. McKneely initially turned the gun over to someone else, but then seized it and fired at McCollum two times.

"Instantly he leveled it on McCollum and fired one barrel," the *Constitution* reported. "Eight buckshot entered his breast, severing the jugular vein and causing the blood to spurt out nearly a foot. As he staggered, McKneely fired again, but the load passed over the falling man's head. McCollum fell prone on his face, and died in a few seconds."

Within a few minutes, McCollum's wife and four children, including Evelyn, were at his side, the *Constitution* reported.

"McCollum was hardly cold in death before his wife and four children had heard the dreadful news," the *Constitution* reported. "They rushed frantically to the scene, and in the blood kneeled to cry in their passionate grief. The scene was one which moved strong men to tears, and added fresh horror to the tragedy."

McKneely was able to escape the scene and fled to Indian Territory, in present-day Oklahoma. He was never arrested or prosecuted for killing McCollum.

Heisman was initially enamored with Willie Tuggle, Evelyn's older sister. She also was a stage actress and had "extremely pretty golden hair, bright blue eyes and a rather small face with a chic figure."[6] But Tuggle was already involved with another man, so Heisman and Evelyn were married less than two years after meeting. Carlisle Cox, Evelyn's son, told *Atlanta Magazine* in December 1964 that his mother, who had divorced her first husband, Edwin W. Cox, married Heisman without his knowledge. The announcement came in a letter from his mother, Cox said.

"I didn't like it at all," Cox told *Atlanta Magazine*. "I just didn't like it. I was an only child, deeply attached to my mother, hard-headed and probably spoiled. I didn't like the idea a bit of someone coming in and poaching on my property . . . taking my mamma away. But it was the coach who broke the ice. His gentility and sense of fair play eventually won me. And he went out of his way to bring this condition on."[7]

Cox was attending school at Gordon Institution in Barnesville,

Georgia, when his mother returned to Atlanta with her new husband. The family settled in a rented home at West Peachtree and Pine Streets in Atlanta. Along with his new wife and stepson, Heisman shared the home with "Woo," the family's poodle. Woo was fond of ice cream, so every night Heisman would send out for dessert for the family dog. In many of his team photographs at Georgia Tech, Heisman is holding the white poodle in his lap.

Heisman's stepson eventually attended Georgia Tech and played football for his stepfather, although at a meager 139 pounds, Cox described himself as "the eternal scrub." Cox became a US Army cavalry officer and served on the Mexican border and in France during World War I. He was chief of staff of US forces in central Africa during World War II. Cox died at Fort McPherson in Atlanta on April 30, 1968. Despite Cox's initial reluctance at having another man in the house, he grew to be very fond of Heisman.

"The coach was not eccentric," Cox said. "Away from home or on certain occasions, he might have been a little on the theatrical side. But this was purely for effect. He was, of course, a professional actor—he even had his own summer stock companies—but he was simply not eccentric. I knew the man and observed him closely. I never once saw him do a thing other than what you would find any absent-minded professor doing."

Heisman's fondness for acting and drama was nurtured at a young age, when he accompanied his parents and brothers to several performances at theaters in Titusville, Pennsylvania. For Heisman, coaching wasn't a year-round profession. During his early coaching career, he joined summer stock companies as soon as the college baseball season ended. He would then return to campus a few weeks before the football season was scheduled to begin. Lorenzo Woodruff, who was known as "Fuzz" Woodruff to thousands of southern newspaper readers and who authored the book *A History of Southern Football* in 1928, once wrote that Heisman was a "great coach and a terrible thespian."

Actually, Heisman was a very well-rounded and gifted actor, even performing on Broadway and in numerous theaters across the South. It appears that his first serious foray into acting came in 1898, while he was still coaching at Auburn. On May 20, 1898, Heisman appeared in *Diplomacy* with the Mordaunt-Block Stock Company at the Herald Square Theatre on Broadway.[8] Later that summer, he performed in *The Ragged Regiment* at the Herald Square Theatre and *Caste* at the Columbus Theatre in Harlem, New York.[9]

After finishing his final season as Auburn's coach in 1899, Heisman joined the Macdonald Stock Company, which produced a pair of multiweek engagements at Crump's Park in Macon, Georgia. Crump's Park was owned and operated by the Macon Railway and Light Company and featured a trolley line, casino, dancing pavilion, and roller coaster. Initially, Heisman had only character parts in the acting company, including the role of Dentatus in the Roman tragedy *Virginius*.[10] When the Macdonald Stock Company took a hiatus in June 1899, Heisman joined another acting troupe, the Thanouser-Hatch Company of Atlanta. Heisman performed in at least two plays for the company, playing a rather significant role in Martha Morton's *Brother John* comedy at Grand Theatre in Atlanta. Heisman played the role of Captain Van Sprague in the comedy, about a wealthy hat manufacturer who attempts to save his brothers and sisters from joining "society."[11]

In 1901, after Heisman's second season at Clemson, he joined the Dixie Stock Company, which produced nearly two dozen plays at Dukate's Theatre in Biloxi, Mississippi. The Dixie Stock Company allowed Heisman to display the full range of his acting skills. He played myriad roles in Biloxi, including Bernard Kavanagh, an aristocratic landlord in the Irish drama *Kathleen Mavourneen*; Ivan Ironlink, a villain of the deepest dye in the English nautical drama *Ben Bolt*; Jack Worthington, the charming hero of the southern melodrama *A Noble Outcast*; and Simon Slade, the evil owner of the Sickle and Sheaf saloon in the Prohibitionist drama *Ten Nights in a Barroom*.

Ironically, while Heisman was performing in the French tragedy *Camille* with the Dixie Stock Company, he played the role of Armand Duval, a young provincial bourgeois who falls in love with a woman suffering from tuberculosis. The role was much like Heisman's real-life experience with Edith Cole only a few years earlier. On July 6, 1901, the *Biloxi Daily Herald* reviewed *Camille* and said "J. W. Heisman showed to advantage as 'Armand Duval' and the character appeared to fit him to a nicety."[12]

Near the end of the Dixie Stock Company's run in Biloxi in 1901, Heisman delivered a prologue of adapted scenes from *Hamlet* before a performance of the comedy drama *David Garrick* at Dukate's Theatre. "Mr. Heisman will assume the role of Hamlet, a part with which he is perfectly familiar, having most successfully portrayed the character of the melancholy Dane many times," the *Biloxi Daily Herald* reported. "The scene will be properly costumed and will serve to show the wide scope of the atrical [sic] entertainment of which the company is capable."[13]

When Heisman returned to Crump's Park in Macon in the summer of 1902, he was managing the Crump's Park Stock Company and working as its leading man. The *Macon Telegraph* reported on May 24, 1902, that Heisman "gives the assurance that Macon will be treated this summer to a higher class of theatrical entertainment than has ever yet been presented at the park theatre. All the plays will be produced under his personal direction, and they are to include some of the latest metropolitan successes and many that the patrons of Crump's Park have never seen anywhere before."[14] Heisman hired Vera Renard of New York as his leading lady and DeLoss Edsall of Indianapolis as his comedian. Evelyn Barksdale played the roles of juveniles and ingenues, according to the *Telegraph*.

According to reviews written by the *Macon Telegraph* that summer, Heisman certainly backed up his lofty proclamation. On June 16, 1902, a packed house of more than fifteen hundred people watched Heisman play the lead role of Monsier Derblay in the French drama

Wife in Name Only. The *Telegraph* said Heisman "again appeared to an excellent advantage, accepting numerous opportunities to display dramatic force of a superior order, which he undeniably possesses. His work is easy, calm, impressive and above the standard, and certainly unlike the swaggerish, overdone attempts sometimes witnessed." Barksdale played a smaller role in the performance, and the *Telegraph* said she was as "pretty and dainty as usual. Her manner is always sweet and impressive, while her costuming of the various parts she has played shows careful attention and good taste."[15]

Just over a week later, the *Telegraph* complimented Heisman for his role of Judge Hustle in the farce comedy *The Cheerful Liar*, reporting that he was "extremely funny and the manner in which he shrewdly extricated himself from the numerous complicated situations into which his utter disregard for truth had placed him was highly amusing."[16]

While still coaching at Clemson in 1903, Heisman started his first acting troupe, Heisman Dramatic Stock Company, which spent much of the summer performing at Riverside Park in Asheville, North Carolina. Newspaper advertisements from that summer indicate Barksdale and Heisman were the main attractions.[17] Shortly after coaching Georgia Tech's baseball team in the spring of 1904, Heisman and Evelyn left for Montgomery, Alabama, where he managed the Casino Theatre at Pickett Spring's Resort for eight weeks. By then he was operating another acting troupe, the Heisman Stock Company. It didn't take him very long to win fans on his new stage. After the troupe's first two performances of the comedy *Because She Loved Him So*—Evelyn Barksdale played the role of Señora Gonzalez—the *Montgomery Advertiser* reported on June 5, 1904, "Jack Heisman may be a better football coach than he is a repertoire actor, but from the two performances of his stock company at the Casino Theatre there is room for doubt on this point. The laughable comedy the Heisman Stock Company gives is a performance that puts them in a class that few similar organizations attain."[18]

Even at the close of the Heisman Stock Company's run at Pickett Spring's Resort, they were packing the Casino Theatre. The *Montgomery Advertiser* reported: "The consistently good patronage which has been extended the Heisman Stock Company is a matter of some surprise. The company has held the boards at the Pickett Springs play house for eight weeks, but the Montgomery public continues to find its performance diverting and entertaining."[19]

Heisman's stay in Montgomery was so successful that the theater invited him back the next summer. The Heisman Stock Company opened the summer of 1905 performing at the Grand Opera House in Augusta, Georgia, where the troupe and its leading man once again received sterling reviews. After watching Heisman's performance as Mortimer Mumbleford in the comedy *A Natural Mistake*, the *Augusta Chronicle* called him "undoubtedly one of the very funniest and most natural light comedians we have ever seen. His style is unique but absolutely convincing, and time and again touched off the audience in roars upon roars of laughter."[20]

Heisman returned to Crump's Park in Macon for the entire summers of 1906 and 1907, when he leased the Casino Theatre from the Macon Railway and Light Company. By then Evelyn had been elevated to the troupe's leading lady, according to the *Macon Telegraph*: "Miss Evelyn Barksdale, the leading lady, is a most beautiful Southern girl. She has occupied the position of leading lady in Mr. Heisman's companies a number of years, and is of the light, airy type, particularly adapted to the kind of plays to be presented. Mr. Heisman says he has no need of an emotional tragedy queen in 'the good old summer time.'"[21] Heisman's stock company also performed regularly at the Thunderbolt Casino in Savannah, Georgia.

Heisman was as meticulous in assembling a cast of actors as he was in building a football team. The *Augusta Chronicle* said he had "hundreds of applications from performers of ability and repertation [sic], embracing all lines of work and coming from all parts of the United States and Canada. This wide range has rendered it possible for him to exercise great care in selecting the members of the company and it is now a certainty that everyone will be a headliner in his or her particular line of work. The average repertoire actor will not do for this work as they have none of the essentials—a quick, sure study, versatility, an ample and diversified wardrobe, nor yet sufficient ability. A city stock such as Manager Heisman not only presents a much higher class of plays than the average repertoire company, but charges a higher gate and must therefore put forward a more capable company of players."

As manager of the Casino Theatre, Heisman offered his audiences a variety of performances, from Westerns such as *Deadwood Dick* and *Jesse James* to serious dramas, comedies, and vaudeville acts. Heisman also was adept at keeping in tune with the innovations in theater. In 1906 he purchased an Edison kinetograph, "the most expensive machine made, to show the people the pictures in up-to-date style." The *Telegraph* reported that Heisman wanted to present "moving pictures between two of the acts, displaying a whole reel of 1,000 feet nightly and changing the entire reel along with the play every Monday and Thursday." [22]

Heisman enjoyed his summers in Macon so much that he nearly agreed to become coach at Mercer University. The Bears had a rich football tradition, playing their first game against Georgia in January 1892. The *Telegraph* reported on June 18, 1907, that Heisman would "consider the offer of Mercer very carefully before he signs any contracts and it may be that he will be seen at the head of Mercer athletics when the institution opens next fall." On September 1, 1907, Georgia Tech announced that Heisman had signed a five-year contract to remain with the Yellow Jackets. Mercer dropped its football program during World War II in 1941. After a seventy-two-year hiatus, the Bears will bring back a nonscholarship team.

Near the end of one theater summer season, the *Telegraph* commended Heisman for his work at the Casino Theatre: "There were those of his friends who advised him that he was buying a gold brick.

Others said he was going to find he had an elephant on his hands. Mr. Heisman listened to these words of advice, winked his other eye, and proceeded to lease the Casino, nevertheless and notwithstanding. Now, Mr. Heisman is winking both eyes. He has done what others of probably greater experience have tried and failed. The people have learned that Manager Heisman intends to give them good shows, and Manager Heisman has learned just what the people are 'hankering for.' If they don't 'hanker' for what he has, he teaches them to 'hanker' properly. This is a trick of the trade, and Mr. Heisman, with all his frankness, seriousness, and conscientiousness, may, in this sense, be called a second Hermann."[23]

Heisman eventually walked away from the stage, but remained involved in theater and the evolving business of moving pictures. In 1908, Heisman and his partner George Greenwood operated Empire Theatrical Exchange in Atlanta, which served as a booking and casting company for stock companies throughout the country. In 1917, Heisman worked with the Triangle Film Distributing Company in New York.

Heisman's notoriety as an actor wasn't as great as his reputation as a coach, but it seems pretty clear that "Fuzz" Woodruff knew more about football than theater.

Chapter Ten

Georgia Tech

A s Heisman enjoyed winning football with Auburn and Clemson, one opponent that had played his habitual victim hatched a plot. If it couldn't defeat a Heisman-coached team, it would make him its coach. Those were the desperate straits in which Georgia Tech found itself when it sent a delegation of alumni, faculty, and boosters to offer him the head coaching position in Atlanta near the end of the 1903 season.

By the end of the 1903 season at Clemson, Heisman was a highly sought commodity. No fewer than four southern colleges—Auburn, Clemson, Georgia, and Georgia Tech—were trying to secure his services for the following season. Georgia Tech might have been the most aggressive in pursuing Heisman. The Yellow Jackets (they were actually known as the Blacksmiths at the time) desperately wanted to improve their football team, which had won more than two games in a season only once in eleven years and had been embarrassed in a 44–5 loss to Clemson in 1902 followed by a 73–0 rout in 1903. Clemson couldn't afford to match Georgia Tech's financial offer to Heisman. In early November 1903, Georgia Tech's student body held a meeting on its campus, where many of the five hundred students agreed to pledge at least $5.00 to help in hiring him. The students raised about $2,000, and the school's faculty also pledged money as an emergency fund to secure Heisman.

"With an enrollment of 500 students Tech possesses as fine material as there is in the south," the *Atlanta Constitution* reported on November 3, 1903. "She has always had excellent baseball teams, and is determined to have as equally good football team if Heisman with the help of the students can make it so. In raising money at Tech the students are allowed to sign sixty-day notes for such amounts as they can afford to give. If this is not paid, the amount is taken out of the general expense [account] deposited by each student. There is little doubt but that sufficient money will be raised."[1]

As luck would have it, Heisman spent three hours in Atlanta while his Clemson team's train to Montgomery, Alabama, was delayed on November 25, 1903. Georgia Tech boosters cornered Heisman at the Atlanta train station. Heisman agreed to accept the job, but the Georgia Tech boosters had to promise not to announce his hiring until after Clemson played Cumberland College of Williamsburg, Kentucky, in the Southern Intercollegiate Athletic Association championship game the next day. One has to wonder if Clemson's players didn't already know their coach was leaving; the Tigers played Cumberland College to an 11–11 tie. Clemson had to rally from an 11–0 deficit in the second half and was undone by a handful of fumbles and penalties.

On the same day that Heisman coached his last game at Clemson, his hiring was announced during Georgia Tech's 16–0 loss to South Carolina on Thanksgiving Day in Atlanta. Georgia Tech's students were so excited they announced the news with a long banner that read, "Heisman, Coach of Tech, 1904."

"Already the students at the Tech are dreaming of a championship team for next season and of a great and crushing victory over Georgia," the *Atlanta Constitution* reported on November 27, 1903. "The announcement that Heisman had been secured to coach the Tech team for the coming year was made yesterday afternoon during the progress of the game with the South Carolina men. A huge sign was stretched out on the field telling the story of the Tech's great victory in the fight for a good football coach, and the Blacksmiths went wild with delight when they learned that the successful southern coach had been secured."[2]

Securing Heisman came with a hefty price tag for Georgia Tech. The school agreed to pay him a salary of $2,250 annually, plus 30 percent of the net gate receipts from its varsity baseball and football games, according to Heisman's first contract, a copy of which was found in Georgia Tech's archives. Heisman agreed to the same financial terms when he signed a three-year contract to coach at Georgia Tech from 1904 to 1907, and his salary increased to $3,000 annually when he signed a five-year contract with Tech from 1908 to 1912 (his income from ticket sales was omitted in this agreement and all subsequent contracts through 1919). At the end of his coaching tenure at Tech, Heisman was paid $4,000 during the 1919 season.

It turned out to be a match made in heaven. Both Evelyn and John Heisman were attracted to the cosmopolitan city of Atlanta and its numerous theaters and acting stock companies. While attractive from the very start, Georgia Tech's offer was sweetened as negotiations drew out. In a 1973 interview with former Georgia Tech player Chip Robert, then ninety-three years old, he recalled:

Coach Heisman was offered $2,000 a year to come to Atlanta. At first he was hesitant, stating that in a big city there would be more expense than this increase would cover. The Institute couldn't stand him more money but suggested that there were other "perks." He requested two things. First, would there be a newspaper that he could write a weekly column for? Of course, there was the *Atlanta Constitution*. Second, could he see the playing field for the school? They took him to the site wondering what he had in mind. After surveying the open field, Heisman announced that he wanted the field enclosed by a 10-foot fence with seating set up inside. Admission was to be charged and he would take 30 percent of the gate fee. This somewhat floored the recruiters. They didn't know if such a thing could be done, how to get it cleared, or how to find the funds to do so. Heisman smiled and said that if they would have the Institute authorize the erection of the fence and seating, then he would get it built.[3]

Heisman knew that his 30 percent of gate receipts wouldn't be worth much if tickets to football games weren't being sold. After accepting the Georgia Tech job, he contacted some old friends, now superintendents in the Georgia prison system, and arranged for inmates to be his labor force. He also volunteered his time at the state prison, and brought along some of his players to teach football to the inmates. By 1905, Piedmont Park was abandoned as Georgia Tech's home field, and the Hollow on campus was converted into the Flats, the future site of Grant Field. Georgia Tech students, under the supervision of a couple of professors, erected a wooden fence around the playing field. Georgia Tech players such as Robert, George McCarty, Cherry Emerson, Bob Wilby, and E. H. Rogers were among the students who drove nails into the wooden planks.[4] Georgia Tech's players showered in Knowles Dormitory across the street, and visiting teams dressed at their hotels.

While writing a column with the *Atlanta Constitution*, Heisman showed his mastery of the English language. The *Constitution* readily agreed to take Heisman on at a rate of some 3 to 5 cents per word, figuring how much could a coach really write about football? The newspaper's management apparently hadn't dug deep enough into Heisman's background to know that he had a law degree, was rather long-winded in even his personal correspondence, and had the vocabulary and attention span to write volumes about something as trivial as a toaster. Over the next several years, Heisman penned a very good weekly column that increased circulation for the *Constitution* and turned into a very lucrative sideline for him.[5]

At Georgia Tech, Heisman was quick to make his reputation of being a sound football strategist and disciplinarian stick. He insisted that all undergraduates know how to sing their alma mater and could sing it as well as their fight song. He would prod them to greater vocal heights by having the school custodian sing out the same songs with gusto. Heisman believed it was the duty of the student body to attend football games, to cheer on Tech, and to create the proper spirit for the home team. He even forbade his players from showering with hot water during the week because he believed it was debilitating. He took over the diet of his team, removing coffee, hot bread, pastries, and especially apples from the training table. He instructed the cooks to serve meat that was nearly raw and unseasoned. "They [apples] didn't agree with him," said Al Loeb, who played center for Heisman from 1911 to 1913, "so he felt the same reaction when we ate them."[6] Heisman outlined his other dietary beliefs in his 1922 book *Principles of Football*:

(4) Ice cream, if pure, a couple of times a week is all right.

(7) Most any meats are good except fresh pork and veal. Beef, mutton, lamb, chicken and fish are all splendid, especially broiled or roasted. No fried meat of any kind should be eaten by an athlete.

(8) Nearly all vegetables get the stamp of approval except cabbage, which should not be eaten in any form.

(9) Potatoes are best when baked. Mashed potatoes and stewed potatoes will do—but never fried potatoes. In fact, fried vegetables of any kind should be carefully avoided as fried meats. Rice, beans, peas, spinach, lettuce, parsnips [and] carrots may all be freely eaten.

(11) Most kinds of fruit are all right. Bananas that are the least bit green had better be left alone. Dates and prunes are especially good and can be eaten to advantage in fairly large quantities. All kinds of nuts are bad.

(14) Food for a football player should never be highly seasoned and

all condiments must be pretty generally side-stepped. I refer particularly to pepper, vinegar, mustard, catsup, horseradish and the like.

(16) Soups do no special harm but, contrary to general belief, there is very little nutrition in them.[7]

Heisman "believed a footballer should retire not later than 10:30 p.m., unless it is absolutely necessary for him to stay up a bit later for study. But in any event he must get at least eight hours sleep every night, undisturbed by noises or interruptions of any kind."[8] Heisman laid out his other ground rules for his players in *Principles of Football*: "On a properly organized team every man must conform absolutely to a very rigorous system of training. It is against the coach's rules to smoke, to chew tobacco, to drink liquor, to stay out late at night, to frequent improper resorts, to gamble, to bet on the games, to eat candy or to drink the ruinous messes that the average non-playing boy pours hourly into his stomach. His indulgence in cake, pie, pastry, and other foods of questionable value is kept at a minimum. He is obligated to study and to satisfy his teachers, because failure to do so not merely injures himself but jeopardizes the chances of the team and the hopes of the whole college."[9]

Heisman also had a list of stringent rules for how his players were supposed to conduct themselves on the field. His list of axioms was hung in Georgia Tech's locker room:

DON'TS

Don't try to play without your head.
Don't fumble the ball.
Don't tackle high.
Don't stop running because you are behind.
Don't forget signals.
Don't be late in lining up.

Don't have your feet in the way of the snapback.
Don't let your opponent get the charge on you.
Don't look toward where the play is going.
Don't jab your fingers into a snapped ball.
Don't catch it on your wrists.
Don't let it hit you on the chest.
Don't coil your arm around the ball's belly.
Don't hold it on your stomach.
Don't stick it out in front when you are downed.
Don't hesitate about falling on it ever.
Don't forget to pull it loose from an opponent.
Don't forget to stiff-arm.
Don't go into the line with your head up.
Don't see how light you can hit, but how hard.
Don't cuss.
Don't argue with the officials.
Don't lose the game.

ALWAYS

Always play with your head.
Always listen for the signal.
Always block your opponent at any cost.
Always start as fast as you can.
Always be where the ball is.
Always win the game.

CAN'TS

You can't play football without brains.
You can't play too aggressively.
You can't afford to waste time talking.
You can't play ball with a swelled head.
You can't win without using these principles.

NEVER
Never drop the ball.
Never get excited.
Never give up.
Never forget a football player may be a gentleman.
Never lose a game.[10]

Perhaps more than anything else, Heisman despised fumbling and cursing by his players. Before each football season, he carried out the same ritual with his team. He would gather his players around him and hold out a football.

In Heisman's best stage voice, he would rhetorically ask, "What's this?"

No player dared to respond, as everyone sensed imminent danger. If a player new to the team began to speak he was elbowed, kicked, or otherwise silenced by the nearest upperclassman, though not a man took their eyes off Heisman. It was a hallowed moment.

Heisman would slowly explain what he was holding: "This is a prolated spheroid—that is, an elongated sphere in which the outer leathern casing is drawn tightly over a somewhat smaller rubber bladder."

And then, after briefly pausing for dramatic effect, Heisman would explain in an even lower stage voice, "Better to have died as a small boy than to fumble this football."

Heisman's mandate applied to everyone. The penalty for a game fumble was not only running extra laps in practice the entire following week, but also a dexterity building exercise of bouncing and catching a football off a fence. The *Atlanta Constitution* reported on November 2, 1907, "Coach Heisman, of Tech, seized upon a unique method of doing away with fumbling among the Yellow Jackets during the past week. Whenever a man couldn't hold the ball he would give him a pigskin and send him over to the fence with instructions to bound the ball against the barrier and to receive it in his arms about four hundred times and if a fumble occurred to begin counting all over again." [11]

Heisman forbade his players from cursing in practice, or worse, during games, and although he usually barked instructions from a little red megaphone, he abstained from cursing at his team to get a point across. Heisman often preached, "Being a good football player is not half so important as being a gentleman." [12]

The father of one of Heisman's players once asked his son, "Harry, does the coach ever swear on the field? Does he ever cuss you boys out?"

"No, he doesn't swear, but he might as well," the player replied. "What he says cuts to the bone as bad as any swearing."

"Well, do you always deserve what he says to you?" the father asked.

"Hmm, I'll say we do," the son answered. "Guess that's one reason his line of talk hurts so. He can give you everything that begins with 'H' without mentioning it once." [13]

The coach's nephew William Lee Heisman once provided details of an incident at Tech in which an opposing player on defense jumped offside across the line of scrimmage. The premature start resulted in the defender stepping on an offensive lineman's fingers. At least one of his fingers was broken and possibly three. The Georgia Tech player jumped from his three-point stance and shouted a string of obscenities. Heisman quickly walked out onto the field, grabbed the player by his collar, marched him to the sideline, and ordered him to the showers in front of a home crowd.

"But, Coach, my fingers are probably broken!" the player pleaded.

"That's no excuse for a gentleman and especially one who plays football and represents his school!" Heisman responded. "Even if we could set and wrap your misshapen fingers, you're done for the day!" [14]

Heisman had broken his nose in a football game and seen many young men painfully hurt in competition, but he held no sympathy for vulgarities on the field, especially before a crowd of students,

families, and members of the sporting community. He considered it
an embarrassment to degrade oneself with profanity. For Heisman it
was pure and simple mental laziness. In *Principles of Football*, he wrote
about the responsibilities that came with coaching:

> Whatever the coach says goes with the impressionable young
> pupil. The coach's word is the law and the gospel, and that
> not merely as regards football but as to most anything under
> the sun. At that age a boy's mind is plastic. Certain things
> are much more apt to get control of his mind, his heart, his
> emotional nature than others. One of these is football, and
> through the medium of this wonderful game the coach, quite
> unintentionally, gets control of the boy. The coach says, "Do
> this!" and the boy does it, though his own father or mother
> might not have been able to get compliance. And so it comes
> that that boy at just that time of life is likely to be taught
> things by the coach and to get into habits engendered and
> fostered by the way his coach acts and thinks that will stick
> to him for the remainder of his life. If the coach is a worth-
> less, reprehensible fellow, a man of bad character or none, he
> is bound to do the boys enormous harm. If, however, he is a
> high type of man with lofty ideals and firm principles of right
> and truth, one who recognizes his power and his responsibili-
> ties, then it's well he coaches football and it's well for the boys
> that play football under him that they went to that School.
> Such a man will do more downright character building for the
> boys than can 19 ministers out of 20, or 99 fathers out of 100.
> Why? Because he has the influence over them that counts at
> the impressionable age.[15]

Heisman also expected his players to attend classes regularly and
fulfill their duties as student-athletes. Lee Heisman once recalled
one of his favorite stories about his uncle and a Georgia Tech player.

It seems the player had not kept his grades up to acceptable levels as Saturday's game approached. The player had the gifted ability of kicking long field goals with deadly accuracy. Before the game, Heisman burst into the locker room to confront him.

"Red, you're out of the lineup for the game," Heisman shouted at him. "I just got the dean's list and you didn't make your grades!"

"Now, Coach, haven't you read the newspapers?" the player asked. "They're saying I've got the $5 million toe!"

As the player pointed at his foot, Heisman shot back: "Yes, so what good is it if you only have a nickel head?"[16]

Red, the "nickel head," reapplied himself to his studies and made the grade, both on and off the field.

With Heisman providing that kind of coaching and mentoring, Georgia Tech's confidence was at an all-time high heading into the 1904 season, according to the *Atlanta Constitution*: "For the coming of a new year, Heisman, the most successful coach in the south, takes charge of the Tech athletics, and a successful future is assured. Tech can not expect to win every game in which she takes part during this year, even with the assistance of her well known coach, for she has no past to serve as a foundation for new victories. In order to win victories in any kind of athletic games, a past, filled with hard-fought battles and well-merited victories, is necessary in order to inspire the players of a team, and to fill them with the needed confidence at those very moments when defeat seems to be inevitable."[17]

It didn't take Heisman long to produce a winning team at Georgia Tech. Only thirty players showed up for the first day of football practice—about eighty tried out for Tech's baseball team—but Heisman was able to mold them into a strong squad. The Yellow Jackets went 8-1-1 in 1904, although Heisman couldn't have been too pleased with his new team's performances against his former ones, losing to Auburn 12–0 and tying Clemson 11–11. Georgia Tech won its first game under Heisman, defeating a team of soldiers from Fort McPherson in Atlanta 11–5 on October 1, 1904. The Yellow Jackets also defeated rival Georgia 23–6 at Piedmont Park on November 12, 1904. It was Georgia Tech's first victory over the Bulldogs since a 28–6 win in 1893; Heisman would win his first five contests against Georgia.

"For the first time in ten years the red and black of old Georgia had yielded in defeat in football struggle to the old gold and white of Tech," the *Constitution* reported on November 13, 1904. "Ten years had passed since the Georgia Techs had experienced the pleasure of crossing Georgia's goal line four times in succession and feeling safe that the victory was theirs."

An unusual play in the 1904 game against Georgia reminded Heisman of how far football still had to go. Late in the game, Bulldogs punter "King" Sullivan prepared to punt out of his team's end zone and then chaos ensued:

It was last down and their ball, but they were so close to their own goal line that "King" Sullivan had to get back nine yards behind the posts to punt. Holding signal drill on that Piedmont Field the day before I had noticed how close the high fence was to the east goal posts and pondered: "What would happen if the ball were to fly over that fence during a game?" I even warned my men what might happen. It happened. "King" spanked the ball hard and true and up it flew squarely against one post and bounded right back over the fence. Instantly, my men ran to the fence and leaped for the top. The Georgians, at first a bit dazed, now came running also, grabbing the legs of the Tech men and pulling them down from the fence. In turn, they started to climb and were pulled down. Along the fence there took place exactly ten fence climbing duels. My eleventh man, "Red" Wilson, ran for a high stump in one corner of the field. Man alive! You can't imagine the excitement or the incitements. It was a mad house. At long last,

"Red" and the referee got over first, and "Red" found the ball. The referee announced: "Touchdown for Tech." [18]

Georgia Tech went 6-0-1 in Heisman's second season, in 1905, defeating Georgia 46–0 and tying mighty Sewanee, 18–18. A rather lackluster 5-3-1 campaign followed in 1906, and then the Yellow Jackets went 4-4 in 1907, which was the closest Heisman came to having a losing season at Georgia Tech. Quarterback Chip Robert, who played at Tech from 1905 to 1908 and captained the '08 team, became one of the school's legendary players and remained one of Heisman's closest friends. After becoming a highly successful architect in Atlanta, Robert became one of Georgia Tech's biggest benefactors and was instrumental in elevating the school's athletics.

As one of Heisman's first quarterbacks, Robert was thrust into the evolution of the game. When Heisman arrived at Georgia Tech in 1904, the memory of Richard Von Gammon, the Georgia football star who died of a brain injury in a game against Virginia in 1897, was still very much alive in the state. Nationally, academics and politicians were mounting serious attacks on the sport. A University of Chicago professor called football "a social obsession—a boy-killing, education-prostituting, gladiatorial sport. It teaches virility and courage, but so does war. I do not know what should take its place, but the new game should not require the services of a physician, the maintenance of a hospital, and the celebration of funerals." [19] After *McClure's* published a two-part condemnation of football in 1905, President Theodore Roosevelt—an admitted fan of intercollegiate football—summoned representatives of Harvard, Princeton, and Yale to the White House in October 1905. The president told them it was time to clean up the sport once and for all.

Less than two months after Roosevelt's football summit, Heisman wrote a column for the *Constitution* in which he criticized the powerful Intercollegiate Rules Committee for its inaction and the sport's archaic style of mass play. Ironically, Heisman's column was published next to three stories detailing the deaths of football players at Union College in New York and at high schools in Indiana and Missouri. Once again, Heisman offered solutions in how to make his beloved sport safer:

> To revise, or not to revise. To reform, or not to reform. To abolish, or not to abolish—that is the question, and a burning one it is in the realm of college football. . . . At the close of the season of 1904 the demand for radical changes became so widespread and insistent that it seemed a heavy impression would surely be made upon the committee members and startling legislation would be the result. But, though the members really sat up and took notice, really took an interest in the discussion, pondered much and discussed more, the absolute result of their deliberations was nil—the changes made proved trifling in the extreme and the game this year is just about as it was last year.[20]

Heisman then offered two solutions: changing the sport's rules to require offenses to gain at least eight yards in three plays (instead of five yards for a first down) and legalizing the forward pass.

"The first thing that is, right now, the matter with football is that it demands the largest, strongest men obtainable; the little man has no chance, no place in or against modern mass playing," Heisman wrote. "This should not be. Any varsity game should be able to use a man no matter what his weight so he is supple and quick, has brains and a stout heart. His right to earn the rousing 'rah-rahs' of his comrades ought not to be dependent on the size of his shoes and shirtband. There is no brutality in football, if by that is meant a player becomes brutal or that it often happens that one brutally— that is, knowingly and purposely—strikes or injures another. For all that, there is a kind of brutality, to my mind, in all mass playing."[21]

A year earlier, Heisman suggested to the rules committee that the forward pass be legalized, which he believed would put less emphasis on mass play. Heisman said his proposal "was finally dismissed for the reason that it would make the game too much like basketball." Heisman didn't think that would be such a bad thing, as long as serious injuries were eliminated as much as possible. The next season, the forward pass was legalized and college football would never be played the same again.

For whatever reason, Heisman had only modest success in his first decade at Georgia Tech; after two stellar seasons in 1904 and 1905, the Yellow Jackets lost at least two games in each season from 1906 to 1914. The 1907 season was perhaps the worst campaign of Heisman's career. The Yellow Jackets finished 4-4, and pressure was mounting on their coach. After Tech defeated Georgia 10–6 at Ponce de Leon Park on November 2, 1907, legendary sportswriter Grantland Rice, who was working at the *Nashville Tennessean*, wrote an article accusing the Bulldogs of using four "ringers" or professional players in the game. "Of all the bare-faced and flagrant violations of collegiate sport, the stunt perpetrated by the University of Georgia in her game against Tech sets a new limit," Rice wrote. "The evidence has been turned over to us from several sources, absolutely reliable, that Coach [W. S.] Whitney used at least four ringers and probably more in the Atlanta conflict."[22]

More serious charges against the Bulldogs followed, with the *Constitution* reporting that "the charge being made all over Atlanta, and not denied by the Georgia men, that the whole scheme was engineered and planned by a lot of gamblers, who hoped to reach a rich harvest off an unsuspecting Atlanta public by springing on Tech a team a great deal stronger than the one which has been representing Georgia in the games previously played."[23] Within days, the Southern Intercollegiate Athletic Association suspended Georgia's entire football team. The Bulldogs didn't wait long to hurl their own allegations against the Yellow Jackets. On November 17, 1907, the SIAA also suspended Tech's football team after Heisman was accused of arranging improper cash payments and inducing another player with illegal benefits (football scholarships weren't yet allowed under NCAA rules). Heisman immediately dismissed the charges, telling the *Constitution*, "I defy any charges that have been made against me and challenge anyone who has them to confront me with them at any time or place he sees fit. And I'll tell him what I think about them, then and there. It is out of the question for anyone to bring charges against me that I cannot refute, and all I want to know is just what they are."[24]

Heisman learned the scope of the accusations during a hearing before the SIAA executive committee at Atlanta's Piedmont Hotel on November 22, 1907. Heisman's longtime friend Walter Riggs was one of the executive committee members. According to a transcript of the hearing that was found in Georgia Tech's archives, Heisman was accused of establishing a scholarship for four players through Daniel Brothers, an Atlanta clothing store. Heisman also was accused of paying a player $14 to play in a game in 1905, and offering inducements to another player to transfer to Tech from Dahlonega (Georgia) Agricultural School (now North Georgia College). After a hearing lasting more than sixteen hours and during which Georgia and Georgia Tech players and boosters testified before the committee, Heisman and his players were cleared of any wrongdoing. W. S. "Bull" Whitney was fired as Georgia's coach for using illegal players and was banned from ever coaching in the SIAA again.[25]

Although Heisman was cleared of any wrongdoing, his teams' struggles at Georgia Tech were beginning to take a toll on him. After the Yellow Jackets finished 5-3 in 1910, losing to rivals Auburn, Vanderbilt, and Georgia, Heisman was criticized in several columns in the *Atlanta Journal*, which accused him of being occupied by other interests, including being president of the Atlanta Baseball Association and being the manager of an African American theater. Heisman survived the attack, but two years later, after the Yellow Jackets finished 5-3-1 and again lost to Auburn and Georgia, Heisman wrote Riggs, who was then president of Clemson College:

> My present contract with Tech expires at the end of this football season. For many reasons—too numerous to mention here—I am ready for a change, and will be on the market at that time. Our prospects here this fall are quite the worst I have ever been called upon to face, and it is impossible that we should have other than a most inglorious season. Prospects for future years are even worse, so far as I can judge, and, frankly, this is one of the reasons why I prefer to leave here. Of course, this letter is written in the strictest confidence. I could have beaten about the bush, but you and I are too old and too good friends for anything of that sort. The thing to do was write you frankly and say what I had to say. If you think you may be able to use me the sooner we get together the better.[26]

Fortunately for Georgia Tech, Clemson didn't have a coaching vacancy at the time. Over the next five years, Heisman would rebound with the force of a tornado.

Chapter Eleven

Rout of the Century

The three-paragraph story was buried in the middle of page ten of the *Atlanta Constitution* on October 7, 1916. Even though Georgia Tech's football team was coming off a 7-0-1 season in 1915 and had blistered Mercer University 61–0 in the 1916 opener, its game against Cumberland College barely registered a blip on the radar. Instead, America's sports world was focused on the opening game of the 1916 World Series between the Brooklyn Robins and the Boston Red Sox, who were led by a powerful pitcher named Babe Ruth.

"This game should be a practice romp for the Jackets," the *Constitution* reported.[1]

It might have been the biggest understatement in journalism history.

What transpired over forty-five minutes at Grant Field in Atlanta on October 7, 1916, is still the subject of both fascination and ridicule nearly a century later. The Yellow Jackets rolled over Cumberland College 222–0, which still stands as the most lopsided score in college football history. The game's statistics alone are astonishing: Georgia Tech didn't even record a first down in the game because it never needed more than two plays on offense to score a touchdown; didn't attempt a single pass; and scored thirty-two touchdowns and kicked thirty extra points. The Yellow Jackets broke national intercollegiate football records for most points in a game (222), offensive yards (978), extra-point kicks (18), and points in a quarter (63).

Cumberland was actually an unlikely victim to end up on the wrong end of the worst loss in team sports history. Cumberland College, which was then a one-year law school in Lebanon, Tennessee, started playing intercollegiate football in 1894 and produced several quality teams. In 1903, the Bulldogs upset Vanderbilt 6–0 and then, in the span of only four days, defeated Alabama 44–0, Louisiana State 41–0, and Tulane 28–0. At the end of the 1903 season, Cumberland College played Clemson to an 11–11 tie in Montgomery, Alabama, in Heisman's final game as the Tigers' coach. The Bulldogs were awarded the 1903 southern championship.

But by 1916, interest in football began to wane on the Cumberland College campus. Cumberland president Samuel A. Coile resigned in the spring of 1916, and the new president, Dr. Homer Hill, eliminated funding for the varsity football team as part of budget cuts. Heisman scheduled a game against the Bulldogs out of spite more than anything else. The Bulldogs had defeated his Georgia Tech baseball team 22–0 in the spring of 1916, and Heisman was convinced they'd used ringers to do it. He offered Cumberland College $500 to play a football game against the Yellow Jackets in Atlanta. When the Bulldogs tried to back out of the game a few months later, Heisman told them he would impose a $3,000 penalty for breaking the contract. Heisman seemed hell-bent on getting revenge.

Cumberland College manager George A. Allen, who later served under US president Franklin D. Roosevelt and advised two other presidents, Harry S. Truman and Dwight D. Eisenhower, scoured the Cumberland campus to assemble a team. The Bulldogs actually played four or five games in 1916—there are records of a 100–0 loss to Sewanee—but without university funding, they participated in little more than intramural contests. J. D. Gauldin, who later worked as an attorney in Dallas, told the *San Antonio Light* in 1955 that many of the Cumberland players were members of the Kappa Sigma fraternity.[2] Gauldin recalled a courier delivering a telegram from Heisman to the fraternity house. The telegram was actually addressed to the school's athletic director, a position that didn't exist at the school.

Gentry Dugat, who later became a newspaper columnist in Texas, said he was recruited to the Cumberland team because he weighed about 175 pounds. Dugat had never played organized football, but wasn't going to pass up a free trip to Atlanta.

"The football recruiters on the Cumberland campus looked me over and decided I would make a good left guard," Dugat said. "I was incautious enough to admit I had never been beaten running in high school. They signed me up. It was my first chance to go to Atlanta, the home of my idol, the late Henry W. Grady, Southern orator and journalist. And the jaunt would net me my first experience in a railway Pullman car. So I went."[3]

It was a trip none of the Cumberland players would soon forget. They departed the campus the day before the game and changed trains in Nashville. Allen hoped to pick up a couple of Vanderbilt University players during the stop, but he actually lost three of his own team members when they missed their connecting train. According to a play-by-play account of the game, which was archived by the *Atlanta Journal*, the Bulldogs reported to Atlanta with a roster of fifteen players, along with Allen and their self-appointed coach, a law student named Butch McQueen. Thirteen of the players were Cumberland College law students—at least their names appeared in the *1916–1917 Bulletin of Cumberland College of Tennessee*—and one player, Dow R. Cope, was a music student. Law school student H. A. Pogue made the trip to Atlanta but couldn't play in the game because of injury.

Georgia Tech won the coin toss and performed its first act of charity by choosing to kick off to the Bulldogs. From there, the game turned into a historical comedy of errors. Cumberland College quarterback Charlie Edwards was knocked out of the game while attempting to block on the opening kickoff. Morris Gouger replaced

Edwards under center, and he gained three yards on the first play from scrimmage. It would be Cumberland's longest run of the game. Cumberland College punted on its first possession, and the Yellow Jackets returned the ball to the Bulldogs' twenty-yard line. On the next play, Everett Strupper ran around left end for a touchdown. Jim Preas kicked the extra point, and Tech led 7–0. The Bulldogs received the ensuing kickoff and then lost a fumble on the next play. The Yellow Jackets scooped up the fumble and ran into the end zone for a touchdown. Preas kicked the extra point for a 14–0 lead.

After the Yellow Jackets took a 28–0 lead early in the first quarter, Cumberland College decided to try to change its luck. Every time the Yellow Jackets scored, the Bulldogs elected to kick the football back to them instead of receiving it, which was still allowed under the rules. But the first time the Bulldogs attempted the maneuver Georgia Tech returned the kickoff to Cumberland College's ten-yard line. On the next play, Strupper broke free around right end, but suddenly stopped running at the one-yard line. The Yellow Jackets wanted left tackle J. Cantey Alexander to score, but his teammates wanted to make him work for it. During each of the previous two seasons, Heisman had given Alexander opportunities to score. Against Mercer the previous week, Alexander failed to score on three runs from inside the five-yard line. Heisman recalled Alexander's comical attempt at reaching pay dirt against Cumberland College:

Many forwards, doomed to spend their playing lives down in the muck of the line, ardently wish they could score just one touchdown before their career's end. Of that number was Cantey Alexander, the clumsiest player I have ever seen in action, yet as courageous as men are born. A "fighting fool" they called him down at Georgia Tech. It was in 1916 we lined up against a team from whom we were sure to win with ease, and I promised Cantey that after we had scored a hundred (his own proposition) he might take the ball over for a touchdown. How that boy worked to roll up that hundred! 'Twas done at last and Cantey began to register excitement. Strupper takes the ball, runs [nine] yards, stops and puts it down on their one-foot line. Each man coaches [Alexander] differently, which "rattles" him more. On the first snap Cantey is trembling, so he muffs the ball. A halfback falls on it. No gain. The second snapped ball Cantey holds, but doesn't understand where to go. He hesitates, and he barely gets back to the line. On the third down our linemen purposely let the opponents through, and Cantey is nailed for a slight loss. By this time the boy is frantic with anxiety. They calm him. [Quarterback Albert] Hill takes the snap and puts the ball in his stomach. The line opens a cavernous hole, the backs protect him, and Cantey muddled in and then goes down under an avalanche of players. The referee—who is in the know—makes a critical inspection of the ball and the goal line, with Cantey prompting: "It's over, ain't it, Mr. Referee?" Finally, he is awarded a touchdown, and his heart starts again to beat. He murmurs, "I never knew it was so hard to buck the line before."[4]

Cumberland College had fifteen turnovers, losing ten fumbles, and had minus twenty-eight yards of offense. The Bulldogs completed a ten-yard pass late in the game, but it came on fourth-and-twenty-two. The Yellow Jackets led 63–0 after the first quarter, 126–0 at the half, and 180–0 at the end of three quarters. Heisman agreed to shorten the second half by fifteen minutes to save the Bulldogs from further embarrassment. Even though Heisman made many concessions by allowing the Bulldogs to substitute freely, one can only imagine how badly the Cumberland players must have been outclassed and manhandled in such a cataclysmic walloping. It could have been no great fun for any Cumberland back to try to carry the ball against such a whirlwind. On one occasion, Bulldogs halfback B. F. "Bird" Patey carried the ball but immediately fumbled, and the ball rolled toward another Cumberland player.

Patey wanted no business in recovering the ball, so he did the next best thing, yelling, "Fall on it, Pete!"

The other Cumberland player glanced at the ball and then back at Patey before replying, "Fall on it yourself—I didn't fumble it!" [5]

Late in the game, Heisman looked at his bench to see if there might be anyone he had not put into the game. He was surprised to see a Cumberland player sitting at the end of the bench, trying to be as invisible as possible. Heisman thought that the player might have gotten turned around in the melee of a recent play and had mistakenly come off on the wrong side of the field after his substitution.

Heisman walked up to the player and gently said, "Son, you're on the wrong bench; yours is across the field."

The Cumberland player shook his head and answered, "No, sir, Mr. Heisman, this is the right bench. If I go over there, they'll put me back in the game!"

Heisman smiled, threw him a blanket, and told him to cover up. Heisman then walked back to his usual position and let the boy stay.

Somehow, Georgia Tech's historical rout barely made a ripple nationally the next day. There was a one-paragraph brief in the *Washington Post*, but only the score was mentioned in other national newspapers such as the *Chicago Tribune* and the *New York Times*. Even the *Atlanta Constitution* buried its game story on page three, reporting that "Tech tired out a good deal towards the close of the game. Otherwise, the score would have been larger than it was." [6] It wasn't until more than a week later that the *Constitution* reported that Georgia Tech's victory was actually the most lopsided outcome in intercollegiate football history, surpassing Florida's 144–0 victory over Florida Southern in 1913. [7]

While Heisman might have been upset with Cumberland's baseball team for using illegal players the previous spring, his real beef was with several local sportswriters who seemed focused on points scored when determining the strength of teams. Indeed, the *Constitution*, to which Heisman was still a regular contributor, published point totals for the South's best teams on its sports pages each week during the season.

After the 1916 season, Heisman explained why the Yellow Jackets defeated Cumberland College so badly:

> [I have] often contended that this habit on the part of sports writers of totaling up, from week's end to week's end, the number of points each team had amassed in its various games, and comparing them one with another, was a useless thing, for it means nothing whatever in the way of determining which is the better of an evenly grouped set of college teams. Still the writers persisted and some at each season's end would still presume to hang an argument on what they claimed it showed. So, finding that folks are determined to take the crazy thing into consideration, we at Tech determined this year, at the start of the season, to show folks that it was no very difficult thing to run up a score in one easy game, from which it might perhaps be seen that it could be done in other easy games as well.[8]

Heisman wrote that he was trying to make a point to sportswriters that Georgia Tech was capable of running up scores as often as a lot of other teams did, but he didn't see the reason in doing it:

> Accordingly, in the Cumberland game the Jackets set their souls to make a record run, and for the first time in our football career we turned loose all we had in the way of scoring stuff, and the result was a world's record of 222 points rolled up in 45 minutes of play. Now, we don't take particular credit

in doing that. If that were all we were after we could have followed exactly the same line of action and, while not compiling
as many points as against Cumberland, we could nevertheless
have so heaped 'em up as to have been able, I dare say, to add
at least another 100 or so to our season's grand total of 421.
But even this 421 was a record for the entire country for the
season, and here we find a lot of people and papers all over the
country once more making much of it and printing our name
in big type at the top of columns of Flub-Dub. My, my! But it's
easy to fool some folks!

Unfortunately, the Bulldogs were on the wrong end of Heisman's
joke. Not everyone agreed with Heisman's method of proving his
point. Heisman was heavily criticized for what many viewed as an
unsportsmanlike act, and Noye Nesbit, one of Heisman's players,
even wrote the words "Tech's Disgrace" above a photograph of the
game in his scrapbook.[9]

The 1916 Yellow Jackets team seemed to personify Heisman. It
was relentless and focused, fought hard in every game, and thought
quickly on its feet. While the Yellow Jackets rolled up a staggering
421 points to the opponents' 20, only a 7–7 tie against Washington
and Lee prevented them from winning a national championship.
Tech's backfield featuring Hill, Strupper, team captain Froggy Mor-
rison, and Tommy Spence was largely unstoppable, and the backs
were supported by great line play from tackle Walker "Big Six" Carpenter, guard Bob Lang, and center Pup Phillips, most of whom were
All-Southern selections. Each player contributed leadership on and
off field.

The tie that marred the unbeaten season had its lighter as well as
dramatic moments. The Yellow Jackets were forced to play the game
without Spence and star end Jim Senter, who were hurt in a 10–6 victory over North Carolina the previous week. Against Washington
and Lee, both teams scored touchdowns and extra points in the first

period, but the rest of the game was a defensive standstill. Heisman recalled:

> Since the first five minutes, when both teams had scored, no further scoring was done, and the score stood 7–7, with four minutes left to play. Our quarterback, Albert Hill, tried a goal from the field at this point and the ball flew straight at the right goal post. The ball hit the upright but slightly on its inside edge. The forward flight of the ball was stopped, and it dropped slowly on the inside of the upright and came down on the crossbar. What agony of suspense! If it dropped beyond the bar we would win the game; if it fell off inside the field it would continue a tie. I'll take an oath today that the ball, wobbling along that bar, rolled a full yard before it finally lost balance. Which way? Inside the field, confound it! The game ended a tie.[10]

The Yellow Jackets had a 6-0-1 record heading into their game against Georgia in 1916. Heisman used a unique method in motivating his team to play its in-state rivals. He kept his players isolated on the train ride from Atlanta to Athens. At the hotel in Athens, "one might have more easily obtained an audience with King George or the Pope than with one of my players," Heisman wrote.[11] After his players were fully dressed for the game, Heisman had them hoarded into a large ballroom of the hotel.

The coach's nephew Lee Heisman recalled details of what his uncle told him of the affair: "The coach wasn't entirely happy with the relaxed attitude of the team. After putting them in the reserved dining room of the hotel, he and the assistant coaches excused themselves and upon exiting the room, quietly closed and locked the big oaken doors. Heisman went over to the hotel manager and handed him an envelope of cash money saying this should cover his costs. The manager scratched his head wondering what this could mean."[12]

The manager soon found out. Finding the doors locked, Carpenter, the Yellow Jackets' mammoth tackle, took matters into his own hands.

"Hell's Bells, bullies, what we here for?" Carpenter asked his teammates. "To lick this Athens bunch to a frazzle! And it's going to be done if I have to do it alone! I'll tell you right now, if we don't win this game, I'm not going back to Tech, nor Atlanta, nor home. I'll be getting out of Georgia and out of the South! Oh, to hell with talk. Come on, let's do something!"

At that moment, Tech's players charged through the thick oak doors, knocking them completely off their hinges. The manager now knew what the envelope of money was for.

"The coach and his assistants paced the sideline of the Georgia field wondering if the 'isolation gamble' had its effect," Lee Heisman recalled. "The clock was getting on to kickoff time, only minutes away. A Tech player had yet to take the field. The crowd was stirring, and catcalls from the Georgia fans were on the rise, challenging Tech to have the courage to show. They sprinted down the street to the playing field and entered just in time for kickoff. Heisman turned around at the roar of the crowd to see the flushed and furious faces of his players as they sprinted to their positions for the kickoff. He knew at that moment his plan had worked."[13]

The Yellow Jackets trounced Georgia 21–0 at Sanford Stadium, avenging a 0–0 tie from the previous season.

After defeating Auburn 33–7 in the Thanksgiving Day game at Grant Field, the Yellow Jackets finished the season with an 8-0-1 record. For several weeks there was an effort to schedule a game between Georgia Tech and Tennessee, which also finished 8-0-1, to decide the Southern Intercollegiate Athletic Association championship. But after an agreement couldn't be reached, alumni members of Tennessee's athletic council conceded the championship to Georgia Tech. One member of the athletic council told the *Atlanta*

Constitution, "I think it will show the proper sportsmanship on our part to make this concession immediately. We do not want to take a position that will bring us into ridicule and make us the objects of uncomplimentary remarks. It is nothing more than true sportsmanship spirit that we concede the title to Tech." [14]

That was the kind of press even Heisman could agree with.

CHAPTER TWELVE

Golden Tornado

When Heisman grabbed his morning newspaper on April 6, 1917, he had to be greatly concerned about the bold headline across the top of the front page of the *Atlanta Constitution*: HOUSE, AFTER NIGHT OF DEBATE, DECLARES U.S. IN STATE OF WAR. For three years, the United States had taken a stance of nonintervention in the Great War in Europe. But after German submarines sank seven US merchant ships and then sent the Zimmermann Telegraph to Mexico's government, encouraging the Mexicans to join them as an ally against the United States to recoup their lost territories of Arizona, New Mexico, and Texas, US president Woodrow Wilson couldn't stand idle any longer. Within a few weeks, the United States was an active participant in World War I, and more than 2.8 million American men were drafted into military service.

Some of the newly enlisted GIs were college football players, many of whom interrupted their college education to help defend their country overseas. As a result, many of the nation's top college football programs were suspended. Northeastern powerhouses such as Harvard, Princeton, and Yale played abbreviated schedules and fielded only informal teams in 1917. Traditional southern powers such as Georgia, North Carolina, Tennessee, and Virginia dropped football altogether. When Georgia announced on September 27, 1917, that it wouldn't field a football team that season, Dr. Stedman V.

Sanford, a future UGA president, told students that "he had a thousand times rather these gridiron warriors be serving Uncle Sam than playing football when their services were needed by their country."[1]

Georgia Tech's attitude about whether football should be suspended during the war was much different. Heisman believed that football, more than any other extracurricular college activity, prepared young men for military service through physical conditioning, discipline, teamwork, and commitment. It was a position that was later supported by Secretary of War Newton Baker and Secretary of the Navy Josephus Daniels. The Yellow Jackets lost their share of football players to the military draft—only ten of thirty-one players from the 1916 squad returned to school—but a strong nucleus was coming back in 1917. Quarterback Albert Hill was returning, along with the All-America halfback Everett Strupper. There were also two very significant additions: halfback Joe Guyon, who had played for Pop Warner at the Carlisle Indian Industrial School in Pennsylvania in 1912 and 1913, and freshman fullback J. W. "Judy" Harlan of Atlanta. Guyon, who had blocked for the legendary player Jim Thorpe at Carlisle, enrolled at a Chicago preparatory school before transferring to Georgia Tech in 1916. Guyon was ruled ineligible to play for the Yellow Jackets' varsity team during the 1916 season under transfer rules. Guyon, a Chippewa Indian who was born at the White Earth Indian reservation in Minnesota, was named second-team All-America by Walter Camp after his second season at Carlisle, in 1913.

With so many weapons in the backfield, opponents couldn't focus on one Tech ball carrier. Any one of the Yellow Jackets' backs would have been an all-star in any backfield in the country. With the four runners together, and coupled with Heisman's genius for misdirection, instantaneous shifts, quick-hitting plays, and lateral passing, it was essentially impossible to hide a weak link in a defensive scheme. Against Georgia Tech, there could be no double teaming or double coverage, or gambling on the direction of play or blocking. The field had to be approached evenly and without partiality.

Despite Guyon's exceptional talent, Heisman's assistants had to persuade him to take the player, who wanted an assistant coach's job at Georgia Tech for his older brother. The assistant coaches descended on Heisman one day in his office and, in an interview fifty-seven years later, Chip Robert recalled their conversation with him:

> Now, you had to understand the coach. Assistants did what he said. Suggestions might be made, but directions and orders came from Coach. He hated having too many people around as "assistants." He preferred a small, controllable staff, not the huge coaching machines you see today with special team coaches and offensive and defensive coordinators and their assistants as well. Word came that Guyon wanted to come to Tech, and most of the scouting crew, led by Bill Alexander, had seen him play, though the coach had not. We were anxious to call Joe and give him the go ahead, but there was a fly in the ointment, a *big* fly. Joe wanted a job guaranteed for his brother as an assistant coach! Now, this wasn't a violation of any recruitment standards of the day, only a violation of the temperament and veracity of Coach Heisman. We all knew this so we collaborated how best to put this to Coach. It was decided that Bill Alexander, Coach's right-hand man and who would be next head coach at Tech, would break the news at the right moment when I gave him the high sign.[2]

According to Robert, the assistants' meeting with Heisman went something like this:

"Coach, Joe Guyon wants to come to Tech," the assistants told Heisman as they walked into his office.

"Guyon, Guyon," Heisman repeated to himself. "I've heard the name, is he any good?"

"Oh, Coach, he can run like the wind, fast as a jackrabbit," one of the assistants said.

"Is he strong?" Heisman asked.

"As an ox, Coach," another assistant said. "Plows through the line like a bulldozer!"

"Can he make his grades?" Heisman asked.

"Held steady at a B+ average at Carlisle, Coach," Alexander replied.

"Hmmm, can make the grades, has some experience, fast, and strong," Heisman said. "Sounds good!"

Heisman began to resume his reading, and then Robert nodded to Alexander, giving him the signal to break the news to Heisman.

"What is it?" Heisman asked.

"It's his older brother," Alexander said.

"Does he want extra tickets?" Heisman asked.

"No, Coach, Joe wants a job for him," Alexander said.

"Well, I'm sure we can refer him to the maintenance department," Heisman said.

"As an assistant coach," Alexander carefully slipped in.

"There was a long, silent pause and we all sucked in our breath and steeled ourselves for the storm we knew would break," Robert recalled.

"No! No! Nooooo!" Heisman yelled. "The last thing I need is another nitwitted assistant that thinks he knows something about this game! There isn't enough tea in China or on the Serengeti Plain to induce me to hire another assistant! They get underfoot and can't keep their heads on straight. And, and, you say he's fast?"

"Like the wind," Alexander said. "He was timed at one hundred yards in low ten seconds in full gear!"

"No! No! No!" Heisman shouted while shaking his head. "Assistants get underfoot, send in the wrong plays, are a distraction, get in the way. You think he's pretty strong, eh?"

"I watched him carry three defenders into the end zone at Carlisle's freshman game, Coach," Alexander replied.

"Concern it!" Heisman said. "I won't hire an assistant just to get a player—no matter what. He can make the grades and play pretty well, you say, Bill?"

Heisman was actually using his assistants' names now, which they believed was a sign that a deal was close to being done. Suddenly Heisman stood up, put his hands over his ears, and stormed out of his office.

"I don't know anything about this!" Heisman shouted while walking out the door.

Georgia Tech's assistant coaches grinned at one another and called Guyon. During the next couple of seasons, Guyon's brother was seen roaming the sidelines at Georgia Tech games.

"We gave him a raincoat and a whistle that he hung 'round his neck, and we assigned a manager to keep him far away from Coach Heisman," Robert recalled. "We wanted him out of sight, out of mind. Every so often, Coach would look down the ranks and see Joe's brother pacing the sidelines, tooting his whistle and acting the big shot. A small scowl would begin on Coach's face, but would soon disappear when Joe would break loose for a long run. Then, Coach would seem to almost grin, shake his head, and resume his duties."[3]

Even after so many veterans left, Heisman scheduled Georgia Tech's games aggressively in 1917, starting with an ambitious Saturday doubleheader against Furman and Wake Forest to start the campaign. Never before had a college football team played two games on the same day. A few days before the doubleheader, Heisman was still unsure how he would divide his team, since the agreement called for the Yellow Jackets to use only varsity players in both contests. "Double bills are common enough affairs in baseball, but this afternoon's attraction is the first time a football team has attempted to put over two wins in one day," the *Constitution* reported on Septem-

ber 29, 1917. "The general opinion seems to be that Wake Forest has
the better eleven of the two visiting teams and as such will be treated
by the Tech coaches, who plan to send against them their best men,
composed mostly of the varsity of last year. The team that opposes
Furman will most likely be made up of second string men and scrubs
from last fall." [4]

In the end, it didn't matter how Heisman distributed his players in
the two games, because the Yellow Jackets easily overmatched both
opponents. Georgia Tech defeated Furman 25–0 in a driving rain-
storm at Grant Field, and then beat Wake Forest 33–0 on a soaked,
straw-covered playing field. It didn't take Guyon long to make an
impression, as he ran for a seventy-yard touchdown in the opening
minutes of the Wake Forest game.

Georgia Tech faced a much more formidable opponent the next
week when it hosted the University of Pennsylvania, Heisman's alma
mater, at Grant Field on October 6, 1917. It was the Quakers' first-
ever trip to the South to play football, and All-America halfback
Howard Berry was one of the best players in the country. Days before
the game, oddsmakers were taking bets on which player would run
for more yards in the head-to-head matchup—Berry or Strupper.

Heisman believed that Strupper, a native of Columbus, Georgia,
might have been the best player he ever coached. Strupper played
football at Riverside Military Academy in Gainesville, Georgia,
before he enrolled at Georgia Tech in 1915. Strupper was about five
feet seven inches and weighed only 148 pounds, and a childhood illness had left him slightly deaf. Because of his condition, Strupper
called signals in the Tech backfield instead of the team's quarterback.
Strupper's mother was also overly protective of her only son, according to Heisman. She did not want her precious son to play the ruf-
fians' game. It was a test of Heisman's oratory and persuasive skills
to turn Mrs. Strupper's fancy to the manly benefits of the game and
the gentleman's behavior that Heisman demanded. Finally, it was
agreed that after every game, Strupper would call his mother to let

her know that he was all right and give her the benefit of hearing her loving son's voice.

From that day forward after every Georgia Tech game, Strupper was hauled to the telephone, no matter his condition.[5] Strupper called his mother and recounted the merry little football contest and all the fine fellows from the other team with whom he made friends. Sometimes, with teammates propping him up on either side, and with court plastering and wraps around his abdomen and ribs, he would make the call. The conversation would last until Mrs. Strupper was satisfied her son was all right. Heisman later described his speedy halfback, who was also a standout baseball player and sprinter at Georgia Tech: "Strupper radiated brilliance in every department. His game was without flaw. Were I compelled to risk my head on what one absolutely unaided gridster might accomplish with a football under one arm and facing eleven ferocious opponents, I would rather risk what this phantom could do in the way of running the gauntlet and coming out unscathed than any other ball carrier I have ever seen in action."[6]

The Yellow Jackets ran all over Pennsylvania 41–0 in front of a packed crowd of fifteen thousand fans at Grant Field that day. It was the first time a southern team had defeated a member of the Big Four of the Northeast—Harvard, Pennsylvania, Princeton, and Yale. It was a monumental football victory for the South. "Vanderbilt held Yale to a tie score several seasons ago and boosted southern football stock considerably in the eyes of the eastern and western critics," the *Constitution* reported after Tech's shutout. "The Tech victory should further emphasize the fact that southern elevens have made wonderful strides in the great college sport and should receive the credit that is their due."[7]

Strupper, who was affectionately called "Stroop" by his teammates and coaches, was not much of a factor against Penn after he was involved in a car accident earlier in the day. Berry also was held in check, and the Quakers were caught completely off guard by

Heisman's new mode of attack. Sometime before the 1916 season, Heisman introduced the Heisman shift, which was a precursor of the T formation. Heisman's tricky maneuver called for his team's center to stand over the ball. The other linemen would stand in a tight formation about a yard behind the center, and the backs would stand in a "T" formation behind them. When the center twisted his body, giving the other players the signal to shift, the other ten men would jump into a single-wing formation to the right or left. But Heisman abandoned the Heisman shift against the Quakers, and "the linemen took their regular positions behind the center. The four backs lined up directly behind the center, and the ball being snapped directly to the man expected to carry it on the play."[8]

A week later, Georgia Tech defeated Davidson 32–10 at Grant Field, and for the first time the team was called the "Golden Tornado." In his October 7, 1917, story of Tech's victory in the *Constitution*, Hal Reynolds wrote, "While no credit must be taken from Davidson for the game fight they put up in the face of big odds, it was evident that the Golden Tornado, as the Tech team has been dubbed, was not the whirlwind that it was one week ago against Pennsylvania."[9] The fetching moniker stuck throughout the rest of the 1917 season and became a tradition at Tech for more than a decade. The last known reference to the Golden Tornado at Tech was after its memorable 8–7 victory over California in the 1929 Rose Bowl.

While Reynolds might have been impressed, Heisman was so disappointed in his team's defensive effort he ordered his players through the "longest and hardest scrimmage of the year" four days after the game, according to the *Constitution*.[10]

Heisman knew his team had to be motivated for its next opponent, Washington and Lee, which had tied Georgia Tech 7–7 in 1916, spoiling the Yellow Jackets' chances of winning a national championship. Heisman had no such worries after the game started, as the Golden Tornado defeated the Generals 63–0 at Grant Field on October 20, 1917, their worst loss in school history. Hill was the star of the game, picking up a fumble and running thirty yards for a touchdown and then scoring on a forty-four-yard run. Hill also recovered a muffed punt in the end zone for a safety. Heisman later called Hill, a native of Washington, Georgia, one of the most intelligent players he ever coached:

One time my Georgia Tech team was playing Washington and Lee. At defensive left half I had one of the most alert chaps to have ever spurred the turf with leather cleats. Albert Hill was his cognomen, and he was playing football in his second year only. Once Washington and Lee started a run around their own left end, away from Hill. Yes, it might have developed into a double pass to eventually swing back to the right, or it might have been a fake end run to the left culminating in a forward pass to the right. By such means are defensive halves decoyed out of position. But they never pulled Hill away from the proper guardianship of his own territory. I never knew him to be fooled by anything of the sort. If the ball came his way, Hill was there. Well, our right end smashed the interference on this play, and our right half tackled their runner, giving him such a jolt that the poor fellow dropped the ball. The spheroid fell to earth, bounced, and before it could drop a second time some Tech player had grabbed it on the bound and made off along our right boundary line 30 yards and a touchdown. It was Hill, who had remained long enough at his post on the left side of the field to make sure his territory was not threatened and had then crossed the right side behind his line fast enough to get that fumbled ball on the first bound and outrun any defensive man. Yes, smart following of the ball. But it was surpassed by what this same Hill did in the second half of the game. Washington and Lee tried exactly the same play and exactly the same thing happened over again—with one exception. This time the fumbled ball popped two feet up into the air but it never had time to fall all the way to earth. While still in midair a Tech player was seen to shoot under it, snatch it out of the ether, and make off with it down the right boundary line for a 35-yard run and another touchdown. And, against it was this man Hill! Any beholder who was keen enough to get the point of these two plays received his money's worth in those two plays alone. But not one in a hundred of the average onlooker would have noted that the merit of the plays lay in the fact that it was not merely a Tech man who recovered the ball, but the one defensive player who was the farthest away from the ball at the instant it went into play.[11]

Georgia Tech won its next three games to improve its record to 8-0, blasting Vanderbilt 83–0, Tulane 48–0, and Carlisle Indian Industrial School 98–0. During the Yellow Jackets' game against Tulane in New Orleans on November 10, 1917—their only road game of the season—Guyon didn't play particularly well. It was the only time in his career that the Indian star disappointed his coach.

"While we were playing Tulane in New Orleans, it was frightfully hot, and I was amazed to see Tulane tacklers nail Joe time and again before he could get out of his tracks," Heisman recalled. "I had to take him out."

After the game, Heisman asked Guyon what was wrong.

"Joe's grin was as fleeting as a ferry boat paddle," Heisman recalled.

"Well, Coach, you see, they had the biggest oysters in New Orleans I ever saw," Guyon told him.

"How many did you eat, Joe?" Heisman asked.

"Not so many—four or five dozen and raw," Guyon answered.

"Good were they?" Heisman asked.

"Going down they were fine," Guyon said.

"How were they coming up?" Heisman asked.

"Hmm, like my game, not so good," Guyon admitted.[12]

Because Guyon had played at Carlisle Indian Industrial School four years earlier, some journalists again accused Heisman of using ineligible players. There also were accusations that Harlan, who had played at Tech High School in Atlanta, was previously a star player at Washington & Jefferson College. But Georgia Tech produced birth records proving that Harlan was only nineteen years old and had attended Tech High for four years.

J. V. Fitzgerald, a sportswriter with the *Washington Post*, defended Heisman in his column on November 11, 1917: "The Georgia Tech football team, which is making such an enviable gridiron record this season, has been accused of harboring players who are really professionals—a charge which is unjust and untrue. The eligibility rules at the Atlanta institution are as strict as those at any college or university in the country and they haven't the degree of elasticity, which prevails in certain places. The fact that Joe Guyon, former Carlisle star, is playing on the Atlanta team has caused comment of an unfavorable nature. Guyon entered Tech a year ago, but was ineligible to play in 1916 on account of the one-year residence rule. Even among Eastern colleges Carlisle is classed only as a prep school. Tech lived up to the spirit as well as the letter of the rule in the Indian's case."[13]

By the end of the 1917 season, Georgia Tech was considered one of the country's three best teams, along with Ohio State and Pittsburgh. Both Pittsburgh and Georgia Tech hadn't lost in three seasons. The Golden Tornado didn't lose in thirty-three consecutive games (there were two ties) from 1914 to 1918; the Panthers won thirty-two consecutive games during that time. Pittsburgh was the defending consensus national champion after finishing 8-0 in 1916 under Pop Warner, who had left Carlisle after the 1914 season. The Panthers would finish 10-0 in 1917, outscoring their opponents by a combined score of 260–31 (a statistic Heisman surely would have loved). Although the Panthers were a dominant team, led by All-

America guards Jock Sutherland and Dale Siles and end H. C. Carlson, they survived a couple of close calls that season. Pittsburgh defeated rival West Virginia 14–9 in its opener and then narrowly achieved a 14–6 victory over Penn (the same Quakers squad the Golden Tornado defeated 41–0) and a 13–10 win over Washington & Jefferson.

The American Red Cross, of all organizations, tried to settle the debate of which college football team was No. 1 in 1917. The Red Cross proposed having the Golden Tornado and the Panthers play in a benefit game on November 24, 1917, in Pittsburgh or New York to support the war effort. Georgia Tech dean Dr. Kenneth G. Matheson was initially opposed to the idea, but later sent a telegram to Pittsburgh officials that read, "Georgia Tech offers to play University of Pittsburgh on November 24 for the benefit of the Red Cross, the place of game to be agreed upon later."[14] The Panthers, who would have been forced to play three games in twelve days, never sent Matheson a reply, and the benefit contest was never played.

Five days before Georgia Tech played Auburn in the Yellow Jackets' Thanksgiving Day finale in 1917, Heisman and several of his players traveled to Montgomery, Alabama, to watch the Tigers play Ohio State. The Buckeyes were an overwhelming favorite over Auburn, which had lost to Davidson 21–7 in Atlanta two weeks earlier. Buckeyes halfbacks Charles "Chic" Harley and Pete Stinchcomb were two of the most feared players in the country. Betting on Ohio State was running four and five to one, with as many as thirty points being given to Auburn supporters. It seemed clear that the Tigers didn't have a chance. Early in the game, Ohio State recovered a fumble on Auburn's one-foot line but could not stick it in the end zone. Heisman and his Tech players cheered on the Tigers, who put up several hard-fought stands. Auburn held Ohio State out of the end zone six times in the game, with the Tigers' "Duke" Ducote safely punting out of danger from his end zone after each stop. Behind the furious plunging of George Revington, Auburn moved the ball to

Ohio State's thirty-yard line just before halftime. Ducote dropped back to attempt a field goal, but time expired before the snap could be made. It was the last scoring opportunity for either team, and the game ended in a 0–0 tie. It was a bitter loss for the Buckeyes nonetheless. "The outcome of the contest is considered generally as an Auburn victory, and the Auburn student body which attended the game are so celebrating tonight," the *Constitution* reported.[15]

The next week, Auburn traveled to Atlanta to play Georgia Tech on Thanksgiving Day. The only obstacle standing between the Golden Tornado and an undefeated season and a national championship was its coach's former team. Perhaps still recovering from their physical contest the week before, the Tigers were never in the game. Auburn's only score came in the fourth quarter, when Ducote circled around end for seventeen yards and then lateraled to William F. Donahue, who ran down the sideline for a sixty-yard touchdown. Guyon scored four touchdowns, leading the Yellow Jackets to an easy 68–7 victory, which secured a perfect 9-0 campaign.

With Ohio State suffering a tie against Auburn, and Pittsburgh dodging a game against Georgia Tech, the Golden Tornado was largely hailed as college football's national champion. Even New York newspapers quickly jumped on the Tornado's bandwagon, and the *Atlanta Journal* published their declarations in early December 1917:[16]

The *New York Sun*: "Georgia Tech looms up as one of the truly great teams of all time. It was decidedly unfortunate that Jack Heisman got together such a powerful aggregation in a season of lacklustre football. We believe that the supremacy of Georgia Tech would have been even more pronounced in peace times, for strengthened by those veterans who went away to enlist, the Tornado would have been much more formidable if such a state were possible. Football, once an Eastern specialty, now is a national sport, and in recognition of that fact we are glad to acclaim Georgia Tech the greatest eleven in the country."

The *New York Evening Mail*: "Georgia Tech stands revealed as the most sensational football eleven of the year. There is no question about it. The University of Pittsburgh, Ohio State and Minnesota have great football teams this year. But the record of the Golden Tornado of Atlanta is a bit beyond that of all of them."

The *New York Globe*: "The one spike needed to clinch Georgia Tech's claim to the war-time football championship of the universe was driven home on Thursday when the Yellow Jackets smothered Auburn under a 68 to 7 reckoning. This performance dissipated the last lingering doubt as to whether Heisman had a really great eleven or merely a lucky one, and definitely established the Golden Tornado's rightful place in the gridiron community."

And the *New York Telegram*: "The distinction of being the greatest scoring machine in the country goes to the football team of Georgia Tech, which wound up its third undefeated campaign. It is no mean honor this brilliant aggregation from below the Mason and Dixon line has achieved. The points acquired by Tech will go down on record as one of the most remarkable features of a season of upsets."

Of course, the *New York Times* waited a couple of weeks to deliver its endorsement, calling the Golden Tornado a "football machine proclaimed by competent observers as the greatest team which has ever been developed in the South and which was unquestionably the leading eleven of the last season."[17]

Even the *Red & Black*, the University of Georgia's student newspaper, wrote an editorial offering the Golden Tornado congratulations on its fine season (although a reader might be able to decipher a hint of sarcasm): "Our hats go off to the 'Golden Tornado,' the wonderful eleven from Georgia Tech. Unrivaled and unequaled the team has swept down the field past all contenders until they now stand undisputed and as yet undefeated champions of the south. Although Georgia has not found time for football this fall on account of extensive war preparations, it holds no grudge or criticism for those who can find time to carry on the pigskin and war game both at the same time. Tech has undoubtedly one of the best teams this year the south has ever produced and although conditions are such that is perhaps impossible to judge fairly of the relative strength of the various college teams, it is a safe bet that the Yellow Jackets would rank high with the best America could produce." [18]

Georgia and Georgia Tech's conflicting policies on athletics during World War I created quite a bit of tension between the rivals. The Bulldogs didn't field football teams in 1917 and 1918. When the schools played a baseball series in 1919, Georgia students produced parade floats that featured UGA students in foxholes in the Argonne Forest and Tech students playing games on Grant Field. Tech's administration was so upset by the display that the two schools wouldn't compete against each other in athletics again until 1925.

After fourteen seasons at Georgia Tech, and all the near misses along the way, Heisman had finally won a national championship. He had resurrected a fledgling football program that had long been rivals' doormats and transformed it into a national powerhouse. During the 9-0 campaign in 1917, the Yellow Jackets outscored their opponents, 491–17. Davidson College (10 points) and Auburn (7) were the only opponents who scored against them. From November 14, 1914, to November 10, 1918, Georgia Tech went thirty-three consecutive games without losing (it tied Georgia 0–0 in 1915 and Washington and Lee 7–7 in 1916). Along with the record-breaking rout of Cumberland College, Georgia Tech defeated Furman 118–0, the Eleventh Cavalry 123–0, and North Carolina State 128–0.

The 1918 season was set against a backdrop of national emergency. The late summer of 1918 marked the worldwide deadly flu epidemic's entry into the United States. The epidemic began in Boston and seemed to follow railroad lines east and south to New York, over to Philadelphia, and then into the Midwest, and finally into the Rockies. It was baffling to medical researchers and identified all too late as influenza. The country would lose more than five hundred thousand citizens to this epidemic, most of them between ages twenty-one and twenty-nine. At the same time, the country had been at war with Germany since April 1917, and the American effort was escalating.

On December 1, 1917, Heisman agreed to a one-year contract to coach Georgia Tech's football team in 1918. The development contradicted an earlier report by the *Constitution*, which said "the South's football wizard will not be signed up to a new contract in 1918. Our informant advises that Coach Heisman has under consideration offers from schools in the east and west, which he is considering, and that these offers are of such nature that the local football mentor is giving them serious consideration." [19]

A week later, the Golden Tornado celebrated its national championship season during a team dinner at the Druid Hills Golf Club in Atlanta. Each member of the team was presented with a gold football emblem that was inscribed with "National Champions." Five of the team members—William Mathes, William Thweatt, Dan Welchel, Theodore Shaver, and William Higgins—had already enlisted in the marines. Four other players—Robert Bell, Jim Fellers, Pup Phillips, and Charles Johnson—were leaving for the marines a week later. [20]

On December 28, 1917, delegates of the National Collegiate Athletic Association voted, on the recommendations of the secretary of war and the secretary of the navy, to continue playing intercollegiate sports. Secretary of the Navy Josephus Daniels, in a letter to the delegates, wrote that "most colleges have added military instruction, and with this training college athletics will make the youths fit for the service calling for strength and ability to endure hardship." [21]

Heisman would coach football again in 1918, but most of his Golden Tornado team wouldn't be with him.

CHAPTER THIRTEEN

Return to Penn

T here are defining moments in a person's life, and like his coaching style, Heisman's often were dramatic. His innovations had already resulted in wide and sweeping rules changes in American football: introducing the center snap; starting a play with the audible signal of "hike"; inventing the first scoreboard; dividing the game into quarters; and, of course, helping legalize the forward pass. He won conference titles and a national championship at Georgia Tech, earning him the respect of his peers across the country. On matters of debate over rules and the game's development, Heisman was often sought out for his perception and keen discernment. Over a quarter century, he had worked as an accomplished actor and successful stage director, and newspapers across the country were now publishing his writing. At age fifty, it should have been the golden moment of his life.

But on a cold afternoon in January 1920, Heisman called his closest friends to his home. Chip Robert, Heisman's former quarterback who later founded a successful architecture firm, Robert and Company, which is still in operation in Atlanta today, recalled the shocking details of the meeting:

The Coach had called several of us from the athletic staff to come to his house that afternoon. Bill Alexander and I arrived within a few minutes of each other. Neither of us knew the reason for the meeting. Mr. and Mrs. Heisman were inside and greeted us warmly. They brought us into the dining room, where on the table were 10 to 12 large envelopes. The Coach instructed us that this represented his and Mrs. Heisman's holdings and investments. What he asked of us was to make an equal divide of the portfolios. If any of it looked like it should belong with another holding, fix it so that it was, but only have two piles that are equal in value when we finished. We did this not knowing what he had in mind. Over the years we had become used to Coach doing the unexpected and didn't question anything. We finished our task inside of a half-hour and then turned to Coach and Mrs. Heisman.[1]

"Now," Heisman told his friends, "as you may have guessed a most unfortunate thing has happened. Mrs. Heisman and I have decided to divorce. There are no hard feelings, however, and I have agreed that wherever Mrs. Heisman wishes to live, I will live in another place to avoid social embarrassment. If she decides to stay in Atlanta, I will leave."

"We all gripped something for support and turned to Mrs. Heisman," Robert recalled. "She chose to live in Atlanta, and Georgia Tech lost her coach. I went home and cried myself to sleep that night."

What Robert and Heisman's other friends didn't know at the time was that Heisman and his former wife had actually been divorced for nearly six months. On June 10, 1919, Evelyn and John Heisman were granted a divorce by Judge Thomas F. Moran in the Second Judicial District Court in Reno, Nevada. Their divorce was published in the *Nevada State Journal* the next day.[2] Why the Heismans were divorced in Nevada isn't exactly known. They were quietly married on October 29, 1903, in Columbia, South Carolina, and lived together in Atlanta for sixteen years. Although Heisman's chosen professions were very public—he coached in front of thousands of fans every

Saturday, performed in front of hundreds of spectators on the stage, and had thousands of subscribers reading his weekly columns—he preferred to keep his personal affairs very private throughout his life. By divorcing in Nevada, the Heismans were able to keep it from becoming front-page news in Atlanta. After their divorce, John completed his final season coaching at Georgia Tech while they presented a facade that everything was pleasant at home.

Why were they divorced after more than sixteen years of marriage? A very independent person, Heisman had married an equally autocratic woman in the former Evelyn McCollum. Heisman wanted to continue to achieve in his various business endeavors—writing, sales, advertising, and even land speculation. He deeply desired to relocate to New York, where he believed his writing career and other business ventures would flourish. But Evelyn was a southern woman, who grew up in Atlanta and still had several family members living close by. Evelyn supported Heisman's football coaching career and wanted her husband's success to continue—but only in Atlanta. Heisman endeavored to always be a gentleman, and likewise Evelyn was ever a woman of grace. They were never antagonistic toward each other, even as their marriage crumbled. Their respect for each other was uncommon. Each felt reflected in the other's ambition and character. After several years of discussion, they came to a mutual decision to divorce, and John prepared to leave Georgia Tech.

It didn't take Heisman long to find work. On February 2, 1920, he was named coach at the University of Pennsylvania, his alma mater. The Quakers pushed their former coach, Bob Folwell, out the door to bring back one of their favorite sons. When Heisman was a player, he helped lay the foundation for what would become one of the country's most dominant programs at the turn of the twentieth century. Under coach George Woodruff, the Quakers won national championships in 1895 and 1897. Carl Williams, who played quarterback for Heisman at Oberlin College and then transferred to Penn on his advice, led the Quakers to a national title in 1904, and Sol Metzger accomplished the feat in 1908. But Penn hadn't been a powerhouse for nearly a decade when Heisman returned to his alma mater.

It's said that if you find the pattern you will find the man. In 1895, Heisman went south to get a fresh start, to heal his broken heart by throwing himself into his work. Twenty-five years later, he returned to the Northeast for a fresh start, to renew his heart by once again throwing himself into his work. When Heisman coached in the South, the game was young and lawless. He also was young and ambitious, and free to write his own rules of the game. With Heisman's wide-open style, he transformed the way football was played in the South. He was used to his team *being* the program. Georgia Tech was grateful for Heisman's work, and he usually received what he wanted. The southern football world had been his oyster. But when Heisman returned to the Northeast in 1920, he found established programs, rules, and conventions that had been in place for several years. For the first time, Heisman joined an established program and was expected to fit in. In many ways it was culture shock for the fifty-year-old coach.

In his first meeting with his Penn players, Heisman laid out his expectations: "Teamwork is my long suit, boys. Anybody can run with a ball, if there are 10 men to open the way for him. But it is interference that counts, and I will want every man to aim to be a 'blocker,' not a star end runner or something else. That is what I have found will get the results, so by the time November rolls around, every man will fill his place with the precision of clockwork. That is the thing on which I will stress now. I may not win a game, or I may win all the games. That is not the thing. For there is a big handicap which I have to overcome. I do not know the players. I do not even know the dozen or 20 best men. I must pick out from all of the men reporting the players to develop into a machine."[3]

Heisman also made it clear there wouldn't be any favorites in his regime. Returning varsity players would have to work for their places on the team, just like the new scrubs. "I would not have gone

Michael Heisman co-owned and operated a cooper shop in Titusville, Pennsylvania, where he supplied oil barrels to many of the world's first oil producers. (© *Drake Well Museum*)

ABOVE: Coopers stand outside the Stephens & Heisman Cooper Shop, which supplied barrels to oil producers during the great oil rush in Titusville, Pennsylvania, during the late nineteenth century. (© *Drake Well Museum*)

LEFT: After his family moved from Cleveland, John Heisman grew up in Titusville, Pennsylvania, which was the site of the world's first flowing oil well. (© *Drake Well Museum*)

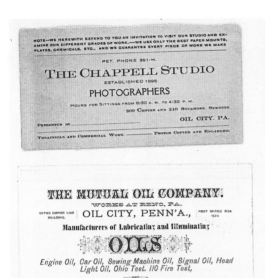

Michael Heisman co-owned a cooper shop, which supplied barrels to oil barons such as John D. Rockefeller and Andrew Carnegie. (© *Steve Kinch*)

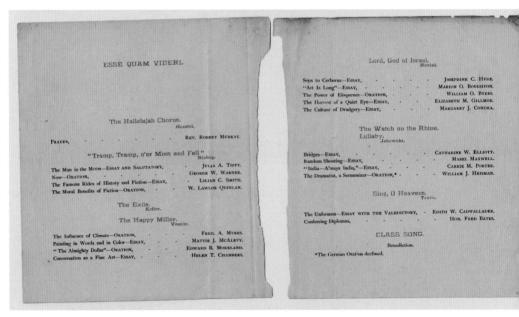

John Heisman was a top scholar and athlete at Titusville High School, where he played on the school's varsity football team. (*Heisman family photo*)

John Heisman stands with his brother Mike in the 1930s. Their brother, Daniel, was tragically killed in a work accident in 1892. *(Heisman family photo)*

John Heisman with his family in Curtice, Ohio, around 1930. Left to right: Heisman's sister-in-law Ida; brother Michael C.; nephew William Lee; wife, Edith; and Heisman. *(Heisman family photo)*

Heisman's nephew William Lee Heisman climbs an oil derrick in Titusville, Pennsylvania, where John W. Heisman grew up as a child. *(Heisman family photo)*

After graduating from Titusville High School, Heisman attended Brown University in Providence, Rhode Island, for two years, before transferring to the University of Pennsylvania to play football and attend law school. *(Heisman family collection)*

John Heisman (second row, far right) graduated from Penn's law school in 1891 but never became a practicing attorney after his eyesight was damaged in an accident. He went into coaching a year after graduating. *(Heisman family photo)*

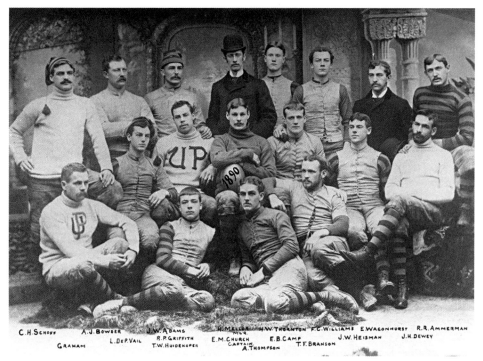

C.H.SCHOFF   A.J.BOWSER   J.W.ADAMS   H.MELLOR   H.W.THORNTON   F.C.WILLIAMS   E.WAGONHURST   R.R.AMMERMAN
GRAHAM   L.DEP.VAIL   R.P.GRIFFITH   E.M.CHURCH   E.B.CAMP   J.W.HEISMAN   J.H.DEWEY
T.W.HUIDEKOPER   CAPTAIN.   T.F.BRANSON
A.THOMPSON

Although John Heisman was undersized, he was a rugged lineman on Penn's football team from 1890 to 1891. *(© University of Pennsylvania)*

While coaching at Buchtel College in Ohio, Heisman fell in love with a student named Edith Maora Cole. Cole nearly died from tuberculosis, but they were later married in 1922. *(© University of Akron)*

Heisman (second row, far left) coached his first team at Oberlin College in Oberlin, Ohio, in 1892. He returned to Oberlin College in 1894 and guided the Yeomen to a 4-3-1 record. *(Heisman family photo)*

Heisman poses with the 1895 Auburn football team at Brisbane Park in Atlanta, the site of Auburn's annual battle against the University of Georgia. *(Heisman family photo)*

Although Heisman is mostly remembered as a legendary college football coach, he also coached baseball throughout his career. *(© Clemson University)*

Heisman coached at Clemson University from 1900 to 1903. He guided the Tigers to a 6-0 record and a conference championship in his first season. *(Heisman family photo)*

While coaching at Georgia Tech, Heisman was often seen with his family poodle, Woo, who had a fondness for eating ice cream. *(Heisman family collection)*

Photo by Will F. Nelson.
COACH HEISMAN,
In His Arms Is the Mascot of the
Tech Team.

Throughout his coaching career, Heisman often barked instructions to his players through a megaphone, which he seemingly carried everywhere. *(© Georgia Tech)*

Heisman's first contract at Georgia Tech paid him an annual salary of $2,250, plus 30 percent of gate receipts from varsity baseball and football games. It was one of the highest salaries in coaching at the time.

(Heisman family photo)

NTRACT between J. W. HEISMAN and THE ATHLETIC ASSOCIATION

of The GEORGIA SCHOOL of TECHNOLOGY

Tht Athletic Association of the Georgia School of Technol-
.es hereby agree to pay J. W. Heisman the sum of Two Thousand

Two Hundred and Fifty Dollars ($2250.00) and 30% of the net gate
receipts for Baseball and Football games played by the Varsi ty teams
as salary; in return for which J. W. Heisman agrees to give his
entire services for year I904 as Coach for Baseball and Football teams
of this organization.   Tht Two Thousand Two Hundred and Fifty Dollars ($2250.00) is to be paid in twelve equal installments, payable
at the end of each calendar month.

By net gate receipts is meant the net sum after the Two
Thousand Two Hundred and Fifty Dollars ($2250.00) as Coach's salary
expenses of uniforms, and other incidental expenses of the teams are
paid.   This 30% is to be reckoned at the end of the year and paid
over to the Coach at that time.

Witnesses   J. W. Heisman----Coach.
M C Curlis   Frank C Turner----for the
W A Jackson Jr   Athletic Association of the Georgia
                                  School of Technology.

Signed in duplicate this --- day of --------- , I903, at Atlanta , Ga.

After nearly losing his eyesight as a player at the University of Pennsylvania, Heisman wore bifocals throughout the rest of his life.
(© Georgia Tech)

Georgia Tech's 222–0 victory over Cumberland College of Kentucky on October 7, 1916, still stands as the most lopsided victory in college football history.
(© Georgia Tech)

ABOVE: Halfback Joe Guyon, a Chippewa Indian who was born on a reservation in Minnesota, was one of the biggest stars on Georgia Tech's "Golden Tornado" team, which won a national championship in 1917. *(Heisman family photo)*

LEFT: William "Bill" Alexander (left) was one of Heisman's most trusted assistants and succeeded him as Georgia Tech's coach in 1920. Alexander had a 134-95-15 record as the Yellow Jackets' coach from 1920 to 1944. *(Heisman family photo)*

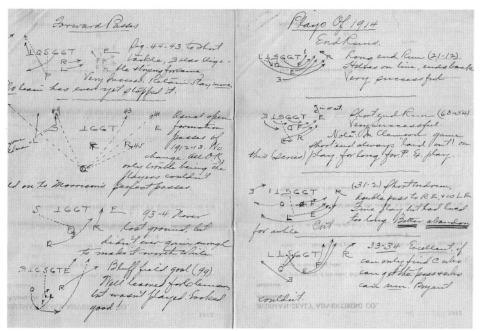

Heisman designed most of his teams' offensive plays and at least one of them was conceived while he was dreaming. He was one of the strongest proponents of legalizing the forward pass in college football. *(Heisman family photo)*

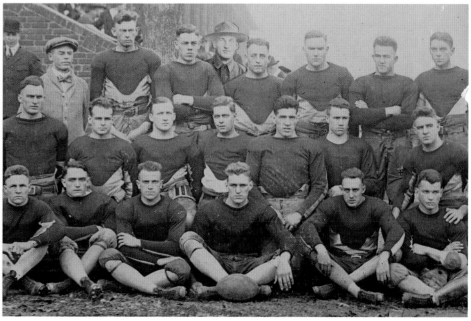

Georgia Tech's "Golden Tornado" team of 1917 finished 9-0 and was a consensus choice for college football's national champion. The Yellow Jackets outscored their opponents 491–17 and blasted Penn, Heisman's alma mater, by a 41–0 score. *(Heisman family photo)*

ANNOUNCEMENT EXTRAORDINARY
---FOR---
PICKETT SPRINGS CASINO
WEEK BEGINNING JULY 31.

TWO GREAT SHOWS NIGHTLY

THE POPULAR

HEISMAN STOCK COMPANY

Will Open the Program Each Night with New Plays of
Superior Merit, and a Stupendous Vaudeville Bill
will follow to close, consisting of

1. **Newest Moving Pictures.** (The, Battle of Mukden.)
2. **Mdlle, Nalada & Co.** European Spectacular Dancing
   Sensation.
3. **The Musical Bennetts.** The World's Greatest Novelty
   Comedy Musical Act.

A Superb Dramatic Company. Unsurpassable Comedies
and Plays. An Excellent Orchestra. Feature Vaudeville Acts. The Finest Program Ever Offered
In a Southern Summer Park.

Heisman and his first wife, the former Evelyn Barksdale, spent eight weeks during the summer of 1904 performing at Pickett Springs Casino near Montgomery, Alabama. (© The Montgomery Advertiser)

Heisman and Evelyn Barksdale were the leading man and leading lady, respectively, for the Heisman Stock Company, one of the coach's early acting troupes. (© The New York Clipper)

CASINO

Monday, Tuesday and Wednesday.

Greatest Comedy of Years.

Will be presented
by a cast of actors
unequalled in
comedy. The fol-
lowing is the cast.

Mortimer Mumbleford...John Heisman
Christopher Blizzard....William Roth
Rupert Sunberry......Joseph Bernard
Dr. Bartolomew Jones...........
....William Richards
James ....Len Morris
Muzzle ....William Fiorello
Maria .... Amelia Fiorello
Violet ....Miss Isabelle Lowe
Lucretia...........Miss Ethel Wynne
Rose Mumbleford..Miss Lebie Morris
Rose Mumbleford..Miss Louise Morris

In addition to
the above, moving
pictures will occu-
py the time be-
tween the rise of
the acts.
Prices as usual 10
and 25 cents.
Seats at the Savoy

One of Heisman's most successful dramatic ventures was managing the Park Casino theater in Macon, Georgia, for several summers. (© The Macon Telegraph)

Even during the early twentieth century, one of Heisman's primary responsibilities as a college football coach was recruiting high school players to his team. *(Heisman family photo)*

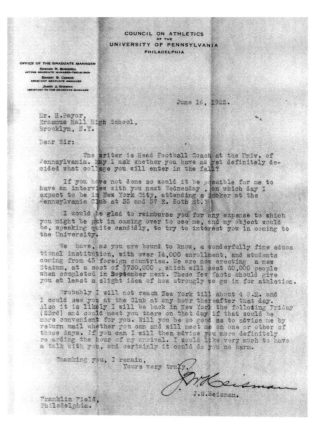

Heisman returned to the University of Pennsylvania, his alma mater, as coach in 1920 and compiled a 16-10-2 record in three seasons. *(Heisman family photo)*

ABOVE: Jonathan "Poss" Miller was one of Heisman's star players at Penn. Miller was later the head coach at Franklin & Marshall College in Lancaster, Pennsylvania. *(Heisman family photo)*

LEFT: Heisman instructs a new man at the University of Pennsylvania. Heisman laid out many rules for his players, including what they should eat and how often they should sleep. *(Heisman family photo)*

ABOVE LEFT: Charles "Pruner" West was one of Heisman's star players at Washington & Jefferson College and was the first African American quarterback to start in the Rose Bowl on January 2, 1922. (*© Washington & Jefferson*)

ABOVE RIGHT: After retiring from coaching, Heisman and his wife, Edith, moved to New York. Heisman was hired as athletic director of the Downtown Athletic Club and helped organize the Touchdown Club of New York. (*Heisman family photo*)

While writing for national magazines such as *Collier's Weekly* and *American Liberty Magazine*, Heisman did much of his reporting through questionnaires to coaches such as this one.
(*Heisman family photo*)

JOHN W. HEISMAN
34 Pondfield Road W.
Bronxville, N.Y.

November 26, 1928

Dear Coach Hubka:

Do you owe anything to football? If you do here's where you can square it.

To round out and preserve certain phases of the history of our great American game, I desire to chronicle true tales of the gridiron:

Incidents of lofty sportsmanship
Humorous episodes and sayings
Freak and unusual occurrences

-- that took place either in games or in practice.

Do you enjoy human interest narrations from your favorite game? Then make a "clearing house" of me for swapping these delightful tales. Won't they make wonderful reading for the next generation?--to say nothing of the present crop of old timers and youngsters.

Think just a moment! You're bound to know of some interesting girdiron happenings never before published. Won't you write and tell me of one or two you have heard or that came under your personal observation? I ask you to help me build up, in permanent form, the literature of our glorious game.

Make it as terse as you like but, where possible, give full names, addresses, teams, date and place, how it came about, what followed--such details as a reader would like to know. If you can't furnish them tell me where or from whom I could get them.

And, if you're willing, I'd like to give you credit for your story. In any case drop me a line--I'll gladly reply: Who knows, maybe someday I'll be able to do something for you. Try me.

In advance and many times I thank you.

Yours, in football brotherhood,

JOHN W. HEISMAN

May 26, 1930.

Mr. W. P. Holcombe,
Brooklyn Edison Company, Inc.,
380 Pearl Street,
Brooklyn, N.Y.

Dear Mr. Holcombe:

We sincerely feel that in the selection of Mr. John W. Heisman as Athletic Director the Downtown Athletic Club of New York is to be sincerely congratulated.

In this respect at least it seems that the Club intends to offer its membership only the best.

In our opinion there are few, if any, men better equipped for this work than Mr. Heisman. He undoubtedly brings to the position qualifications of character, ability, personality, industry and reputation of a very high order.

We wish for the Club great prosperity and for Mr. Heisman a most successful and satisfactory administration.

Very truly yours,

Robt. T. Jones Jr.

Legendary golfer Robert Jones Jr. and his father were among the prominent people who recommended Heisman for the athletic director position at the Downtown Athletic Club of New York. *(Heisman family photo)*

Coach John Heisman, 1923.
(© Washington & Jefferson)

anywhere else than back here to Penn," Heisman told his players. "But I want you men to understand that I will do my very best. I am not the representative of any clan and will play no favorites. Influence will have no effect with me. I don't care what fraternity, society or other affiliation you may have. You must show me that you are the best man to play for Penn next fall."

Teaching the Quakers his intricate system was more arduous than Heisman believed it would be. He also was disappointed in the number of men and the quality of players who reported for the team in his first season. When the Quakers left for a two-week training camp at the George School in Bucks County, Pennsylvania, in late August 1920, there were only thirteen players and three returning varsity members.[4] DeBenneville "Bert" Bell, star quarterback of the 1919 Penn team and future owner of the Philadelphia Eagles and NFL commissioner, left after graduation the previous spring. Danny McNichol, one of the team's best halfbacks, quit the team to focus on his engineering studies. Heisman built his squad around captain Bob Hopper; halfback Joe Straus; and Rex Wray, his smallish quarterback. Overall, Heisman was disappointed in his team's depth and lack of size.

"I don't know whether it is a lack of college spirit here or what is the trouble," Heisman said before the 1920 season.[5]

The Quakers' plight would get worse, and it never really improved much during Heisman's three-year tenure. Optimism was high after Penn won its first four games of the 1920 season—shutouts over Delaware, Bucknell, Swarthmore, and Lafayette. But then the Quakers inexplicably lost their next four games. The team was ravaged by injuries, and Heisman was frustrated with the athletic culture—or "college spirit," as he called it—of the school. His team rarely practiced together because many of his players attended classes until dark. A 28–7 loss to Penn State on October 30, 1920, seemed to be his tipping point.

"I have no fault to find with the team for its many misplays,"

Heisman said. "How am I to conduct practice when only half the squad is able to be there? One day I have one group of players and then the next day some of them are called to classes. It is teamwork which the team needs badly now, and I don't see how they are going to get it when the players are not able to be on the field until just before nightfall."[6]

Heisman's new players also seemed less receptive of his unorthodox coaching methods than his players at Georgia Tech. The accustomed "awe" of the coach was lacking, and Heisman seemed to be nothing more than a new oddity for his players. Questions concerning his methods and harsh intensity were sometimes raised in practices. According to Edwin Pope, author of *Football's Greatest Coaches*, "there was plenty of impatience to go around," and Heisman was often left to shout, "I have taught you all that I know, and still you know nothing!"[7]

A Penn substitute named Hughie King was a miserable blocker, and Heisman liked to stab him with the line, "Hughie, why don't you work as other men do?"

"How the hell am I going to work when there is no work to do?" shouted King, who rarely played.

"Ah, Hughie," Heisman said blandly, "you must be vicious. You must be like a bull in a china shop."[8]

Heisman seemed to be more critical of his players than ever before. After an ugly 44–7 loss to Dartmouth on November 13, 1920, he told reporters, "If anyone can tell me why the team played so well in the Pitt game, and then a week later did just exactly the reverse, I would like to know. This team has had more coaching and instruction than any other team I've ever had anything to do with, but still the men will not tackle."[9]

Pope also wrote that other Penn players were becoming frustrated with Heisman's complicated scheme: "Halfback Frank Dewhirst lost patience with Heisman's strategies and cried, 'C'mon guys, just hand me the pumpkin and let me run!'"

Heisman quickly corrected him, saying, "No, Frank, no! You must learn to hop like a chickadee."[10]

While Dewhirst probably shook his head in disbelief, Heisman's intricate system of misdirection in the backfield was designed to send everyone in motion in one coordinated swoop. As a halfback, fullback, or quarterback landed in his "start" position, the center snapped the ball before the defense could adjust. The "chickadee hop" entailed strong but fluid jumps forward, laterally, and diagonally to assigned positions that disguised where and to whom the center snap was going. One of Heisman's players at Georgia Tech recalled everyone watching the center, whose responsibility was to size up the defense as the backs stood in a straight I formation, perpendicular to the line of scrimmage. When the center swooped down over the ball, the backs "hopped," and in one motion the center snapped the ball straight to the designated back, whose job was to carry, pass, or punt. As a result, the backfield formation was disguised until the last possible instant.

The scheme became known as the Heisman shift, and it was largely unstoppable at Georgia Tech, which piled up 491 points in its national championship season in 1917. However, Heisman's offense proved to be ineffective at Penn, where his teams never scored more than 167 points in a season. Bill Roper, a highly successful coach at Princeton at the time, wrote that rules changes prevented Heisman's system from being as explosive. Under new rules introduced in 1921, players in motion had to come to a complete stop before the ball was snapped. It was a drastic change at the time, and it's a rule that is still observed in football today.

"I have never had to face a situation where at the eleventh hour my entire plan of attack was swept away by a changed interpretation placed upon a rule, that really did not seem to need any such interpretation," Roper wrote. "This is exactly what happened to John Heisman. For years he has believed in the 'shift play,' which has been his offensive dogma. At the end of the 1920 season and after the

Rules Committee had passed on the 1921 code, Heisman planned his attack for the coming season based upon the shift. The coach who has to change his style of attack after the season has really begun is at a disadvantage. A rightly equipped eleven goes on the field with a set of formations and developments growing out of them, carefully considered several months before the actual opening of the season. No coach can throw his team on the field one day and on the same devise his formations and plays." [11]

Only after Penn won its last two games in 1920, defeating Columbia 27–7 and Cornell 28–0, was Heisman assured of returning to Pennsylvania. Struggling for the first time in his coaching career, Heisman was determined to make his system work at his alma mater. He brought in new assistant coaches before the 1921 season and spent even more time explaining the details of his shift system to his players. Even though the Quakers lost the nucleus of their 1920 team—Hopper, Straus, Herman Harvey, and Carl Thomas graduated—they were optimistic about their chances. "This squad has ten times the pep, life and ambition that the boys had last year," Heisman said before the season. "No other word will do, they are ambitious now. Last year, they were listless; yes, and even lazy. The crowd seems to know more what it is here for—it is more together— helping one another. The men are not worrying whether they can make the team, but more whether they can help make a team." [12]

Heisman had reason to be optimistic at the beginning of the season, after Penn blasted Delaware 89–0 in its opener and started 4-0-1. But there were still signs of trouble. After Penn's 20–0 victory over Franklin & Marshall on October 1, 1921, Heisman demoted eight players from the varsity team for poor performances. After that game, he instructed all of the players who had not played a full quarter to run four laps around the track. [13] After a 7–0 victory over Gettysburg the next week, he threw end Ed McMullin off the team for rough play. Heisman's motivational ploys didn't seem to work. The Quakers lost three of their last four games and finished 4-3-2.

Even after two lackluster seasons, Heisman wasn't ready to give up on his alma mater. Heisman's dear friend Walter Riggs, now the president of Clemson College, was trying to hire him to coach the Tigers again. In a November 18, 1921, letter to Riggs, which Heisman wrote six days before Cornell blasted Pennsylvania 41–0 in the Quakers' last game, Heisman explained why he couldn't leave his alma mater:

They have found that I run football with system, with order and with discipline; that the players are good students, gentlemen and sportsmen always, and that they will fight with dogged courage to the last gasp, no matter how badly they are beaten. This has made me many friends, some of powerful influence, who insist it makes no difference whether we are beaten badly five years in succession so long as we are sure that football is at last being built on the right kind of foundation here at Penn. Not only is this the view of the alumni but I have won over the Provost and all the faculty, and I get no end of letters from alumni all over the country encouraging me and holding out strong moral support. Of course all this helps. I did think for some time that they would surely ask me to resign, and I was quite ready to do so. In fact I was disgusted beyond words; not for only was there no material but the place is singularly lacking in college spirit. Such players as I had had no real love for the game, and play only for the glory and fame they expect to get from participation. Of course there are a few exceptions, but the football morale of the entire squad is frightfully low. In short there appears just now no chance but that I will be back here next season, which will finish up my contract. What will happen after that of course I have no way of knowing. One hates to give up, and I must not quit so long as they actually want me, for it is still *my* university and I must be loyal whether everybody else is or not.[14]

Riggs responded to Heisman more than a month later, telling him, "Toward the close of next football season I want you to let me know how you are fixed. I do not know what the situation here will be, but if we should be looking for a football coach, needless to say we would think ourselves in great luck if we found you available."[15]

Drastic times call for drastic measures, and Heisman didn't hold back anything heading into the 1922 season. Even before the 1921 season ended, he announced that the Quakers would participate in year-round football. He borrowed the idea from Penn's rowing coach, and encouraged freshmen and new players to join the team for off-season conditioning in November 1921. By the beginning of the 1922 season, Heisman planned to have four separate teams: varsity, scrub, junior varsity, and freshman squads. In an interview with the *Philadelphia Inquirer*, Heisman explained his reason for expanding the football program:

> To produce a football team, the fundamental thing is to have football players. A football player I conceive to be something above the average individual. A person is not a football player merely because he weighs 200 pounds; nor because he can run 100 yards in 10 seconds; nor because he can catch a ball. A football player must have brains. He must have more than the usual amount of brains. And in addition he must also have speed and power, fight and skill. He must be something out of the ordinary. Penn was sorely lacking this year. We had men who were trying hard, but they had only ordinary ability.[16]

Over the next several months, Heisman worked overtime to whip his teams into shape, calling on one group to quicken its pace, admonishing another to hit harder, and yelling for managers to bring another bag of footballs. His eyes constantly roamed the field, and he held the always-ready, small, red megaphone as though it were adhered to his hand.

One day, a monkey wrench was thrown into Heisman's well-oiled practice regimen. From the far end of Franklin Field, a single critic was heard. Who would dare interrupt Penn's practice? Heisman's players were perplexed and looked to their coach for direction. Heisman's blood seemed to boil with each thunderous shout. Heisman began to make out the catcalls.

"You bag of lazy bones!" the person shouted. "How do you expect to beat a girl's chorus let alone Franklin and Marshall? Do any of you know the meaning of hustle?"

"Who in thunder?" Heisman thought. "How dare they! This is untenable, unimaginable; of all the impertinent, presumptuous absurdities. This is a mackerel's nose whisker. By Jupiter! They are in for my icy-cold dressing down, in tune with the blast of last year's Nor'easter! Great eyes of the underworld!"

Heisman's pace to the far end of the field quickened, and now he could hear his own name being called.

"What's the matter, Heis?" the person shouted. "Don't you have it anymore? Or do I have to come down there to instruct you in the finer points of the game?"

By now, Heisman's players had fallen in step behind their coach as he walked across the field. With each step, the young men anticipated the thunderous scolding they knew was coming.

Instead, after Heisman finally reached the stands, he stood in complete disbelief. He looked into the stands and wiped his eyes to make sure he wasn't mistaken. It was Edith Maora Cole, the woman he had left on her deathbed in Ohio nearly three decades earlier. Stricken with tuberculosis, Cole recovered but later suffered mysterious bouts in which she would lose her voice for weeks at a time. Cole's physician believed that higher altitude would help repair her throat and lungs, so she moved to Denver, and her condition improved. But after returning to Ohio to visit her mother in 1898, Cole lost her voice again. Her physician recommended a peculiar remedy—inhaling the fumes from a battery plant in Cleveland. For several days, Cole sat in the factory, and eventually her voice returned for good.[17]

Cole told Heisman that she had followed his coaching career through the newspapers. She learned of his marriage to Evelyn McCollum and refrained from contacting him, not wishing to create confusion or turmoil.[18] In June 1898, Cole married Melvin Stone of Denver, who was described as a "millionaire broker" by the *Norwalk (Ohio) Chronicle* in their wedding announcement.[19] According to US passport records, Stone was apparently quite wealthy, traveling to Europe for months at a time. When they divorced in 1921, Cole decided to find Heisman.

After Heisman's emotional shock passed, it took him very little time to rekindle his relationship with Edith. With their marriage, they picked up and completed their lives together. Among the many well wishes that poured in was one unexpected, heartfelt letter. It was from Evelyn McCollum and her family in Georgia, who were glad that there was "someone to see after him at this stage of the game."[20]

While Heisman's personal life was back in order, he spent the 1922 season attempting to restore his coaching reputation. Once again the Quakers opened the season strong, winning their first four games, including a 12–0 victory over Maryland. Early in the season, Heisman became the first coach to put a player in the press box, phoning plays to him via a telephone on the sideline. On October 28, 1922, Penn played the US Naval Academy in front of a crowd of more than fifty thousand fans at Franklin Field. The Quakers stumbled over themselves in the first half, falling behind 7–0 after the Midshipmen scored a late touchdown. When Heisman reached Penn's locker room, he called out captain Jonathan "Poss" Miller.

"Poss," Heisman told him, "I'm going to talk to you straight from the shoulder. If the team plays through the second half in the same manner that it played during the first half, I am through as your coach. I shall pack my bag tonight and catch the midnight train back to Atlanta, Georgia. I can stand defeat, if defeat must come, but I won't endure a defeat that is taken lying down. The team has been fighting after a fashion, but it's not the kind of fight that men who are determined to win put up. I want you to tell the boys inside. That's all!"[21]

Heisman turned around and left the field house. Miller limped back into the locker room, tears streaming down his dirt-covered cheeks.

"Boys," Miller cried, "the coach implies that we're yellow. He tells me that if we can't show more fight during the second half he's going back to his southern home. This is the last game he will ever coach. Are you willing to let it be? Will you let anyone call you yellow and get away with it? Men of Pennsylvania, the hour has come to give your answer. In five minutes from now, we're due to go back there on that field. Are you going to act the part of the helpless victim of a Roman holiday? There are fifty thousand people out there looking down to see us slaughtered. Men of Penn, if you ever fought, fight now! Fight as you never fought before to prove that no Pennsylvania team ever lays down! If there is anyone here who feels like quitting, let him speak out now—if not, come on and fight like men!"[22]

The Quakers responded with two touchdowns in the second half—both scored by Miller—and they stunned the Midshipmen, 13–7. Miller, the Penn player who delivered Heisman's message, was the one inspired the most, according to the *Philadelphia Inquirer*:

"Playing like a man possessed, scintillating with the strength and worthiness of an All-American, he really led Penn to a superb victory through the matchless individual fighting spirit he imported to his fellows and in the power of his own efforts. Twice he ravished the opposition for the touchdowns that spelled a triumph for Penn and twice he exborted [sic], he implored, he led his men to deeds of glory and efforts of might. Miller's spectacular exhibition has not been seen on Franklin Field in many a day. He seemed unstoppable, a little whirlwind on attack and a juggernaut beneath which Navy's hopes were crushed, and her joys smashed."[23]

Heisman actually coached his last game at Penn about a month later, when the Quakers lost for the third time in four games, falling to Cornell 9–0 on November 30, 1922. After finishing 6-3 in his third season at Penn, Heisman elected not to have his coaching contract renewed by his alma mater. He had been living in the Normandie Hotel in West Philadelphia for quite a while, and yearned for a fresh start with Edith. Even though a 16-10-2 record at Pennsylvania was a stain on his otherwise sparkling coaching résumé, Heisman was still a highly sought commodity.

Within weeks of resigning as Penn's coach, letters and telegrams from colleges across the country poured into Heisman:

From J. Y. Sanders Jr., an attorney and Louisiana State University booster: "In confidence I will state that the Alumni of LSU in co-operation with the University authorities are very anxious to secure as football coach a man with the acknowledged capacity and splendid reputation such as your record has established for you. Would you consider an offer from the Louisiana State University?"[24]

From J. A. C. Chandler, president of the College of William & Mary: "I am in a position to offer you $10,000 a year provided we can agree on the work to be done. I will arrange for an interview in which to draw upon contract. Wire me at once whether you are available after thinking the matter over."[25]

From A. R. Tiffany, chairman of the committee athletic council of the University of Oregon: "The position of football coach at the University of Oregon for next season is open. I am writing you this letter because I thought you might be interested personally in the position."[26]

From Harold Hirsch, a former University of Georgia player and Coca-Cola executive: "Are you in a position and would you be willing to consider an offer to coach Georgia? Please advise by wire and keep entire matter strictly confidential."[27] It didn't take Heisman long to turn down Georgia's offer. His close friend Kenneth G. Matheson, a former acting president at Georgia Tech and then-president of Drexel University in Philadelphia, found it ironic that Georgia would offer Heisman a job, after the Bulldogs had accused him of so much wrongdoing when he was coaching at Auburn and Georgia Tech. In a letter to Heisman on February 16, 1923, Matheson spelled out the point:

> It seems that you have made an admirable disposition of your affairs in every way, and I congratulate you and Mrs. Heisman very cordially. Wasn't it a turn of the worm to have you approached by Georgia, said worm, of course, being Georgia? After having attacked you for every conceivable crime through the years, it does seem remarkable that they should wish you in that pure and saintly pot! Really though, it is exactly like Georgia. I congratulate you that you decided not to accept the offer.[28]

Among Heisman's numerous letters and telegrams was a letter from Penn provost Josiah Penniman, who wrote, "I am glad that you think I was helpful to you when you were carrying what I knew to be a very heavy burden, made unnecessarily heavy, by the lack of cordial cooperation on the part of those from whom you had the right to expect it. I regard your achievements at the University of Pennsylvania as in many ways extraordinary. Intimations of this lack of loyalty to you reached my ears, and I promptly condemned the situation as thoroughly unsportsman-like. When a man is doing his work the best he knows how, and when it is evident to competent observers that he does know how, he ought to receive absolutely united support or else he ought to be told that his services are no longer desired. I agree with your opinion that the work of your three years will show plainly in the future, even though there may be few who realize it as clearly as I do."[29]

Two years after Heisman left his alma mater, former Penn player Louis Young guided the Quakers to a 9-1 record and a national championship in 1924. Clearly, Young benefited from the foundation Heisman had laid before him.

Even though Heisman's career was taking another unexpected turn, his life had foundation again, and he left Pennsylvania in search of a new life with his first love.

CHAPTER FOURTEEN

Washington & Jefferson College

O n paper, at least, the 1922 Rose Bowl game might have seemed
like the biggest postseason mismatch in college football history. The University of California, the so-called wonder team
of the West, was the defending Rose Bowl champion, having de-
molished Ohio State 28–0 on New Year's Day 1921. The Bears went
undefeated again in 1922. Washington & Jefferson, a school of only
450 students in Washington, Pennsylvania, about thirty miles south
of Pittsburgh, was such an unlikely choice to play California in the
Rose Bowl that *San Francisco Chronicle* columnist Jack James famously
wrote: "The only thing I know about Washington & Jefferson is that
they are both dead."

But after the aptly named presidents made a six-day train trip to
Pasadena, California, stopping to practice in Kansas City and visit
the Grand Canyon along the way, it didn't take them long to put a
huge scare into the Bears. Playing in front of fifty thousand fans on
January 2, 1922, at Tournament Park in Pasadena (the "granddaddy
of them all" didn't move to the Rose Bowl stadium until 1923), the
Presidents took the game's opening kickoff and drove to California's thirty-five-yard line. Washington & Jefferson halfback Wayne
Brenkert scored on a thirty-five-yard run, but the touchdown was
called back because the Presidents were offside. It was the only time
a player from either team would cross the goal line. The Presidents

missed two field goals and squandered another scoring chance when speedy Hal "Swede" Erickson broke away for a long run, but slipped on the muddy field at California's twenty-yard line. The game ended in a 0–0 tie.

Although the resolution may have been anticlimactic, the Presidents "outrushed, outgeneraled and generally outplayed the California Bears," the *New York Times* reported on January 3, 1922. When the Presidents returned to Washington, Pennsylvania, more than a week later, they were greeted at the train station "by [the] entire undergraduate body of the college, the pupils of the Washington schools, which had been dismissed for the occasion, and several thousands of townsfolk. The members of the football party were loaded into automobiles and, headed by a brass band and followed by thousands of cheering enthusiasts, a parade from the railroad to the Court House Square, in the centre [sic] of the business district, was staged."[1]

After the Presidents slipped to 6-3-1 in 1922, coach Earl "Greasy" Neale, who was the Cincinnati Reds' leadoff hitter in the infamous 1919 World Series against the Chicago White Sox, was forced out. Neale left for the University of Virginia, and Washington & Jefferson announced a new coach would be hired "only after the most careful consideration and deliberation; that when a man is chosen he will be one who is known to be 'orthodox' in his fundamental football, and one who can be depended upon to insist on the playing of the game on the soundest basis only."[2]

On January 4, 1923, Heisman was hired as Washington & Jefferson's new coach. After signing a three-year contract to coach the Presidents for $10,000 annually, Heisman left for his new off-season home in Miami on the same day. By all accounts, Washington & Jefferson graduate manager Robert "Mother" Murphy and line coach David Morrow oversaw the football operations for much of the summer until Heisman returned to the campus on September 2, 1923. Well rested and rejuvenated, Heisman jumped headfirst into coaching his new team. Even though the results had not been as good as expected, Heisman's return to Pennsylvania had benefited him in several ways. Psychologically, he returned to something familiar. Emotionally, he was reunited with Edith Cole, though he certainly hadn't known it would happen at the time. Professionally, Heisman maintained his calling with a recognized football program, one whose history he had contributed to, as it was *his* alma mater. Financially, he received a pay increase that set him on the road to recover his savings, which had been greatly reduced by his divorce from Evelyn McCollum. Now another increase in pay, at Washington & Jefferson, seemed to "loom up" the most, as Heisman would say.

The Washington & Jefferson team returned solid material for Heisman to mold into a well-oiled machine in 1923. The Presidents were only two years removed from their trip to California and still smelled the sweet aroma of roses. With Heisman on board, the Presidents' alumni and boosters figured they would win the Rose Bowl when they went back again. The highly charged "college spirit" of Washington & Jefferson was refreshing to Heisman, and harkened back his memories of coaching at places such as Auburn, Clemson, and Georgia Tech.

Not everything went smoothly from the start. The rules of the day prohibited sending in a play for the next down, though sending in a signal was permitted, as long as it wasn't called until the following down. Heisman recalled sending a new player into an early-season game for the first time in 1923: "I had on the squad a chap by the name of Lyle who had never been in a real game before. One day, while playing [Bethany College of West Virginia], I sent him in to take [William] Thomas's place."[3]

"And don't forget to report to the referee!" Heisman yelled before sending Lyle onto the field.

"Report?" the player asked nervously. "What do I say?"

"Why, you tell him you are to take Thomas's place," Heisman instructed.

"Well, what do I say?" the player asked, apparently still puzzled.

"Oh, simply say, 'Lyle for Thomas,' and after one play tell Cap to run forty-eight quickly," Heisman said.

Lyle ran onto the field, repeating "Lyle for Thomas, Lyle for Thomas," to himself over and over again.

Washington & Jefferson right tackle Chet Widerquist, the team's captain, steered Lyle up to the referee and then left him.

"Who are you?" asked the referee.

"Lyle for Thomas!" Lyle shouted.

The referee grabbed the small notepad in his pocket and wrote, "Lyleford Thomas."

"Well, whose place do you take, Thomas?" the referee asked.

"Why, Lyle's place," Lyle answered. "No, I mean Thomas takes. No, I take Thomas's place. And Coach says for us to run forty-eight quickly."

The referee finally smiled and said, "Well, you can tell him that yourself after the first play, you know."

"I know!" Lyle said excitedly. "But I'm afraid I'll get it knocked clear out of my head by then, so I thought I'd better tell you about it while I can still remember it."

Despite Lyle's confusion, the Presidents opened the 1923 season with a 21–0 victory over Bethany College, a small liberal arts college in Bethany, West Virginia. The Presidents were scheduled to play Washington and Lee University of Lexington, West Virginia, at home on October 6, 1923. Shortly after the Generals arrived on campus, Murphy sent them a note that said, "W & J doesn't play unless West plays." Halfback Charles "Pruner" West was the Presidents' best player. West was an African American, and many southern colleges wouldn't permit their teams to play against black opponents until the 1930s and 1940s.

Most northern schools acquiesced to the southern teams' requests, but Heisman would have no part of it.

"Well, I won't," Heisman told Washington and Lee coach Jimmy DeHart.

"Remove him or there will be no game!" DeHart replied, before pointing to the crowd in the stands to emphasize his position, which was obviously the threat of lost revenue.

"If you don't play, you lose!" Heisman yelled.

Heisman made his demand, even though he knew West had a badly sprained ankle and probably couldn't play in the game. Heisman had an opportunity to avoid the confrontation at hand but chose to ignore it.

Heisman quickly met with Washington & Jefferson president Simon Strousse Baker, who supported his coach's position. DeHart and graduate manager Richard A. Smith telephoned Washington and Lee dean Harry Campbell, who told them that "athletes of the institution had never participated against negro athletes, and that this tradition would not be violated at this time."[4] The Generals forfeited the game by a 1–0 score. Washington & Jefferson officials handed DeHart enough money to pay for the team's train ride back to Virginia, and the "squad literally had to sneak out of town," the *Richmond (Virginia) Times-Dispatch* reported on October 9, 1923. According to the report, some players even took connecting trains to Pittsburgh so they could get out of Washington, Pennsylvania, as quickly as possible.

Smith told the *Times-Dispatch* that the Presidents had agreed to leave West off the field when the game was scheduled months in advance.

"When I made the contract with Washington & Jefferson, I did not know they had a negro player," Smith told the newspaper. "So the contract contained no reference to a situation of that character. Later, when I learned from Coach DeHart that there was a negro on Washington & Jefferson's varsity squad, I asked Coach DeHart to explain our position to the Presidents, on the occasion of the Washington and Lee's basketball trip to Washington & Jefferson last February. Coach DeHart talked with Graduate Manager Murphy and was assured, he tells me, that West would not be played against Washington and Lee."[5]

Smith sent a letter to Murphy a week before the game, reminding him of Washington and Lee's policy of not playing against African American opponents.

"I had better mention the matter which Mr. DeHart spoke to you about concerning your man West playing against us," Smith wrote. "I feel that it is useless to mention this to you, as I know you realize our geographical location and of course will not attempt to play this man. The faculty here would not allow us to schedule this game if they knew we would play against him. We realize the feeling here is different than at your school, and of course hate to bring the matter up on that account and are leaving the proposition in your hands to handle as you see fit."[6]

Murphy never responded to Smith's letter, but Heisman made the Presidents' position known before the game. Baker continued to support Heisman even after southern newspapers criticized Washington & Jefferson.

"I am sorry the unfortunate condition arose," Baker told the *Times-Dispatch*. "I respect the tradition which Washington and Lee followed in refusing to play the game, but Washington & Jefferson College is a northern school with traditions, too. It has never made any distinction against color or creed in controlling its students. Charles West, who was the cause of the controversy, has been one of the best students in the college for the last three years. He has been an honor to the school, both as a student and as an athlete, adding to its prestige by his gentlemanly conduct and his efforts as an athlete."[7]

West, who grew up in Washington, Pennsylvania, was the first African American to play quarterback in the Rose Bowl when he led the Presidents against California. West also was a nationally ranked runner and javelin thrower, coming out of nowhere to win the pentathlon at the prestigious Penn Relays at Franklin Field in Philadelphia on April 27, 1923. In addition, West was an alternate on the US track-and-field team at the 1924 Summer Olympics in Paris. After playing professional football for a couple of seasons, West enrolled in medical school at Howard University in Washington, DC, where he helped pay for his education by coaching the school's football team. He practiced medicine for nearly fifty years in Alexandria, Virginia, until his death in 1979.

Not everyone, of course, supported Heisman's decision at the time. Three days after the canceled game, the *Times-Dispatch* published an institutional editorial that said, "No Southerner blames Washington and Lee for the stand it took. Social equality has not been extended to the negro here. The negro understands that perfectly and appreciates the reason for it. There would not be the slightest difference in playing football with him and in sitting down with him at a formal dinner or meeting him for a game of golf on the country club links. College sports are purely social. And social distinctions necessarily are arbitrary. If the white man of the South declines to admit the negro to his circle, that is his particular business. The question of sportsmanship is not involved, nor is that of political rights."[8] The *Times-Dispatch* reported in the same edition that Washington and Lee had received many letters and telegrams defending its policy from individuals, colleges, and organizations, including a Ku Klux Klan chapter from North Carolina.[9]

Ironically, Heisman faced a similar dilemma while coaching at Georgia Tech. The Golden Tornado considered scheduling a game against Rutgers during the 1918 season, and then was invited to play the Scarlet Knights in a postseason game at the Polo Grounds in New York in November 1918, with gate receipts being donated to the United War Charities Fund. However, there was one obstacle in the plan, according to the *Atlanta Constitution*: "Rutgers has a star end in Robeson, but this gink happens to be of the dark skinned gentry and Tech could hardly play a game with him in the line-up."[10]

Paul Robeson was an All-America end at Rutgers from 1915 to 1919. When the Scarlet Knights hosted Washington and Lee in a game on October 14, 1916, in East Brunswick, New Jersey, the Generals demanded Robeson not play in the game. Rutgers president William Henry Steele bowed to the Generals' request, leaving his team's best player on the bench. But when the same demand was made by West Virginia at a game about a month later, Scarlet Knights coach George Sanford stood by his star player. Robeson became a Phi Beta Kappa scholar and was valedictorian of his graduating class in 1919. He attended Columbia Law School, played professional football, and became an internationally acclaimed actor and singer. He also was one of the most important civil rights activists of the early twentieth century.

Heisman's decision not to bench West, his own African American star, was an important statement of character and principle for Washington & Jefferson College, one that was due and timely. Perhaps it was easier for Heisman to make such a decision at Washington & Jefferson, where Jim Crow laws had not been ingrained in the culture for generations. Nevertheless, the decision was an important personal victory for Heisman. Through the years, Heisman had seen several young African American men aching to take the field in the major college game, only to be denied the opportunity by segregation. At last Heisman had a fine player in West, who justified his belief that anyone of abundant character, grit, and ability was welcomed on the gridiron to test his skills against the best competition. Washington & Jefferson's 1-0 victory over the Generals was recorded with an asterisk, but rather than simply footnoting a forfeit, it underscored an advance in human dignity.

While coaching at Georgia Tech, Heisman also had no patience for anti-Semitism. Al Loeb, who played center for Heisman at Tech from 1911 to 1914, was one of his favorite players. Loeb was a Jewish boy playing at a college in the South. Loeb later recalled, "I came to Georgia Tech wanting to get a degree and to play football. It was difficult, not that I couldn't understand my studies or that I couldn't play well enough on the field, I could do both well enough. It was difficult being a Jewish boy in the Bible-belted South. I took a good deal of kidding, some of it good-natured, some of it not so good, some of it outright mean. I was ready to go home that first year when Coach Heisman pulled me aside and talked with me. He spent time with me, helping me see my way through the slights and offenses, bolstering a pride in my heritage, helping me stand as a man. I wouldn't have stayed were it not for him. As each year passed the taunts became less until they were mostly gone, and only some bittersweet recollections remained. I will always be grateful to my coach for teaching such lessons of life." [11]

Perhaps galvanized by Heisman's decision regarding West, Washington & Jefferson breezed through the early part of its schedule in 1923. With West and freshman fullback Will Amos, a twenty-five-year-old World War I veteran, the Heisman shift was slowly becoming a weapon. The Presidents defeated Brown 12–7, with Amos scoring two touchdowns, and then beat Carnegie Tech 9–7. Washington & Jefferson won at Detroit 6–0 on October 27, 1923, with West scoring the game's only touchdown.

A week later the Presidents traveled by train to New York to play Lafayette at the Polo Grounds. The *New York Times* reported that the Presidents were "accompanied by the entire student body of 1,500 and the university band." [12] Heisman was concerned because his quarterback, Joe Basista, was injured, along with backup Ray McLaughlin. In front of a crowd of about twenty-five thousand fans, the Presidents took a 6–0 lead on Amos's pass to Al Haddon. But after a couple of stout defensive stops in the first half, the Presidents finally yielded late in the game. Lafayette scored a touchdown in the final minutes, but it also missed the extra-point kick, and the game ended in a 6–6 tie. Without Basista, the Presidents attempted only two passes in the game.

Washington & Jefferson recovered to wallop Waynesburg 40–0,

and then prepared for one of its biggest games of the year, at Pittsburgh on November 17, 1923. It would be the final contest in which Heisman would square off against Pop Warner, who left Pittsburgh after the 1923 season to become the coach at Stanford University. The Panthers were reeling with a 2-4 record, having lost four games in a row, and the Presidents were heavy favorites to win the game. Warner worked all week to stir his players' spirits "and get them into a mental state which would not admit defeat, that turns an ordinary player into a luminary of the first magnitude."[13] Warner brought in marching bands and former Pitt players to inspire his team.

In front of more than thirty-five thousand fans at Forbes Field in Pittsburgh, the Presidents took a 6–3 lead at the half. But Heisman didn't know that Basista, his quarterback and a hard-hitting safety, had been knocked nearly unconscious in the early minutes. Basista never admitted his condition to his coach, and continued to play in the game, even though he could remember only about 20 percent of the signals. The Panthers upset the Presidents 13–6, and Heisman accepted blame for the defeat. Washington & Jefferson's alumni and boosters were incensed by the loss, and their ire was leveled at both Heisman and his players. Heisman was hardened to criticism after thirty-one years of coaching, but his young players were not.

Four days after the loss to Pittsburgh, newspaper reports surfaced that Heisman was asked to resign as Washington & Jefferson's coach—after his *first* defeat at the school.

"This is certainly news to me, but if it is so, and football coaches are asked to resign every time they lose a football game, then there will be very few coaches left in this country," Heisman told the *Pittsburgh Chronicle-Telegram* on November 20, 1923. "I am satisfied here, the players have given me their best and there is no strife or discontentment among the squad. My contract has two more years to run and although I never cross bridges until I come to them, I don't intend to resign, in fact I have never given it a thought. Pitt defeated W. & J. and, as far as I am concerned, the incident is closed. I have lost games before and will probably lose many more before I quit coaching the game, but as far as resigning as coach at Wash-Jeff, I have no such intention." [14]

Widerquist, as captain of the team, received the most blame and was razed, criticized, and thoroughly harassed by boosters after the Pittsburgh game. Widerquist anchored the line at right tackle and was one of the country's finest linemen. Off the field, he was an attentive student and quite sensitive to unjust catcalls. One night shortly after the loss, at the height of the belligerence, Widerquist went out on the town to blow off steam. He ended up drinking all night and felt afterward that he had disgraced himself and his team and was beyond redemption. Widerquist woke up the next morning and began to pack his bags to go home.

Freshman Frank Niehaus saw what Widerquist was doing and ran to Heisman's home. Walking to Widerquist's dormitory room, Heisman thought about the tomfoolery he had witnessed young men get into over the years and knew the Pittsburgh loss and its aftermath had been difficult for his captain. Heisman ordered the rest of players out of Widerquist's room and sat down to talk with him. Heisman's message was simple: "You can leave, and all your critics will be proven right. You can stay and by doing so, let their words fall off of you like water sheds a duck. You fight one more good fight and you may graduate without regret and never wonder 'What if?' West Virginia awaits us and they haven't been beaten in twenty-two straight games. Without you I'm sure it will be twenty-three. With you, nothing is certain for West Virginia."

On Thanksgiving Day 1923, Washington & Jefferson traveled to Morgantown, West Virginia, to play the Mountaineers in the most intense rivalry game of the season. The Mountaineers' star player was halfback Nick Nardacci, who had guided them to an undefeated record and their first postseason game in 1922. Heisman knew the Presidents wouldn't have a chance to win if they didn't slow him down. Heisman recalled:

It had rained steadily for 10 days and they had practiced on it daily in that condition. Imagine its appearance. West Virginia had a great team. They had not met defeat in 22 straight games. The star of a very brilliant backfield was a chap by the name of Nardacci. A whirlwind for speed, and possessing the most poisonous "cutback" inside and outside of tackle to be found, I had repeatedly warned my men of this acute-angled cutback, but still I feared it. Five minutes after the start of the game, the Mountaineers had the ball on their own 45-yard line. The next snap went to Nardacci, and he swung toward his right end with the smoothness and aplomb of a thoroughbred. Every man behind our line promptly raced leftward to head him off. Suddenly the runner swerved and cut down inside our left tackle. He shot through our line with the speed and refraction of a chimney swallow's flight. In a jiffy four of his teammates fell in behind him and they were off for our goal with not an enemy before them. Worst of all, there seemed not to be a single Washington and Jefferson man in pursuit.[15]

But then, out of nowhere, Heisman spotted a Washington & Jefferson player sprinting down the sideline:

Who's that? It's Niehaus, our 160-pound freshman right end. He had first charged across the neutral zone, then saw the play going away from him, and, suspecting the "cutback," had wheeled and taken after the ball. I estimated Nardacci's lead on him at six yards and I yielded all hope. Not so the freshman. Like a falcon he darted after that carrier pigeon. Then ensured a race of sheer desperation, superhuman effort and ecstatic thrills that can have no superior in sport. How that freshman ran! Nardacci's speed, his heart-breaking lead, his four rear guards, and clammy, clinging mud failed utterly to daunt that freshman's soul. No thought of how appallingly silly he would look when bopped about in the mud by those West Virginia blockers had the power to dismay the brave lad. Intrepidly he accepted his responsibility and magnificently he tried the depths alone. Deaf to the noise of friend and foe alike, responsive only to the hammering beats of his own courageous heart, the freshman strove like a "god."[16]

With Niehaus chasing him, Nardacci seemed to run out of gas and slowed. Heisman recalled Niehaus drawing even with Nardacci's blockers and penetrating them "like a searing iron." He pulled Nardacci down at Washington & Jefferson's five-yard line, saving a touchdown. Inspired by the effort of their freshman, the Presidents stiffened and the Mountaineers couldn't score. Washington & Jefferson won the game 7–2, ending West Virginia's long winning streak. Widerquist and Niehaus led several goal-line stands in which Nardacci was stopped short of the goal line. "Nick Nardacci, hero of a dozen West Virginia victories, was weak today," the *New York Times* reported. "It was his fumble on the West Virginia 10-yard line in the second period that put W. and J. in the position to score and on the sixth play Amos crashed through the Mountaineers' line for the only touchdown of the game."[17]

On the way out of Morgantown, West stopped at a store, where he saw a display in the window of a Sambo-like black doll being carried by a stretcher to an ambulance. A sign read, "The ambulance is ready for you, Mr. West." West asked the storeowner if he could have the display when he was done with it. The embarrassed storeowner gave it to him on the spot.[18]

Washington & Jefferson finished 6-1-1 in Heisman's first season, and with its talent and school spirit, it was probably a place where Heisman could finish his career. The Presidents had been adept at learning his Heisman shift, and many of his best players were coming back the next season. Washington & Jefferson's administration realized the benefits of having a strong football program, as the school's enrollment was steadily increasing from the notoriety it received from the sport.

Yet Washington & Jefferson's meddling boosters weren't nearly satisfied with Heisman's work. In late December 1923, Heisman received a letter from his old friend Dr. Kenneth G. Matheson, the president of Drexel University. Matheson wrote:

> I wish also to congratulate you most cordially on the splendid success of your first football season at Washington and Jefferson. To lose only one game by a close score is success of the highest order, and I am sure that the officials and students of your college have sense enough to appreciate your skill and experience. I read some time ago the action of W & J alumni gamblers who were sore over the one defeat suffered by your team this season. I was both very indignant and amused, and I realized that such squealing on the part of the sufferers would not hurt your standing with the college, or even with the sensible alumni, who, let us hope, are in the majority. I hope and believe your career at W & J will be highly successful, and that you will be increasingly appreciated for your exceptional work.[19]

After the season, Cadwallader M. Barr, a former Pennsylvania state senator and president of the Washington & Jefferson College Alumni Association of Western Pennsylvania, was compelled to send a letter to the club's members, asking for patience with Heisman, who by this point must have felt like his first Presidents team finished 1-6-1:

> To me it does not seem that the right hand of fellowship was uniformly extended to the "stranger within our gates." It appears to me that public and press have jumped on Heisman

with unusual severity, forgetting that he was a stranger to this neck of the woods. He had no knowledge of the personnel of our own team, the teams which we played, the people, the papers, the officials nor the working condition which he found among us. It is no easy task to coach at Washington. He met with unusual misfortune in that his players encountered an unprecedented run of accidents almost from the first day of the season. Above all and over all, it seems to me, the question of whether Heisman is or is not a "miracle man" as a coach, is far from being the most important consideration before us. When W. & J. went out to look for a coach last winter, its president and athletic association were unanimously minded that what they wanted was a man who would live and act right, and who would inculcate the correct spirit of sport and sportsmanship. With this idea in mind they searched far and wide before they decided that in John W. Heisman they had found such a man. The best testimony that I am able to secure shows that Heisman came through the past season at W. & J. in fine shape as to the question of moral influence, of right living and of sportsmanly conduct. My information, gleamed from many sources, gives Heisman a 100 percent bill of health in this respect. His influence for good on the players has been fine and wholesome. Their sportsmanship has improved immeasurably.[20]

Without warning, Heisman returned to Washington & Jefferson's campus on February 18, 1924, to meet with members of the school's Council Committee on Coaches and Managers. Heisman requested to be relieved from completion of his three-year contract. The details of his departure were rather vague, although it is clear that he felt he didn't have the full support of the school's boosters, creating a toxic environment for his coaches and players. Later that night Washington & Jefferson released a statement that read:

Mr. Heisman requested that he be relieved from the remainder of his three-year coaching contract. A thoroughly amicable discussion of his request ensued, and, after hearing his reasons the committee acceded to his request. Both the council and Mr. Heisman wish to state that there has been and will be no breach whatsoever in their friendly relations. W. and J. and Coach Heisman go their respective ways, each with the best wishes for the other.[21]

Although Heisman coached at Washington & Jefferson for only one season, he still left an indelible mark on the institution. At a ceremony honoring West in September 2011, Washington & Jefferson president Tori Haring-Smith said the incident with Washington and Lee University in 1923 reflected the school's principles of "uncommon integrity that we teach our graduates to emulate. We tell Charles West's story all the time here, and his picture is all over campus."[22]

West's daughter Linda West Nickens said that her father remembered Heisman's gesture throughout his life. "It took a lot of courage, but W & J stood by its tradition of integrity," she said.[23]

CHAPTER FIFTEEN

Rice Institute

Rice Institute in Houston was the dream of millionaire businessman William Marsh Rice, who made his fortune in real estate,
cotton trading, and railroad development in Louisiana and
Texas in the late nineteenth century. Upon his death, Rice wanted
a school opened bearing his name, in which its students would
receive free tuition. Rice was found dead in his New York apartment on September 23, 1900, and authorities initially believed the
eighty-four-year-old man died in his sleep of natural causes. Weeks
later, Rice's attorney, Albert T. Patrick, cashed a large check from
Rice, and it was soon discovered that the deceased man changed
his will shortly before his death, leaving his fortune to Patrick instead of an endowment for the school. An investigation by New
York's district attorney proved that Rice's valet, Charles F. Jones,
poisoned him with chloroform under Patrick's instructions.[1] After
Patrick's conviction, Rice's fortune of $10 million was finally be-
queathed to the school, which opened in 1912 as the William
Marsh Rice Institute for the Advancement of Literature, Arts, and
Science.

Rice fielded its first football team the same year it opened its
doors, and Phil Arbuckle, a former University of Chicago player
under Amos Alonzo Stagg, guided the Owls to a 3-2 record. The
Owls were charter members of the Southwest Conference in 1915—

after Louisiana State declined an invitation—and had some success in the new league. Rice went 8-1 in 1919, after Arbuckle returned to the sideline for a second time, but finished fourth or worse in the Southwest Conference standings in each of the next four seasons. Arbuckle resigned after a 3-5 finish in 1923. William Ward Watkin, chairman of the Committee on Outdoor Sports, was charged with finding a new coach, and Rice's students and alumni wanted a proven winner who could deliver conference championships and defeat bitter in-state rivals Texas and Texas A&M.

Watkin, an architect and University of Pennsylvania graduate, learned that Heisman was unhappy with his situation at Washington & Jefferson. During a meeting with Watkin in New York on February 3, 1924, Heisman laid out his grandiose demands: He wanted a five-year contract and $9,000 annual salary, but would live in Houston only during the football season and a few weeks in the spring. Because of Heisman's expanding role with a sporting goods business, he wanted to live in New York for most of the year. Watkin was alarmed at the proposal because even though Heisman was willing to accept a $1,000 reduction in salary, he would still be paid more than any Rice professor—and for only part-time work, no less.

Shortly after interviewing Heisman, Watkin sent the following telegram to Rice Institute president Edgar Odell Lovett:

> After conference lasting five hours I have following impression that Heisman is sound steady experienced and anxious to come South. He is now considering two Southern offers and one Western evidently Oregon. These offers are higher than his present salary. I am convinced I stirred his enthusiasm for Texas and the Institute. Have following definite agreement subject to our acceptance. He will come one month for spring practice beginning in March and between three four months in fall and will take general responsibility for all assistant coaches and teams as athletic director. I believe it only a ques-

tion of time till he would decide to withdraw from New York business and stay all year. Salary $9,000 and contract five years with clause providing we may have option on his service after five years for any length of time without increase salary. He wants to change only once again and that for a Southern job. He now gives only three months at Washington [& Jefferson] for $10,000.[2]

On February 7, 1924, Rice bursar J. T. McCants sent a telegram to Watkin on behalf of Lovett: "President is making progress with original recommendation. Trustees favorably impressed but embarrassed by contract feature and age of candidate."[3]

In the end, the Owls couldn't pass on a coach of Heisman's pedigree, and couldn't find a candidate of similar experience and accomplishments who was willing to take the job on a year-round basis. During a meeting with Heisman in New Orleans on February 11, 1924, Patrick agreed to all of Heisman's terms.[4]

The *Thresher*, Rice's student newspaper, produced a special edition announcing Heisman's hiring on February 19, 1924, the day after he resigned as Washington & Jefferson's coach:

Twenty-nine years as boss on the gridiron! That is one of the many things that J. W. Heisman will bring with him to Rice. Heisman has played football, studied football and made football teams. Many elevens have met with phenomenal success under the coaching of the veteran expert who brings to Rice a coaching prestige not enjoyed by many southern institutions. In his years of experience the new Owl coach has learned men—southern men and northern men. He knows his crowd and is especially fond of southern university life. His desire to return to the South was one of the things that enabled William Ward Watkin to secure his services in the face of the bidding of a dozen other schools.[5]

Shortly after Heisman's hiring was announced, he sent a telegram to the *Thresher* that read: "Greetings to Rice and student body. Everybody roll up sleeves and let's go."[6]

The *Thresher* also put out a campuswide call for football players that couldn't have encouraged the Owls' new coach: "Heisman is one of the outstanding football authorities in America today. He ranks with Rockne, Stagg, Percy, Haughton, Glenn Warner and Dobie—BUT does that mean that we are to expect too much of him? Do we realize that the success of next year's athletics depends a great deal upon US—the students? A lot of blowing is not going to help matters any. Men are needed—men who will work, men who are not yellow, men OFF PROBATION, real honest-to-God he-men with a love for Rice and a willingness to do something once in a while besides sleep, study occasionally, and eat in the mess hall. Heisman needs men—Will Heisman get them?"[7]

It didn't take Heisman long to realize that finding those kind of men wouldn't be easy at Rice. Because of the school's stringent academic requirements, finding football players who would be admitted to Rice—and, just as important, stay enrolled—was a very arduous task. In July 1924, while Heisman was living in New York, he received a letter from Edward Wademan, a Rice alumnus, who was in charge of helping the Owls recruit prospective students:

> Just a word today, because I'm busy as thunder preparing to get away tomorrow for a little vacation. I'm sorry to report to you that so far this summer I have done practically nothing on this new athletes job. Somehow, I just haven't been able to stir up the interest and enthusiasm I had for the work last year. When I return in August we will knuckle down for the following three or four weeks and see if we can't do any good. Meanwhile, I hope that you are having a real vacation, and that you will return well rested, recuperated, and invigorated.

Not that you especially need any of those things—but still that's what a vacation is supposed to do![8]

Heisman wrote back to Wademan a few weeks later, trying to stress the importance of recruiting potential football players: "Good teams can be turned out without assistance from the alumni, but not with the frequency that the alumni demand. I have no illusions on this point. I have coached at my share of colleges where nobody manifested concern for the approaching football season. It is hard enough to coach where the material exists."[9]

Going into the job, Heisman knew Rice would have to compete against more established football programs—the Longhorns played football for the first time in 1893, and the Aggies started the next year—with better resources, more alumni, and stronger connections to Texas high schools. Texas colleges such as Baylor, Southern Methodist, Sam Houston State, and Trinity University were getting their share of homegrown players as well. Besides his failed venture into tomato farming three decades earlier, Heisman had spent very little time in the state and knew few of the high school coaches.

The *Houston Post* summarized Heisman's challenge heading into the 1924 season:

> It takes man power in these days of fierce competition to win football championships, and, in comparison with S.M.U. and Texas University, Rice's man power is woefully weak. From time to time, Rice gets a number of star high school athletes, but few can make the scholastic grade. Be it said to the credit of Rice Institution and its officials, that the school maintains high scholastic standards. Scholarship ever should be placed above athletics. Better by far that a University be weak in athletics and strong in scholarship, than that the reverse be the case. If a star football player can't play football and make his

courses, then it's just too bad for the football team. Houston and former Rice students have waited patiently for the development of a winning football team at the Institute. Back in the years prior to the war, Rice gathered a team, which in four years ranked right at the conference top. A.&M. was no nemesis for it, by any means; and the Texas Longhorns were finally beaten. However, there must be a reason somewhere. Is it that a strict abiding by the letter and the spirit of the amateur sports rules keeps Rice at a disadvantage with other schools? Is it that the Rice alumni make less effort to attract athletic students than is the case at other schools? Is it that the severity of entrance requirements at the institution works to eliminate the students who are most interested in athletics? Is it that the scholarship standards are so high that the man giving a good deal of his time to sports fails to meet them? Is it that less favoritism in class is shown the athletes at Rice than at other colleges? No one can ask for victory all the time; but surely this second-rate rank need not be accepted as final, unless indeed Rice is determined not to play the fame of college sports like it is played generally, and in that case she should so announce to the world. If she accepts the rules and the practices of the game, she should win. We have the confidence in her strength to expect that of her.[10]

In the summer of 1924, Heisman tried his best to attract talented players to Rice. He was able to persuade Ed Herting, a bruising fullback from Hartford, Connecticut, to enroll in the school. But as soon as Herting chose to play for the Owls, Alex C. Humphreys, president of Stevens Institute of Technology in Hoboken, New Jersey, objected to Heisman "poaching" high school players from the Northeast. Humphreys complained to the NCAA president, General Palmer E. Pierce, who wrote Watkin a concerned letter. Watkin told Heisman he thought it would be a "great mistake" under the circumstances to bring any athletes from the Northeast to Rice. Even if the Owls recruited the players properly, Watkin argued, they would be accused of improper recruiting. Watkin was a firm believer that there was no room for "proselyting" in intercollegiate athletics.[11] Herting enrolled at Rice and was one of the Owls' best players, but he was one of only three players on Heisman's first team from outside Texas.

With the odds stacked against him, Heisman went to work at Rice, doing what he knew best: teaching, exhorting, prodding, and demanding the best of his team. Despite returning only seven varsity players from the 1923 team, Rice won three of its first four games in Heisman's first season, including a come-from-behind 7–3 victory at TCU and a 19–6 upset of Texas. It was the Owls' first victory over the Longhorns since 1917—Texas had won the previous three games by a combined score of 112–0—and only the second in school history. The Owls won the game even though team captain Harvey Smith was recovering from the flu and had to leave the game after three quarters because of dehydration. "Big" Bill McVey of Cleveland was recovering from the chicken pox, and George Morgan and Joe Heyck were dealing with bouts of boils.[12]

" 'The eyes of Texas' are bleary," the *San Antonio Express* reported on November 3, 1924. "Rice Institute students Saturday afternoon and night shook the equanimity of every Texas University student and alumnus—the Ricers 'painted the town blue.' Coach John W. Heisman of the Owls was the center of more talk Saturday night and Sunday than either candidate for Governor, notwithstanding the fact that Jim Ferguson spoke here. President E. O. Lovett of Rice is in Europe. Some wag remarked, 'If Lovett doesn't hurry back here he'll find Heisman in the president's chair when he returns.' "[13]

Apparently Heisman even had to motivate his players to overcome the color of Texas's jerseys before he could convince them they could win. Heisman later recalled,

In my first year at Rice, we won a remarkable victory from a powerful opponent because I had succeeded in bringing my team to a fighting pitch few opposing teams in the country could that day have overcome. I had frequently been told that the Rice players invariably had the game scared out of them by the very sight of the brilliant orange sweaters the other team wore. Well, the text of my talk was this little matter of school colors. I stated I had been told how they became hopeless the instant they saw that rival team come out on the field in those flashing orange or yellow suits, or whatever colors they were. Then I eulogized their own matchless colors, blue and gray, [which were] noble, historic, resplendent. I scouted the idea that such colors could be routed by any shade of yellow. I refused to believe that any honest wearer of Union blue and Confederate gray could ever "quit" while there was a man of them left alive; those colors must make heroes even of cravens. Splendor of God! What a response they gave! The visitors [were] never in the game at any stage.[14]

Unfortunately for Heisman, upsetting Texas in 1924 would be the high point of his Rice career. The Owls lost to Austin College 6–2 the next week, the first of three consecutive losses to finish the season. Overall, Heisman was pleased with his team's 4-4 record in 1924, given its mediocre level of talent and the fact that it had to absorb his offense so quickly.

"To begin with there was not a great quantity of material, either experienced or inexperienced, in college," Heisman wrote after the 1924 season.

This lack was felt keenly throughout the season. For, though the coaches in the end managed to put up a reasonable looking first line up, the second string men were so far behind the first string players that any substitution instantly spelled a decided weakening in the team's offensive and defensive strength; and it was through such unavoidable weakenings that the team usually went down to defeat in the four games it lost. Then too a large percentage of the regulars were too light for a Varsity team, notwithstanding a few of the men were quite as heavy as players need to be. Still worse was the fact that the team did not have composite speed. As a rule light men are at least fast. Ours were no faster than the heavy man, and compared to the fast men of opposition teams they could not be accounted as being in a class with their foes. Certainly no man in the Rice backfield would have any business on a cinder path.[15]

The Owls would go 4-4-1 in each of the next two seasons, losing each of their four Southwest Conference games in 1926. There were a few bright spots, such as defeating Arkansas 13–9 on October 17, 1925. Center Wash "Heavy" Underwood of Honey Grove, Texas, who was captain of the 1925 and 1926 teams, was one of Heisman's best players. Underwood "could snap on a bee-line of a distance of thirty-three yards and so accurately that the receiver could get it while kneeling. This *is* some snapping," Heisman wrote.[16] Of course, Underwood's talent would catch Heisman's eye as one who had snapped in the middle of the line himself.

With so little talent and depth, Rice struggled to compete against opponents such as Loyola–New Orleans and Trinity, let alone its more powerful Southwest Conference opponents. Adding to Rice's plight was the fact that many of Heisman's players were struggling to remain in school. In the spring of 1925, the *Thresher* reported that of the fifty-two student-athletes of "recognized worth" who lived in dormitories, twenty-three had either flunked out or been placed on academic probation in the previous two academic terms. Conversely, only five of the twenty-six players who lived at home or somewhere else off-campus ran into academic difficulties.[17] Heisman's solution was to place all of his players living on campus in one dormitory. The

Owls took over East Hall, where there were rules prohibiting smoking, drinking alcohol, and entertaining visitors during study hall. It was the first athletics dorm in college sports. Heisman also came up with another method of getting his players to study—he had them grow beards so they would be less attractive to female students.[18]

Heading into the 1927 season, Heisman probably realized that the end of his coaching career was near. Once again, the Owls were undersized and too thin to compete in the rugged Southwest Conference. The Owls opened the season going 1-1-1 in their first three games, then dropped five games in a row, including a 27–0 loss at Texas and a 14–0 loss to Texas A&M.

The writing seemed to be on the wall, *Houston Post* columnist Lloyd Gregory reported late in the 1927 season: "John W. Heisman, head coach of the Owls, and a veteran of something like 37 years in this wearing, tearing game of football, apparently is slated to go as head coach after this fall. We are in no [way] authorized to speak for Mr. Heisman, but we have an idea that he will be ready to step aside, if the Rice athletic council feels that he should. His term at Rice has been filled with disappointments, some of which he himself was responsible for, but many for which he was not responsible. Too, Mr. Heisman has reached an age where he can not hope much longer to coach football."[19]

Before the Owls played their finale, against Baylor at Rice Field on November 24, 1927, Heisman walked into their locker room to give his pregame speech. He told his players:

> Boys, 36 years ago this fall, I coached my first team, and we won from Ohio State University our first game. You are the last team I shall coach and this is my last game as coach. Having started my career with a win, you surely can guess how I would like to close it. I can foresee what it will mean to me in the years to come to be able to look back on this day coupled with a clean victory, rather than a defeat that ended

my life's efforts. Never before have I asked you to play for me, but only for your college. But if I have ever done anything for which you incline to think you owe me so little, I will appreciate it an hundred fold if you will square the debt today by putting forth the best effort of your lives.[20]

It was a day Heisman would remember fondly. After the teams were tied 6–6 at the half, the Owls scored two touchdowns in the third quarter to win, 19–6. Felix "Spud" Braden, playing in his first varsity game, scored a touchdown that put Rice ahead for good.

"They played much their best game of the year and achieved the victory I had asked," Heisman later wrote. "Then they told me it was my talk that did the trick."[21]

Six days later, Heisman submitted a four-paragraph resignation letter to Lovett, in which he expressed his "very deep appreciation of your many courtesies and the high consideration which you and the Trustees have always accorded me."[22]

Just like that, Heisman's coaching career was finished. His love affair with football, however, was far from over.

CHAPTER SIXTEEN

New York

S hortly after resigning as Rice Institute's head coach in December 1927, Edith and John Heisman returned to their home at 28 East Seventieth Street in New York. For the previous several years, Heisman had lived much like a northern snowbird, traveling to the South to coach during the fall and spring and then returning to New York for rest in the winter and a cooler summer. Heisman was never one to sit idle for very long, so he started a project of enormous scope nearly as soon as he retired from coaching. He called it "Heisman's Hundred in the Football Hall of Fame." Heisman compiled his personal hall of fame of legendary college football players, writing a short biography for each player and an overview of his gridiron career. Heisman's hall of fame was published in dozens of newspapers and magazines across the country.

Heisman had always been a prolific writer, and even though his coaching career ended poorly at Rice Institute, he was still considered one of the leading authorities on college football. While coaching at Georgia Tech from 1904 to 1919, Heisman was a regular columnist for the *Atlanta Constitution* and the *Atlanta Journal*, which were competing newspapers in the Southeast's largest media market at the time. Each season, Heisman selected the All-Southern Eleven, an all-star team of the best players from southern colleges, and even ranked teams in the Southern Intercollegiate Athletic Association, including his own. The majority of Heisman's columns were written to be educational for his readers, whether they were about rules changes in football or how to steal bases in baseball. But the *Constitution* even allowed him to write analyses about his own teams, a practice that would certainly be considered a conflict of interest in today's journalism. In one of his first articles for the *Constitution*, Heisman wrote about Tech's 3–2 loss to Mercer's baseball team on March 28, 1903: "As in yesterday's game, Tech greatly outhit Mercer, outran them on the bases, and broke even with them on fielding, and yet she lost. This was largely due to the extreme cleverness of the Mercer batters, who, in both games, contrived to be hit by the Tech pitchers in unheard of numbers."[1]

On October 27, 1907, a day after the Yellow Jackets football team lost to Auburn 12–6 at Ponce de Leon Park in Atlanta, Heisman wrote, "I don't suppose anyone who saw the game doubts that Tech would have won the contest had she not fumbled the ball so atrociously. She was able to go through Auburn's line most anywhere and around the ends for starting gains, but the Tech men just couldn't keep from fumbling and Auburn was always there to fall on it. Of course, Auburn's second touchdown was in the nature of a place of good luck or a fluke, but all those things are in the game nowadays."[2]

So much for objective sports coverage.

More than a decade later, when Heisman was coaching at the University of Pennsylvania, he authored a series of twenty-eight columns for the *Macon Telegraph* during the 1920 season. The newspaper announced the series on October 17, 1920: "John W. Heisman, author of the famous Heisman jump shift, used by Georgia Tech football elevens of the past decade and variously known as the 'wizard of the gridiron' and the 'father of the forward pass,' will, beginning with Monday's edition of the *Telegraph*, begin a series of 28 football articles, written especially for the *Telegraph* and which will deal with every phase of the famous branch of sport, both from a theoretical and practical standpoint. No one coach or football authority in the country is as capable of writing these stories as is John Heisman. His twenty-five years of experience with football machines as player and coach stamp him as an authority extraordinary."[3]

During Heisman's final season of coaching the Quakers, in 1922, his most ambitious literary work, *Principles of Football*, a 376-page book, was published by Sports Publishing Bureau of St. Louis, Missouri. In the book, which was in many ways a football manual for novices and experienced players and coaches alike, Heisman offered instructions on tackling, passing, signaling, and kicking. He also explained the nuances of the Heisman shift and other formations, and offered coaches and players tips on proper training, practicing, and treatment for injuries. A promotional flyer for Heisman's book read, "The book is a perfect compendium of coaching facts, methods, hints, and ideas. In direct and simple language, but in terse form the author discloses the playing principles that he expounds to his players and the methods he employs to bring them that splendid knowledge and superb mental grasp of the games essentials for which his teams have always been noted."[4] The book was reprinted in 1999.

In 1932, Heisman and the legendary sportswriter Grantland Rice, who was sports editor of the *Atlanta Journal* and who had famously depicted Notre Dame's backfield as the "Four Horsemen" for the *New York Herald Tribune* in 1924, coauthored *Understand Football*, a sixty-three-page book published by General Foods Corporation.

Over the years, Heisman's writing also appeared in newspapers such as the *Cleveland Plain Dealer*, the *New Orleans Times-Picayune*, and the *Seattle Daily Times*. At one point Heisman's work was syndicated by the North American Newspaper Alliance. In 1927 Heisman signed with King Features Syndicates, Inc., which syndicated "Heisman's Hundred in the Football Hall of Fame." According to Heisman's records, he signed a contract on the same day he delivered his manuscript.

Collier's Weekly, one of the country's most widely circulated magazines, was impressed enough with Heisman's work to sign him up for two years. Heisman wrote a series of articles for the magazine, nearly all of which consisted of a few thousand words and included anecdotes, funny stories, and his recollections of playing and coaching. Believe it or not, much of Heisman's writing was based on his own reporting. While writing for *Collier's Weekly*, Heisman sent a letter to hundreds of high school and college football coaches and former players around the country, asking them to recall their most cherished moments in the sport. Heisman started each letter the same way:

> Do you owe anything to football? If you do here's where you can square it. To round out and preserve certain phases of the history of our great American game, I desire to chronicle true tales of the gridiron—incidents of lofty sportsmanship, humorous episodes and sayings, and freak and unusual occurrences—that took place either in games or in practice. Do you enjoy human-interest narrations from your favorite game? Then make a "clearing house" of me for swapping these delightful tales. Won't they make wonderful reading for the next generation, to say nothing of the present crop of old-timers and youngsters? Think just a moment. You're bound to know of some interesting gridiron happenings never before published. Won't you write and tell me of one or two you have heard or that came under your personal observation? I ask you to help me build up, in permanent form, the literature of our glorious game. Make it as terse as you like, but, where possible, give full names, addresses, teams, date and place, how it came about, what followed—such details as a reader would like to know. And, if you're willing, I'd like to give you credit for your story. In any case, drop me a line—I'll gladly reply. Who knows? Maybe someday I'll be able to do something for you. Try me.[5]

In some cases, Heisman wanted details of a specific play, game, or incident and would send a questionnaire to a coach or a player. For instance, legendary Notre Dame head coach Knute Rockne replied to Heisman's request for details about George Gipp's famous drop kick against Western State Normal School (now Western Michigan) in 1917. Among the questions Heisman asked Rockne about the kick were: Ball was wet or dry? Was the kick high? Wind was with or against the kick?[6] Michigan coach Bennie Oosterbaan replied to a request for information about his own playing career, and University of Chicago head coach Amos Alonzo Stagg provided details about the Maroons' game against Nebraska in 1906.

Men *and* women seemed to enjoy reading Heisman's stories in *Collier's Weekly* and later *American Liberty.* One female reader asked Heisman for more details about what actually happened in the locker room at halftime and after games: "I have read with considerable interest the various articles you have had in Collier's concerning football, and I have just finished reading 'Hero Stuff,' written in your usual interesting style. But—I've heard a number of my girlfriends complain with me that a girl never gets an opportunity to 'be on the inside.' Know what I mean? What happens between halves in the dressing room? What do boys talk about? How do they regard each other? We want the personal touch, the things you men can find out by dropping in on these fellows once in a while. Being girls, we, of course, cannot do that, and must depend upon second-hand information." She added the following postscript: "The truth, and nothing but the truth, please, Mr. Heisman."[7]

Even the most seasoned journalists make mistakes from time to time, and Heisman was no exception. In a story for *Collier's Weekly* in October 1929, he told the tale of Frank Hertz, a brilliant halfback on the 1925 Carroll College team. In a game against Lake Forest, Hertz clipped a blocker, breaking his own leg in the process. Heisman wrote that Hertz was taken to a hospital by ambulance and was later visited by members of the Lake Forest team. "I don't deserve your sympathy," Heisman quoted Hertz as saying. "You've been too decent to me. All this kindness. You've got to know the truth. The truth is that I clipped him. You can break a fellow's leg that way, you know. I clipped him. See? I don't deserve sympathy."

About a month later, Hertz, who then was the athletic director at Iron River High School in Iron River, Michigan, wrote a letter to Heisman: "I am much in the position of the man—who to the mail-order advertisement—took one lesson on the piano and held his audience spellbound. And again stealing a line from the advertiser, 'imagine my surprise' when recently I learned that, repenting of my sins, I had broken down, before a hospital room full of people, and sobbed out a tearful story of transgression. It was very nice of you, but very awkward for me, because ever since that reference appeared in *Collier's* I have been trying to tell an admiring and constantly increasing army of people that it was all a lot of hooey. What I am particularly interested in, however, is in learning 'how come' all that—where from?"[8]

A correction never appeared in *Collier's Weekly*, but Heisman did respond to Hertz's letter, writing, "Frankly, it's a hard one to answer, but your tone and attitude, both in the letter and in your interview with the newspaper representative disclose you as a thorough gentleman and that will make it somewhat easier. It is, of course, plain to you that I did not see the game of which I wrote. Nor do I know anything of the incident narrated save what was told to me by a highly estimable gentleman living in Lake Forest and who did see the game and was, apparently, most familiar with the details of the alleged incident. You are bound to know I could not make up the incident out of whole cloth. I sincerely trust that you won't suffer too great annoyance from the incident, and I beg to tender you a full apology in the event that your feelings have been injured in any way; I am not that kind of fellow."[9]

In 1929, Heisman was also writing for *Sporting Goods Journal*, a specialty magazine for salesmen of sporting goods. It was a subject Heisman was certainly qualified to write about. For several years while living in New York, Heisman worked with Alex Taylor & Company, which was perhaps the country's first sporting goods firm to sell equipment directly to high schools and colleges with traveling salesmen. The company had a retail store on East Forty-Second Street in New York and also had a mail-order business. Working at Alex Taylor & Company allowed Heisman to keep up with the latest innovations in equipment, which was something he really enjoyed. He helped develop a new valve for footballs, which he introduced at the football rules committee meeting in New York on March 9, 1923. The valve made "it possible to do the lacing and insure a clean job before the ball is inflated. So far as could be judged it is a big improvement over the old method of lacing the ball after it has been blown up. Besides being easy to inflate the new valve distributes the weight more equitably, which makes the ball travel more truly whether from kick or forward pass." [10]

Heisman also invented his own football board game, which was patented on September 19, 1905. The patent application indicates Heisman intended for the game "to provide means whereby the field game of foot-ball can be simulated to a considerable extent in an indoor game." The idea included a game board, mechanical counter for keeping downs and yards, and six receptacles which included "center plays, tackle plays, end runs, tricks, punts, try-at-goal, and kickoff." [11] It appears that the board game was never fully developed.

While writing for *Sporting Goods Journal*, Heisman offered innovative and aggressive ideas for the salesmen, who called on stores, high schools, and colleges, as well as local youth teams. He also had ingenious ideas for getting rid of dead inventory: "Put the idea into the coaches' heads that the overstock in the store (which they can't unload) could be had at a bargain, a few cents on the dollar, and used for the Frosh, the Scrubs, and scrimmages in inclement weather. I always found this to save loads of money, and the boys fought over the bright mismatched colorful jerseys. The coach will be so grateful that you'll get his full order for the rest of the team, including balls, tackling dummies, and larger ticket items." [12]

Just as with his writing career, Heisman knew how to play from both sides of the fence.

Epilogue

L ate in September 1936, on a cool, autumn day, Heisman enjoyed
a round of golf with some friends from the club. He had become
an avid golfer in recent years, thanks to the tutelage of Robert
Jones Jr., who had given Heisman his first set of clubs. After only
a couple of years of playing, Heisman was already nearly a scratch
player. On this day, though, he was not having his best round and
was pestered by a persistent cough. One of Heisman's playing part-
ners suggested that he see a doctor, but Heisman waved it off, saying
the cold was nothing and would clear up soon. As was Heisman's
custom after any exercise, he went home and took a cold shower.
It was a ritual he always insisted of his players at southern colleges,
but places such as Atlanta, Auburn, Alabama, and Clemson, South
Carolina, weren't apt to get cold snaps like New York. Still, Heisman stuck to his spartan-like routine and braved the cold waters. His
cough worsened.

Edith Heisman helped her husband to bed and called for a doctor.
The doctor said Heisman's cough was actually a nasty bout of pneumonia. Penicillin and other antibiotics wouldn't be mass-produced
in the United States until 1942, so there was little a physician could
do besides prescribe rest and the consumption of lots of fluids. The
only medical treatment at the time was taking sulfur pills, which

was a dangerous proposition. If a patient received the right dose of sulfur, it stimulated the body's antigens to fight harmful bacteria. But the wrong dose could make a patient's condition worse or even lead to death. Much like a forward pass, three things could happen after taking sulfur pills, and two of them were bad. Heisman took the medicine.

On October 3, 1936, Heisman lost a nine-day battle with pneumonia. He was sixty-six years old. After a funeral in New York, he was buried in Rhinelander, Wisconsin, near the state's upper peninsula, which had become the couple's summer home. Edith Heisman moved to Rhinelander to live with her sister after her husband's death and died there on November 19, 1963.

John Heisman's obituary in the *New York Times* described him as an "all-around authority on athletics and former football coach. . . . He was the originator of the 'Heisman shift' and was said to be the first to suggest the introduction of the forward pass into football. He was also the inventor of many methods used in modern football."[1]

Perhaps more than any other man, Heisman changed the face of the game America passionately loves. His documented and credited contributions include:

- Seven-man interference—In 1892, Heisman moved the quarterback back to safety on defense and brought the fullback up behind the defensive linemen, essentially creating the position of middle linebacker.
- Tossing the snap—In 1893, because his quarterback was too tall to pick the football from the ground, Heisman had his center snap the ball through the air.
- Hidden ball trick—Heisman's 1895 Auburn team surprised Vanderbilt by hiding the ball under a player's jersey, a trick play that was quickly outlawed.
- Doubling through the center—One of Heisman's favorite plays,

which was first developed in 1896 and which was the forerunner of the counter play.

- Introducing "Hike!"—Until 1898, teams started a play by sight or touch signal. Heisman introduced the audible signal of "Hike!"
- Lateral pass—The play developed in 1899 was a revival of an older offensive weapon, which became the double lateral pass that warped around defensive ends. The play would evolve into the still popular option play.
- The forward pass—Even though Heisman didn't create the play, it was perhaps his greatest contribution to the game. He first approached the rules committee about adopting the forward pass in 1903 and argued for its inclusion in the rules each year afterward.
- The spin buck—First introduced by Heisman in 1910, the spin buck was a play executed through a series of fake pitches, passes, or handoffs until the back promoting the fakes spun into the line, which was then vacated by misdirection. The play became a foundation of the full house, wishbone, and single-wing backfields.
- The Heisman shift—Heisman's most feared offensive system, which, while legal, succeeded in overwhelming defenses by confusion. The shift's success rested on players jumping into a new formation in the split second prior to the snap of the ball. The confusion the shift created for defenses allowed an offense to catch its opponent off guard. The Heisman shift and its imitators were eventually legislated out of the game.
- Scoreboard—He introduced the first scoreboard with downs and distance, which reduced and then eliminated spectators walking onto the field.
- Quarters—Heisman proposed dividing the game into quarters, which gave players times to rest and helped reduce the number of football-related injuries across the country.
- Equipment—He helped develop padded equipment, such as playing pants with pockets for pads, which were specifically

designed according to human anatomy, which Heisman studied extensively.

- American Football Coaches Association—Heisman, with Major Charles D. Daly and Amos Alonzo Stagg, founded the AFCA in 1921. Heisman served as president of the association in 1923 and 1924. The coaches association exists today, working to improve coaches through ongoing education, interaction, and networking. The AFCA membership now includes more than eleven thousand people associated with the sport.

Some of Heisman's best ideas were never approved when he was coaching but became football staples several years later. In 1922 he proposed an extra period known as "overtime" to settle tied games. "Coach Heisman's plan calls for a short period of play after games ending in tied scores, during which each eleven would be given the ball for three plays," the *Baltimore American* reported on December 28, 1922. "The team gaining the most ground on its first three plays would be given an extra point."[2] Overtime wouldn't be introduced in college football until 1996. In the 1920s, Heisman also recommended dividing the country's college football teams into three divisions to make competition more equitable. He proposed dividing the teams into "First Rank," "Second Rank," and "Third Rank," based on "over 40 years of close contact with most of them and through the keeping of a watchful eye of their performances during the past 40 years."[3] Today the NCAA designates its teams under four divisions: Football Bowl Subdivision, Football Championship Subdivision, Division II, and Division III.

In the days after Heisman's death, the Downtown Athletic Club unanimously voted to rename its award the John W. Heisman Memorial Trophy.

The Heisman Memorial Trophy, which Heisman initially rejected and then reluctantly embraced, became his lasting legacy.

Acknowledgments

John M. Heisman

No one controls where they are born or to what family. I have long felt the obligation to present the story of my granduncle to the football public. Discovering the life of John W. Heisman has consumed decades in research, in hopes of gaining some depth of understanding into his personality and character. When told that my publisher, Jonathan Merkh, wanted to bring in a professional sportswriter, I was initially apprehensive. Entrusting one-hundred-plus years of football history to a stranger, gave me a hard gut check. Mark Schlabach handled himself in the only way he could: He was himself, straight-forward, and hugely appreciative of what I laid before him. In the months we worked on Coach Heisman's biography, I never felt that Mark took anything for granted. His considerable additions and professional cleanup of my earlier writing have made this book not just a good read but content-rich and a ready resource for the sports historian. It has been a respected relief and pleasure to work with Mark.

I have so many to thank: my other family, Rich and Doris Shields, who gave me siblings; the late Professor William D. Scott, my mentor who first encouraged me to write this book. The friends who have served as my advisory board, Larry Evans, John Ross, Jack Karsten,

John Cook III, and a longtime friend and true gentleman for many years, Rudy Riska.

My thanks to the professionals at Simon & Schuster: my publisher, Jonathan Merkh; my editor, Philis Boultinghouse. A big thanks to Marilyn Somers, director of living history for the Georgia Tech Alumni Association, and acknowledgments of my great appreciation for the late Dean Griffin, Chip Robert, and Al Loeb, three of the many history-making grand gentlemen of Georgia Tech, whom I was privileged to meet. Thank you to Ursula Cox, granddaughter of Carlyle Cox, who provided so much insight into the glory years of Coach Heisman.

My warm appreciation goes to the good people of Titusville, Pennsylvania. The late Jim Spence, past editor of the *Titusville Herald*, who put me up in the YMCA while I searched the microfiche records of the newspaper.

My deepest appreciation and gratitude goes to my family for putting up with several rooms of clutter and stacks of old manuscripts and to my brother-in-law Mike Wilson for his support in this effort. Finally, with much love, thank you, Elaine, my most excellent spouse. With much pride, to my children: Amanda, Hilary, Sam, and Kara, thank you for striving to be the significant people you are, here is a portion of your heritage. To God be the glory.

Mark Schlabach

When former Southern California tailback Mike Garrett, the first of the Trojans' seven Heisman Trophy winners, was handed the trophy in 1965, he said, "The award is wonderful, but who's Heisman?"

In more than two decades of covering college football for newspapers such as the *Atlanta Journal–Constitution* and *Washington Post* and now ESPN, I have served as a Heisman Trophy voter for many years. I've read dozens of newspaper and magazine articles and books about the Heisman Trophy, and know plenty about the men who have taken the stage in New York to accept sports' greatest individual honor.

But when John M. Heisman entrusted me to help tell the story of his great-uncle John W. Heisman, I pondered the very question Garrett famously asked more than four decades ago: "Who's Heisman?"

While the Heisman Memorial Trophy has grown to become the most recognized and revered honor in all of American sports, very little is known about its namesake. The trophy wasn't named in Heisman's honor until its second year of existence in 1936, only a few months after he died from complications of pneumonia.

A former athletic director of the Downtown Athletic Club in New York, Heisman was much more than a successful college football coach at schools such as Oberlin College, Buchtel College, Auburn, Clemson, Georgia Tech, Pennsylvania, Washington & Jefferson, and Rice. He was a football innovator, introducing many of the methods, formations, and plays that are still used today. Among other things, Heisman invented the lateral pass, quarterback snap, audible "hike" signal, hidden ball trick, and scoreboard.

While Heisman flourished in a very public profession and was never afraid to publicize his teams' accomplishments, his private life was just that—very private. That was the biggest challenge in researching and writing *Heisman: The Man Behind the Trophy*. For all of the material that was handed down to John M. Heisman—and Coach Heisman documented and cataloged much of his professional life—very little was known about his life outside of athletics.

But through the help of archivists at the schools where Heisman worked, and after combing through thousands of newspaper articles dating back more than one hundred years, I'm confident we've pieced together a very accurate and detailed account of Heisman's life—both on and off the field. Along with being a highly successful coach, John W. Heisman was an accomplished thespian, a nationally syndicated sportswriter, and a successful businessman and entrepreneur. His personal life was often complicated, but had many, many layers, including the drama of a Shakespearean romance.

I'd like to thank the following people who assisted in my research into Heisman's life: Nancy Hoites of Whittier, California, and Eva Fintelmann of Germany for their research in identifying the lineage of the Heisman family; Susan Beates of the Drake Well Museum and the staff of the Crawford County (Pa.) Historical Society for their research assistance on Heisman's time in Titusville, Pennsylvania; Henry Timman, a historian in Norwalk, Ohio, for his assistance in researching Edith Maora Cole's life; and Davis McCollum of Marietta, Georgia, for his vast knowledge of Evelyn McCollum Cox and her family's history.

I'd like to thank the following university archivists for their help in researching Heisman's academic, playing, and coaching career: John Ball (Akron), Lauren Meyers (Rice), Raymond Butti (Brown), Mandi Johnson (Georgia Tech), and Nancy R. Miller (Pennsylvania). Clemson historian and professor emeritus Jerome "Jerry" Reel and sportswriter (and close friend) Larry "JoJo" Williams of Clemson, South Carolina, also provided immense expertise.

I'd also like to thank the following sports-information directors for their help in securing many of the archival documents and images you'll find in the book: Dean Buchan (Georgia Tech), Timothy Bourret (Clemson), Steve Fink (South Carolina), Mike Mahoney (Pennsylvania), and Scott McGuiness (Washington & Jefferson).

I'd like to thank Jonathan Merkh, publisher at Howard Books, and his editing and marketing team of Philis Boultinghouse, Amanda Demastus, and Libby Reed for their tireless and detailed work on the project. A writer couldn't ask for a better publisher, one who still understands the importance of the written word and American history.

I'd also like to acknowledge my editors at ESPN.com for allowing me to continue to tackle projects like this one: David Duffey, David Albright, Rob King, Patrick Stiegman, Lauren Reynolds, Brian Kelly, and Conor Nevins. Thank you for trusting me to take on the additional work and balance my duties.

I'm grateful that John M. Heisman trusted me in telling his family's rich story, one that went untold for too long. Hopefully, by working together, we've helped college football fans put a face on American sports' most famous trophy. I'd like to thank the numerous Heisman Trophy winners who have endorsed this book. By understanding the importance of revealing Heisman the man, you once again revealed the honor that comes with being a part of the Heisman fraternity.

Most of all, I'd like to thank my family, my wife, Heather, and our children, Caroline, Jane, and Jack, for their sacrifices while I completed this project. I love each of you dearly.

Notes

PROLOGUE

1. Bill Clark, "The John Heisman Nobody Remembers," *Atlanta Magazine*, December 1964, 32.
2. Note on half-page piece of paper, outlining qualifications for Downtown Athletic Club Award, signed by John W. Heisman and found in Rudy Riska's office at club in 1971.
3. "Berwanger, Great Chicago Back, Honored at Two Functions Here," *New York Times*, December 11, 1935, 1.

CHAPTER ONE: AMERICAN DREAM

1. Herman Weiskopf, "Heisman Trophy or Bogart Cup?," *Sports Illustrated*, January 4, 1971, M3–M4.
2. Mike Jensen, "John Heisman: The Man behind the Famous Trophy," *Philadelphia Enquirer*, December 9, 2010, 1.
3. Bill Clark, "The John Heisman Nobody Remembers," *Atlanta Magazine*, December 1964, 33.
4. Ibid.
5. Johann Michael Heissmann's birth records found at Protestant Archive in Regensburg, Germany, by researcher Eva Fintelmann.
6. Anna Heissmann's death certificate found at Protestant Archive in Regensburg, Germany, by researcher Eva Fintelmann.
7. *Borussia* manifest No. 9235, "Germans to America Passenger Data File, 1850–1897," US National Archives and Records Administration.
8. *Borussia* passenger list, "Passenger Lists, 1820–1957," microfilm serial, M237_185, www.ancestry.com.
9. "Hamburg," *Times* of London, March 7, 1857, 6.

10. Carol Poh Miller and Robert Wheeler, *Cleveland: A Concise History, 1796–1996* (Bloomington, Ind.: Indiana University Press, 2009), 53.
11. Michael Heisman's marriage to Sarah Lehr, license and application, found at Cuyahoga County Courts, Ohio, Vol. 18, 192.

CHAPTER TWO: TITUSVILLE

1. Lee Clayton, John W. Attig, David M. Mickelson, Mark D. Johnson, and Kent M. Syverson, *Glaciation of Wisconsin* (Madison, Wis.: Wisconsin Geological and Natural History Survey, 1992), 1.
2. Fred Anderson, *Crucible of War: The Seven Years' War and the Fate of Empire in British North America, 1754–1766* (New York: Vintage Books, 2001), 56–57.
3. "Petroleum: An Historical Sketch," *American Catholic Quarterly Review*, 1895, 409.
4. Herbert C. Bell, *History of Venango County, Pennsylvania: Its Past and Present* (Chicago: Brown, Runk & Company, 1890), 309.
5. Anonymous, *History of Crawford County, Pennsylvania*, Vol. I (Chicago: Warner, Beers & Co., 1885), 465.
6. Samuel T. Pees, *Oil History* (Oil City, Pa.: Petroleum History Institute), 1.
7. Ibid.
8. Legal advertisement, *Titusville Morning Herald*, October 20, 1879, 2.
9. Pees, 1.
10. Advertisement, *Titusville Morning Herald*, November 27, 1878, 3.
11. "Brevities," *Titusville Morning Herald*, July 20, 1886, 4.
12. Ibid., December 31, 1885, 4.
13. "Crushed to Death," *Titusville Morning Herald*, May 22, 1892, 1.
14. Ibid.

CHAPTER THREE: BROWN UNIVERSITY

1. John W. Heisman, "Signals," *Collier's Weekly*, October 6, 1928, 12.
2. John W. Heisman, "Look Sharp Now," *Collier's Weekly*, November 3, 1928, 19.
3. "High School Commencement," *Titusville Morning Herald*, June 18, 1887, 1.
4. Heisman, "Signals," 12.
5. Ibid.
6. Ibid.
7. Ibid., 12–13.
8. Ibid., 12.
9. Ibid., 13.
10. Martha Mitchell, *Encyclopedia Brunoniana* (Providence, R.I.: Brown University Press, 1993), 237.
11. Heisman, "Signals," 13.
12. Ibid., 12–13.
13. Ibid., 13.

14. Ibid.
15. Ibid.

CHAPTER FOUR: UNIVERSITY OF PENNSYLVANIA

1. Steven Morgan Friedman, "A Brief History of the University of Pennsylvania," University of Pennsylvania Archives and Records Center, 1.
2. "Harvard Beaten," *Boston Daily Globe*, October 23, 1884, 5.
3. John W. Heisman, "Defense in Football" (unpublished manuscript, c. 1928), chap. 4, 5.
4. Ibid.
5. Ibid., 5–6.
6. Ibid., 3.
7. John W. Heisman, "Football of Ye Olden Days: An Uproarious Contrast with Gridiron Sport of Today," *All Sports Magazine*, November 1936, 14.
8. Heisman, "Defense in Football," 5.
9. "A Hard Football Game," *World*, October 16, 1890, 6.
10. Ibid.
11. "Slugging Winked At," *Boston Daily Globe*, October 23, 1890, 10.
12. "Only Six to Nothing," *Boston Daily Globe*, November 9, 1890, 6.
13. John W. Heisman, "Signals," *Collier's Weekly*, October 6, 1928, 12–13.
14. Ibid.
15. Heisman, "Football of Ye Olden Days," 13.
16. Ibid.
17. Ibid., 14.
18. John W. Heisman, "The Story of Football and Other Football Stories" (unpublished manuscript, c. 1928), chap. 2, 8.
19. "Blue Day," *Boston Sunday Globe*, November 16, 1890, 7.
20. Heisman, "The Story of Football," chap. 2, 8.
21. John W. Heisman, "Look Sharp Now," *Collier's Weekly*, November 3, 1928, 32.
22. John W. Heisman, "The Development of the Running Game, Part II" (unpublished manuscript, c. 1928), 3.
23. University of Pennsylvania catalog and announcements, 1891–92, 261.
24. John W. Heisman, "Offensive Part I" (unpublished manuscript, c. 1928), 4.
25. Ibid.
26. William L. Heisman, multiple interviews by John M. Heisman, 1966–1969.
27. Heisman, "The Story of Football," chap. 2, 8.

CHAPTER FIVE: OBERLIN COLLEGE

1. Nat Brandt, *When Oberlin Was King of the Gridiron* (Kent, Ohio: Kent State University Press, 2001), 51.
2. Ibid., 4.
3. Notice posted annually throughout John W. Heisman's coaching career.

4. Brandt, 61–62.

5. John W. Heisman, "Between Halves," *Collier's Weekly*, November 17, 1928, 18.

6. John W. Heisman, "Look Sharp Now," *Collier's Weekly*, November 3, 1928, 19.

7. Brandt, 65–66.

8. John W. Heisman, "The Story of Football and Other Football Stories" (unpublished manuscript, c. 1928), chap. 2, 1.

9. Brandt, 72.

10. Heisman, "Look Sharp Now," 19.

11. Brandt, 74.

12. Ibid., 76.

13. Heisman, "The Story of Football," 3–4.

14. John W. Heisman, "These Are Men" (unpublished manuscript, c. 1929), 3–4.

15. Ibid.

16. Heisman, "The Story of Football," chap. 3, 9.

17. Brandt, 85.

18. John W. Heisman, *Ann Arbor Courier*, November 22, 1892, n.p.

19. Brandt, 86.

20. Ibid., 88.

CHAPTER SIX: BUCHTEL COLLEGE

1. Nat Brandt, *When Oberlin Was King of the Gridiron* (Kent, Ohio: Kent State University Press, 2001), 92.

2. "140th Anniversary: At 140, the University of Akron Honors Its History and Embraces Its Future," University of Akron, 2010.

3. Ibid.

4. "Heisman! Heisman! Rah! Rah! Rah!," *Buchtelite*, c. spring 1893, n.p.

5. "New Era in Athletics," *Akron Daily Beacon*, c. spring 1893, n.p.

6. "Triumphal Tour of the Denison Base Ball Team," *Newark (Ohio) Daily Advocate*, June 6, 1893, 5.

7. "Major Football Change Developed at Buchtel," *Akron Daily Beacon*, n.d., n.p.

8. John W. Heisman, "Fast and Loose," *Collier's Weekly*, October 20, 1928, 53.

9. "Major Football Change Developed at Buchtel," n.d., n.p.

10. Ibid.

11. Ibid.

12. Ibid.

13. Brandt, 96.

14. Ibid., 102.

15. "Stagg's Team Beaten by Oberlin," *Chicago Tribune*, November 5, 1893, 4.

16. Ibid.

17. John W. Heisman, "The Story of Football and Other Football Stories" (unpublished manuscript, c. 1928), chap. 3, 12–13.

18. Ibid.

19. Ibid.

20. Ibid.

21. Ibid.

22. "Play Good Football," *Chicago Tribune*, November 13, 1893, 11.

23. "Ohio State Fair," *Richwood (Ohio) Gazette*, August 23, 1894, 2.

24. John W. Heisman, "Here Are Men" (unpublished manuscript, c. 1929), 12–13.

25. Ibid.

26. Ibid.

27. Ibid.

28. William L. Heisman, multiple interviews by John M. Heisman, 1966–1969.

29. Brandt, 146.

30. "Death Rates by Cause of Death, 1900–2005," *Vital Statistics of the United States*, Vols. I and II (Washington, DC: US Public Health Service, 2005).

31. Edith I. Heisman, interview by William L. Heisman, 1960.

CHAPTER SEVEN: AUBURN

1. "Our Coach," *Orange and Blue*, n.d., n.p.

2. John W. Heisman, "The Story of Football and Other Football Stories" (unpublished manuscript, c. 1928), chap. 3, 20.

3. Ibid.

4. Ibid.

5. "1895: Board Minutes of the Agricultural and Mechanical College of Alabama," Auburn University Libraries Special Collections and Archives, June 10, 1895, 310.

6. "Vanderbilt 9, Auburn 6," *Atlanta Constitution*, November 10, 1895, 11.

7. Heisman, "The Story of Football," 22.

8. Ibid.

9. "After the Game the Victors Were Given a Brilliant Hop," *Atlanta Constitution*, November 24, 1895, 15.

10. Ibid.

11. "A Grand Gala Event!!!," *Atlanta Constitution*, November 24, 1895, 20.

12. "Football Giants," *Atlanta Constitution*, November 28, 1895, 8.

13. "Auburn Victorious," *Atlanta Constitution*, November 29, 1895, 2.

14. "Auburn at It, Too," *Atlanta Constitution*, November 22, 1896, 13.

15. "Georgia Wins Out," *Atlanta Constitution*, November 27, 1896, 12.

16. Ibid.

17. John W. Heisman, "Here Are Men" (unpublished manuscript, c. 1929), 10–12.

18. John W. Heisman, "Between the Halves," *Collier's Weekly*, November 17, 1928, 53.

19. "From Gridiron to the Grave," *Atlanta Constitution*, October 31, 1897, 7.

20. Ibid.

21. "The Game of Football," *Atlanta Constitution*, November 7, 1897, 32.

22. "Football the House Feature," *Atlanta Constitution*, November 2, 1897, 5.
23. George Magruder Battey, *A History of Rome and Floyd County, Georgia* (Atlanta: Webb Vary Company, 1922), 349.
24. John W. Heisman, "Football at Auburn in My Day," *Auburn Alumnus*, n.d., 100.
25. John W. Heisman, "Fast and Loose," *Collier's Weekly*, October 20, 1928, 14.
26. "Georgia Team Leaves Field," *Atlanta Constitution*, November 25, 1898, 1–2.
27. Ibid.
28. "Contest Fierce and Clean," *Atlanta Constitution*, November 19, 1899, 5.
29. Ibid.
30. W. R. Tichenor, "Sewanee Wins from Auburn," *Atlanta Constitution*, December 1, 1899, 3.
31. "Heisman Makes Reply to Taylor," *Birmingham Age-Herald*, December 4, 1899, n.p.
32. Wiley Lee Umphlett, *Creating the Big Game: John W. Heisman and the Invention of American Football* (Westport, Conn.: Greenwood, 1992), 58.
33. "Heisman Makes Reply to Taylor," n.p.

CHAPTER EIGHT: CLEMSON COLLEGE

1. John W. Heisman's contracts, W. M. Riggs Presidential Records, Strom Thurmond Institute, Clemson University Libraries.
2. "Clemson Tigers Too Much for Carolina," *State*, November 2, 1900, 8.
3. "Past Crowds Overshadowed," *State*, November 2, 1900, 1.
4. "How Football Games Resulted Yesterday," *Atlanta Constitution*, November 11, 1900, 9.
5. John W. Heisman, "On Football," *Oconeean*, 1903, n.p.
6. William J. Latimer, *Three Score Years of Football at Clemson* (n.p., November 1956).
7. John W. Heisman, "Development of the Running Game" (unpublished manuscript, c. 1928), 10–11.
8. "Coach Heisman Tells Why His Teams Are Successful," *Atlanta Constitution*, October 19, 1903, 7.
9. Ibid.
10. "Football Notes," *Atlanta Constitution*, November 3, 1903, 9.
11. "Clemson vs. Carolina Here Next Thursday," *State*, October 26, 1902, 11.
12. "Fair Columbia Welcomes All," *State*, October 29, 1902, 1.
13. Ibid.
14. "Tamed Tiger; Twisted Tail," *State*, October 31, 1902, 8.
15. "The Trouble over the Transparency," *State*, November 2, 1902, 16.
16. Ibid.
17. Ibid.
18. John W. Heisman, "The Greatest Feats of Football" (unpublished manuscript, c. 1929), 5–6.

19. "Alabama Wants Heisman," *State*, November 14, 1902, 5.
20. "Clemson Comes to Meet Tech," *Atlanta Constitution*, October 17, 1903, 8.

CHAPTER NINE: HEISMAN ONSTAGE

1. "Cartersville," *Atlanta Constitution*, May 24, 1873, 1.
2. Ibid.
3. "Roundabout in Georgia," *Atlanta Constitution*, October 27, 1877, 3.
4. "Crime and Casualty," *Atlanta Constitution*, January 10, 1879, 1.
5. "The Fatal Shot," *Atlanta Constitution*, May 28, 1889, 1.
6. "Between Parents," *Atlanta Constitution*, July 18, 1895, 5.
7. Bill Clark, "The John Heisman Nobody Remembers," *Atlanta Magazine*, December 1964, 30–34.
8. "Diplomacy," *New York Dramatic Mirror*, May 28, 1898, 14.
9. "The Ragged Regiment," *New York Herald*, June 21, 1898, 14.
10. "Virginius," *Macon Telegraph*, June 27, 1899, 6.
11. "Amusements," *Atlanta Constitution*, June 15, 1899, 9.
12. "Camille Last Night," *Biloxi Daily Herald*, July 6, 1901, 8.
13. "David Garrick," *Biloxi Daily Herald*, August, 16, 1901, 8.
14. "Summer Drama," *Macon Telegraph*, May 24, 1902, 8.
15. "People Turned Away at Crump's Park," *Macon Telegraph*, June 17, 1902, 5.
16. "A Cheerful Liar," *Macon Telegraph*, June 24, 1902, 8.
17. Advertisement, *New York Clipper*, November 22, 1903, 878.
18. "Heisman Company Begins Engagement," *Montgomery Advertiser*, June 5, 1904, 8.
19. "At Casino Theatre," *Montgomery Advertiser*, July 27, 1904, 8.
20. "Excellent Performance at the Grand," *Augusta Chronicle*, June 13, 1905, 4.
21. "The Heisman Stock Company," *Macon Telegraph*, May 22, 1906, 8.
22. Ibid.
23. "Season at Crump's Park Casino Soon to Be Closed," *Macon Telegraph*, September 10, 1906, 3.

CHAPTER TEN: GEORGIA TECH

1. "Coach Heisman Wanted by Tech," *Atlanta Constitution*, November 9, 1903, 3.
2. "Coach Heisman Comes to Tech," *Atlanta Constitution*, November 27, 1903, 4.
3. Lawrence "Chip" Robert Jr., interview with John M. Heisman, June 1973.
4. Al Thorny, *The Ramblin' Wreck: A Story of Georgia Tech Football* (Huntsville, Ala.: Stroude Publishers, 1973), 40.
5. Lawrence "Chip" Robert Jr., interview by John M. Heisman, June 1973.
6. Al Loeb, phone interview by John M. Heisman, June 1973.
7. John W. Heisman, *Principles of Football* (St. Louis, Mo.: Sports Publishing Bureau, 1922), chap. 3, 26–28.
8. Ibid., 29.

9. Ibid., 6.
10. Edwin Pope, *Football's Greatest Coaches* (Atlanta: Tupper & Love, 1955), 119.
11. "Heisman Seized Plan to Abolish Fumbling," *Atlanta Constitution*, November 2, 1907, 11.
12. Pope, 118.
13. John W. Heisman, "Between the Halves," *Collier's Weekly*, November 17, 1928, 18.
14. William L. Heisman, multiple interviews by John M. Heisman, 1966–1969.
15. Heisman, *Principles of Football*, 18–19.
16. William L. Heisman, multiple interviews by John M. Heisman, 1966–1969.
17. "Coach Heisman Takes Charge," *Atlanta Constitution*, January 3, 1904, 8.
18. John W. Heisman, "The Story of Football and Other Football Stories" (unpublished manuscript, c. 1928), 10–11.
19. Wily Lee Umphlett, *Creating the Big Game* (Westport, Conn.: Greenwood, 1992), 89.
20. John W. Heisman, "The Future of Football Involves Many Issues," *Atlanta Constitution*, November 26, 1905, 4.
21. Ibid.
22. "Georgia Used Four Ringers," *Atlanta Constitution*, November 14, 1907, 11.
23. "Was Georgia Team Used as Pawn for Gamblers?" *Atlanta Constitution*, November 14, 1907, 11.
24. "Jackets Coach Says His Say," *Atlanta Constitution*, November 20, 1907, 11.
25. Transcript, Southern Intercollegiate Athletic Association executive committee hearing, November 22, 1907, Georgia Tech Archives and Records Management.
26. John W. Heisman, letter to Walter M. Riggs, September 20, 1912, W. M. Riggs Presidential Records, Strom Thurmond Institute, Clemson University Libraries.

CHAPTER ELEVEN: ROUT OF THE CENTURY

1. "Yellow Jackets Play Cumberland," *Atlanta Constitution*, October 7, 1916, 10.
2. Harold Scherwitz, "Spotlights," *San Antonio Light*, October 9, 1955, 55.
3. Ibid.
4. John W. Heisman, "The Story of Football and Other Football Stories" (unpublished manuscript, c. 1928), 22–23.
5. John W. Heisman, "Not Guilty" (unpublished manuscript, c. 1928), 1.
6. Hal Reynolds, "Yellow Jackets Roll Up Over Two Hundred Points in Beating Cumberland," *Atlanta Constitution*, October 8, 1916, 3.
7. Parke H. Davis, "Yellow Jackets–Cumberland Score Was Record One," *Atlanta Constitution*, October 15, 1916, 3.
8. John W. Heisman, "Coach Heisman Reviews 1916 Season" (unpublished manuscript, c. 1916), 1.

9. Gene Griessman, "The Man behind the Heisman Trophy," *Atlanta Journal-Constitution*, November 25, 1984, 1H.

10. John W. Heisman, "Between the Halves," *Collier's Weekly*, November 17, 1928, 54.

11. John W. Heisman, "Psychology in Coaching and in Playing" (unpublished manuscript, c. 1928), 6.

12. William L. Heisman, multiple interviews by John M. Heisman, 1966–1969.

13. Ibid.

14. "Tech Concedes Title to Tech; Exhibits the Best of Sportsmanship," *Atlanta Constitution*, December 3, 1916, 1.

CHAPTER TWELVE: GOLDEN TORNADO

1. "University Abandons Football This Year on Account of War," *Atlanta Constitution*, September 17, 1917, 10.

2. Lawrence "Chip" Robert, interview by John M. Heisman, June 1973.

3. Ibid.

4. "Tech Will Play Two Games Today," *Atlanta Constitution*, September 29, 1917, 8.

5. John W. Heisman, "The Telephone and the Athletic Director," *Telephone Review*, August 1930, 12–14.

6. John W. Heisman, "Little Giants of the Gridiron," *Intercollegiate Football Pictorial*, 1936, 24.

7. Hal Reynolds, "Yellow Jackets Run Wild over the Penn Eleven," *Atlanta Constitution*, October 7, 1917, 3.

8. Ibid.

9. Hal Reynolds, "Davidson Gives Jackets Another Fierce Battle," *Atlanta Constitution*, October 14, 1917, 3.

10. "Heisman Will Drive His Jackets Hard," *Atlanta Constitution*, October 16, 1917, 12.

11. Heisman, "Little Giants of the Gridiron," 24–25.

12. John W. Heisman, "The Story of Football and Other Football Stories" (unpublished manuscript, c. 1928), 16.

13. J. V. Fitzgerald, "The Round-Up," *Washington Post*, November 11, 1917, 22.

14. "Pittsburgh Delays Answering Tech," *Atlanta Constitution*, November 18, 1917, 3.

15. "Auburn Tigers Play Ohio State to Scoreless Tie," *Atlanta Constitution*, November 25, 1917, 3.

16. "New York Papers for Tech—One and All," *Atlanta Journal*, December 2, 1917, 8.

17. "Georgia Tech's Football Juggernaut; Greatest of the Gridiron Machines of 1917," *New York Times*, December 16, 1917, S8.

18. "Georgia's Paper Sings Praises of Tech Eleven," *Atlanta Constitution*, November 25, 1917, 3.

19. "Tech to Lose Heisman and Bulk of the Team," *Atlanta Constitution*, November 27, 1917, 12.

20. "Everett Strupper Elected to Lead 1918 Tech Eleven," *Atlanta Constitution*, December 9, 1917, 3.

21. "Colleges Refuse to Drop Athletics," *Atlanta Constitution*, December 29, 1917, 12.

CHAPTER THIRTEEN: RETURN TO PENN

1. Lawrence "Chip" Robert Jr., interview by John M. Heisman, June 1973.

2. "Moran Grants Decrees," *Nevada State Journal*, June 11, 1919, 8.

3. "Coach Heisman Down to Work," *Philadelphia Inquirer*, February 5, 1920, 14.

4. "Penn's Footballers Off for Workout," *Philadelphia Inquirer*, August 31, 1920, 15.

5. "Penn's Coach Wants More Candidates," *Philadelphia Inquirer*, September 16, 1920, 14.

6. "Heisman Explains Penn State Debacle," *Philadelphia Inquirer*, November 2, 1920, 16.

7. Edwin Pope, *Football's Greatest Coaches* (Atlanta: Tupper & Love, 1955), 127.

8. John W. Heisman, "The Story of Football and Other Football Stories" (unpublished manuscript, c. 1928), 4–5.

9. "Heisman Raps Penn for Poor Tackling," *Philadelphia Inquirer*, November 11, 1916, 16.

10. Pope, 127.

11. Bill Roper, "Penn's System of Attack Shattered by New Rules," *Trenton (N.J.) Evening Times*, October 9, 1921, 34.

12. Franklin Bates, "Penn Spirit Grand Is Heisman's Praise," *Philadelphia Inquirer*, September 11, 1921, 23.

13. "Eight Penn Players Are Demoted by Coach," *Patriot*, October 4, 1921, 13.

14. Letter from John W. Heisman to Walter Riggs, November 18, 1921, W. M. Riggs Presidential Records, Strom Thurmond Institute, Clemson University Libraries.

15. Letter from Walter Riggs to John W. Heisman, January 10, 1922, W. M. Riggs Presidential Records, Strom Thurmond Institute, Clemson University Libraries.

16. "Here's Heisman's Dope on Penn's Grid Decline," *Philadelphia Inquirer*, November 29, 1921, 16.

17. "Speech Regained," *Norwalk (Ohio) Chronicle*, February 3, 1898, 5.

18. Edith M. Heisman as told to William L. Heisman, 1960.

19. "First June Bride," *Norwalk (Ohio) Chronicle*, June 3, 1898, 6.

20. Ursula Cox, interview by John M. Heisman, June 3, 2009.

21. "Heisman Has Good Method of Putting Pep into Grid Men," *San Diego Union*, December 11, 1922, 13.

22. Ibid.

23. Gordon Mackay, "Penn Sinks Navy in Great Triumph, 13–7," *Philadelphia Inquirer,* October 29, 1922, 19.

24. J. Y. Sanders Jr., letter to John W. Heisman, November 8, 1922.

25. J. A. C. Chandler, letter to John W. Heisman, December 20, 1922.

26. A. R. Tiffany, letter to John W. Heisman, January 15, 1922.

27. Harold Hirsch, telegram to John W. Heisman, November 27, 1922.

28. Dr. Kenneth G. Matheson, letter to John W. Heisman, February 16, 1923.

29. Josiah H. Penniman, letter to John W. Heisman, February 27, 1923.

CHAPTER FOURTEEN: WASHINGTON & JEFFERSON COLLEGE

1. "W & J Eleven Back Home," *New York Times,* January 14, 1922, n.p.

2. "Coach for W. and J. Not Yet Selected," *New York Times,* December 24, 1922, n.p.

3. John W. Heisman, "The Story of Football and Other Football Stories" (unpublished manuscript, c. 1928), 13–15.

4. "Negro in Line-Up, Game Called Off," *Richmond Times-Dispatch,* October 7, 1923, 1.

5. Ibid.

6. "W. and L. Tells Why Game Off," *Tampa Tribune,* October 10, 1923, 8.

7. "Negro in Line-Up," 1.

8. "The Negro in Football," *Richmond Times-Dispatch,* October 9, 1923, 6.

9. "Some Players Took Long Train Routes," *Richmond Times-Dispatch,* October 9, 1923, 8.

10. "Tech May Play Rutgers in Gotham," *Atlanta Constitution,* January 5, 1918, 10.

11. Al Loeb, interview by John M. Heisman, June 1973.

12. "W. and J. Due Here Today," *New York Times,* November 2, 1923, n.p.

13. "Arise W. & J. and Act," *Pittsburgh Chronicle-Telegram,* November 19, 1923, n.p.

14. Havy J. Boyle, "Through the Sports Lens," *Pittsburgh Chronicle-Telegram,* November 21, 1923, n.p.

15. Heisman, "The Story of Football, 13–15.

16. Ibid.

17. "W. and J. Humbles West Virginia, 7–2," *New York Times,* November 30, 1923, n.p.

18. Debra Duncan, "W&J Honors Early Black Football Star," *Pittsburgh Post-Gazette,* September 8, 2011, n.p.

19. Dr. Kenneth G. Matheson, letter to John W. Heisman, December 30, 1923.

20. Cadwallader M. Barr, letter to Washington & Jefferson College Alumni Association members, December 1923.

21. "Heisman Resigns as W. and J. Coach," *New York Times*, February 19, 1924, n.p.
22. Duncan, "W&J Honors Early Black Football Star."
23. Ibid.

CHAPTER FIFTEEN: RICE INSTITUTE

1. "Murdered Man's Estate Founds Great University," *New York Times*, February 25, 1912, 1.
2. William Ward Watkin, telegram to Rice president Edgar Odell Lovett, February 3, 1924, William Ward Watkin Papers, Woodson Research Center, Fondren Library, Rice University.
3. J. T. McCants, telegram to William Ward Watkin, February 7, 1924, William Ward Watkin Papers, Woodson Research Center, Fondren Library, Rice University.
4. Patrick James Nicholson, *William Ward Watkin and the Rice Institute* (Houston: Gulf Publishing Co., 1991), 162–163.
5. "New Owl Coach One of America's Leading Experts," *Thresher*, February 19, 1924, 1.
6. "J. W. Heisman New Coach," *Thresher*, February 19, 1924, 1.
7. Ibid.
8. Edward Wademan, letter to John W. Heisman, July 5, 1924.
9. John W. Heisman, letter to Edward Wademan, July 1924.
10. "Athletics versus Academics," *Houston Post*, 1924.
11. Fredericka Meiners, *A History of Rice University: The Institute Years, 1907–1963* (Houston: Rice University Studies, 1983), 104–5.
12. Campanile Yearbook, *Class of 1925, Rice University* (Houston, Tex.: Rein Printing Co., 1925), 237.
13. "Houston Wild over Victory by Owls on Grid," *San Antonio Express*, November 3, 1924, 10.
14. John W. Heisman, "The Story of Football and Other Football Stories" (unpublished manuscript, c. 1928), 7–8.
15. Campanile Yearbook, 232.
16. Heisman, "The Story of Football," 6.
17. Meiners, 105.
18. "Gridsters Ordered to Grow Beards because of Girls," *Atlantic-News Telegraph*, October 17, 1924, 6.
19. Lloyd Gregory, "Looking 'Em Over," *Houston Post*, November 1927, n.p.
20. Heisman, "The Story of Football," 11–12.
21. Ibid.
22. John W. Heisman, letter to Edgar Odell Lovett, December 2, 1927, President E. O. Lovett's Personal Papers, 1871–1957, Woodson Research Center, Fondren Library, Rice University.

CHAPTER SIXTEEN: NEW YORK

1. John W. Heisman, "Heisman's Team Drops Another," *Atlanta Constitution*, August 29, 1903, C1.
2. John W. Heisman, "Auburn Team Won Deserved Victory," *Atlanta Constitution*, October 27, 1907, 8.
3. "John W. Heisman Begins Series of Grid Stories for Telegraph," *Macon Telegraph*, October 17, 1902, 6.
4. John W. Heisman, promotional flyer, *Principles of Football*, 1922.
5. John W. Heisman, letter to Ladas Hubka, November 26, 1928.
6. Knute Rockne, letter to John W. Heisman, n.d.
7. Nellie E. Mulhern, letter to John W. Heisman, October 25, 1929.
8. Frank Hertz, letter to John W. Heisman, November 14, 1929.
9. John W. Heisman, letter to Frank Hertz, November 19, 1929.
10. "Heisman Springs New Valve for Footballs," *Boston Globe*, March 10, 1923, 10.
11. John W. Heisman, US patent No. 799,848 (Washington, DC: US Patent Office, September 19, 1905).
12. John W. Heisman, "Bonehead Plays You Can Avoid When Selling Spring Football Orders," *Sporting Goods Journal*, March 1930, 81.

EPILOGUE

1. "John W. Heisman, Noted Coach, Dies," *New York Times*, October 4, 1936, n.p.
2. "Would Decide Tie Football Battles," *Baltimore American*, December 28, 1922, 8.
3. John W. Heisman, "A New Method of Classifying College Football Teams" (unpublished manuscript, c. 1928), 2.

Index